The Classic Baptist Heritage of Personal Truth

THE
CLASSIC
BAPTIST
HERITAGE
OF
PERSONAL
TRUTH

The Truth As It Is In Jesus

Frank Louis Mauldin

Foreword by John P. Newport

PROVIDENCE HOUSE PUBLISHERS
Franklin, Tennessee

Printed in the United States of America

03   02   01   00   99   1   2   3   4   5

Library of Congress Catalog Card Number: 98-68603

ISBN: 1-57736-131-8

Cover design by Gary Bozeman

PROVIDENCE HOUSE PUBLISHERS
238 Seaboard Lane • Franklin, Tennessee 37067
800–321–5692
www.providencehouse.com

To

Biff

in whom
truth, grace, and love
meet

Contents

Foreword

This is a unique and important book. Its significance goes beyond its title. According to Martin Marty, the eminent church historian, there is an urgent need for "Baptistification" or an accent on decision, initiation, and decisive identity in the Christian world. In this tradition, Mauldin describes the unfolding, decline, and restoration of the classic personal truth emphasis in seventeenth– and eighteenth–century Baptist life. He uses this dramatic and fascinating particularity of history to provide answers for crucial contemporary problems such as the nature of truth, the distinction between propositional truths and personal truth, the equation of truth with Jesus Christ and the gospel, election and freedom, the balance of faith and reason, the context for understanding the Bible, the urgency of incarnational ethics, and the proper approach for evangelism and missions.

Trained in philosophy at state and semisecular universities, a brilliant Ph.D. student in philosophy of religion, a professor in Christian and state universities, a biblical philosopher, and an active Christian layman, the author has the unique background to give readers a broad biblical framework for personal study and church and denominational life. He moves us beyond Modernism and Postmodernism and provides us with an urgently needed Christian paradigm. The passionate preface alone is worth the price of the volume.

This book should appeal to a number of audiences. For example, it has a strong emphasis on spiritual formation and the importance of incarnational Christian ethics. In the light of Postmodernism, it should appeal to readers in the field of philosophy of religion who deal with the problem of faith and reason. It is an excellent study for use by colleges, seminaries, and local church groups as a basis for conferences and seminars.

A major controversy among Baptists and other evangelical Christians relates to the question of how to create a balance between the objective and the subjective. Throughout this book the author deals with this problem. His emphasis on the fact that biblical truth is relational is very important. Today we have the rationality of Fundamentalism and the subjective emphasis of the Charismatics. The book presents a view which goes beyond and balances these two emphases.

A major contribution of this book is its emphasis on the proper use of the Bible in the total context of the Incarnation, the Trinity, and the Christian walk. Even though reason is not primary, the book emphasizes throughout the importance of proper standards of reasonableness.

John P. Newport
Special Consultant to the President for Academic Research;
Vice President for Academic Affairs and Provost, Retired;
Distinguished Professor of Philosophy of Religion; Emeritus
Southwestern Baptist Theological Seminary

Preface and Acknowledgments

We have no book quite like this one. It is the first of its kind. It examines, and celebrates, the biblical and the historic Baptist understanding of personal truth. We have books that explain Baptist faith and practice, others that consider Baptist history, and still more that examine a particular theological or denominational issue. But no other book undertakes the basic task of this book, that of examining the primary writings of English and American Baptists in the seventeenth and eighteenth centuries with the avowed fourfold purpose (1) of identifying and analyzing the distinctive notion of personal truth present therein, (2) of demonstrating the existence of a classic Baptist heritage of truth, (3) of understanding what it means for Baptists in the classic heritage to equate truth with "the truth as it is in Jesus," and (4) of making the case that the story of personal truth (along with the stories of faith and freedom) constitutes the soul—the essential core and the common ground—of Baptist identity and integrity.

The book achieves its fourfold purpose by teasing out the genius and the substance of the classic Baptist heritage of personal truth in several different yet related ways. It is at once:

1. a historical study of the notion of personal truth forged by Baptists in their formative centuries;
2. a systematic or a philosophical analysis of the biblical and the historic Baptist understanding of the foundations of personal truth;

3. a classic way of understanding truth in terms of gospel realism and personalism, taking with utmost seriousness Jesus Christ's witness, "I am the truth;"
4. an existential engagement of the classic heritage so as not only to preserve but to restore and to embrace, in the late modern and postmodern worlds, the personal truth that is at the heart of what it means to be a Baptist;
5. an establishment of the original text or documents of truth used by American and English Baptists in the seventeenth and eighteenth centuries;
6. a confessional recital of the living Baptist heritage of personal truth;
7. a personal pilgrimage, and at times an odyssey, to that truth which is "the simplicity of the gospel."

In but a few words, in these several yet related ways, ever mindful of its fourfold purpose, the book tells the story of the classic Baptist passion for personal truth, a story full of significance for understanding the identity and the integrity of Baptists, both then and now, and, more importantly, for encountering and knowing the personal truth itself.

A HISTORICAL STUDY

In its telling of the Baptist story of personal truth, the book chronicles the historical unfolding of the classic heritage of personal truth among General, Particular, Regular, and Separate Baptists throughout the seventeenth and eighteenth centuries. It begins by tracing the establishment of the classic Baptist heritage of personal truth in the seventeenth century both in England and the American colonies. It then narrates a turning away from personal truth by English and American Baptists alike in the first half of the eighteenth century. It offers documentary evidence that Baptists negated their seventeenth-century legacy, and did so by covering over personal truth with the impersonal and the propositional truths of reason, experience, doctrines, and facts. Finally, the book records the reaffirmation of the classic view of personal truth by both English and American Baptists in the second half of the eighteenth century.

The historical analysis of the book is thoroughly grounded in a study of the primary sources or the vital documents in Baptist history. It is based upon a study of the confessions, diaries, church covenants, treatises, books, pamphlets, correspondence, circular letters, association reports, sermons, hymns, and catechisms produced by English and American Baptists. It also attends to materials gathered from studies of the major figures in Baptist history, such as Thomas Helwys, John Clarke, John Gill, Andrew Fuller, Dan Taylor, Isaac Backus, William Carey, and the like. Significantly, it brings to the foreground a number of figures who have remained in the background of Baptist history yet nevertheless played a key role in the development of the classic view of truth, for example, Jonathan Maxcy, Elizabeth Backus, John Sutcliff, and Oliver Hart.

The book includes primary sources now in print and readily accessible, for instance, Andrew Fuller's "An Essay on Truth" and Isaac Backus's "Truth Is Great and Will Prevail." It also contains published materials not well-known or readily accessible, such as Edmund Botsford's "On the Duty of Christians in Matters of Controversy" and Richard Furman's "On the Use of Reason in Religion." Some materials in the book can be said to be new. They have not been circulated since their first publication and can currently be found only in archives and on microfilm, including one of the best statements on truth in the classic heritage, that of Paul Hobson in his 1647 work, *A Discoverie of Truth.*

A SYSTEMATIC OR A PHILOSOPHICAL ANALYSIS

This first telling of the classic Baptist story of truth is not only historical but systematic in substance and method. It offers a philosophical analysis of the genius, the fundamentals, the categories, and the networks of truth embodied in the historical documents of Baptists in their formative centuries. Baptists have been studied historically and theologically, but philosophical studies of any kind are rare. Studies of truth do not exist at all, although truth is one of the core values of the Baptist soul. As a first step in filling this void the present study of the original Baptist text of truth makes a unique, albeit modest, contribution.

The philosophical analysis of the classic text of truth shows that English and American Baptists display a particular genius in matters of truth. They are gospel realists and personalists who from first to last equate truth with reality, and who on every occasion equate reality with the gospel story of persons, human and divine, in fellowship within the life-world.

For Baptists truth is not a true belief, a true doctrine, or a true statement of any kind. Truth is not propositional. It does not arise from ways of knowing, out of epistemic starting-points and theories of knowledge, or from a cognitive grasping of facts, ideas, experiences, judgments, or principles. Or, in the language of the book, truth is not truths (throughout the whole of the book, the truth identified by the Baptists with reality is designated by the term "truth," while that truth identified with true statements or propositions is designated by the term "truths").

Baptists rather defend the thesis that truth is someone real, not something true. It is someone encountered, not something known. It is an event in the life-world, not a quality of a statement or a proposition. Truth, which has a face, a name, a story, is the actual person of the Living God—Father, Son, Spirit—and of Jesus Christ, who together fellowship with actual persons face-to-face, name-to-name, story-to-story within the realism of the gospel of grace. It is the dramatic good story of characters and events moving within time and place, through conflict toward resolution, in the chapters of the biography of the Living God, a story told locally in terms of the happenings of contemporary life and language, which are not just vehicles that carry and communicate truths but necessary parts of truth itself. Truth is a tangible happening that comes about, so to speak, as someone dynamic, vigorous, passionate, gracious, and sometimes quite explosive.

In its systematic exposition of the classic genius, the book finds that the language of truth in the Baptist heritage begins with talk of fundamentals, two in number, which give shape to truth: (1) truth is the person of God—truth is what God is and does; and (2) persons can be and do the truth—persons model or participate in the truth that God is and does.

The book also identifies five categories of truth in the classic heritage. The primary function of the categories is to reveal the character of the fundamentals by dividing them into their essential parts. Baptists do this by recounting gospel realities. Their categorical scheme consists of claims that (1) truth is Jesus Christ, (2) truth is the Holy Trinity, (3) truth is the Holy Scriptures, (4) truth is abundant life and liberty, and (5) truth is reasonableness.

Finally, the book finds that the fundamentals and the categories, which give body and beauty to the personal quality of truth in the classic heritage, form a network of relations. Each fundamental and category in the network has it own unique essence and integrity. However, each also has a relational essence and integrity. The language of truth in the classic heritage thus achieves and maintains its unity by a harmonious balancing of diverse elements, and it judges any truth-claim contextually by the full range of fundamentals, categories, and relations.

Preface and Acknowledgments

A CLASSIC WAY OF UNDERSTANDING

The equation of truth with gospel reality is a profound transformation of the ordinary and the modern meanings of truth, but it is the meaning of truth that is primary, true statements being secondary and derivative and always more tentative for the Baptists. And, it is truly the classic meaning. The understanding of truth forwarded by English and American Baptists in the seventeenth and eighteenth centuries is classic in the sense that it was the original and the dominant meaning of truth held in common by Baptists in their formative centuries. It is classic too in the sense that it was not handed down from a center of scholarship or by a prince of the church but literally bubbled up from the bottoms of history. It arose simply, not from the elite, but out of the freedom of the plain people called "Baptists." Among the Baptists there were no special classes. Truth belonged to the whole of God's family. All had equal access to it. What could be more characteristically or classically Baptist?

The historic Baptist view of truth is also classic in the sense that without the notion of personal truth the Baptist way would be meaningless and without history. For the pilgrimage to truth (along with the stories of faith and freedom) was an essential part of the paradigm or the standard case of what it meant to be a Baptist in the seventeenth and eighteenth centuries. It helped set the meaning, as well as the direction, for subsequent Baptist life and thought in the nineteenth and twentieth centuries. It is still at work giving definition to things genuinely Baptist. And, it will always be significant for being a Baptist. This broad, enduring, and extraordinary influence over the 400 years of Baptist history is demonstrable and visible.

Consider too these reasons for thinking of the Baptist legacy of truth as classic. The notion of personal truth reflects a heritage from an older native reform and evangelical spirit derived from Anabaptism, Puritanism, Separatism, and the thought of John Calvin in the sixteenth century. And, although the Baptist approach to truth appeared in the modern era, it was not shaped by modern but by classic biblical patterns of thought. Baptists in the seventeenth and eighteenth centuries thought like the prophets and the apostles, in ways used by Hosea, Jesus, Paul, and John, not in the manner of Descartes, Newton, Hume, and Kant—the contemporaries of the Baptists. That is to say, English and American Baptists took to heart the gospel story and the normative words of Jesus, "I am the truth," and they modeled a realistic and a personalistic approach to truth after them.

In keeping with this understanding of "classic," the book adopts a classic way of understanding the Baptist heritage of personal truth. It attends to the fundamental kind of truth that sprang up in the everyday life-worlds of the plain people called "Baptists," who were ultimately concerned with "the grace and truth that came through Jesus Christ," a concern tempered by the spirit of the radical reformation and a fierce loyalty to biblical and gospel ways of thinking.

AN EXISTENTIAL ENGAGEMENT

My purpose for writing this book is more complicated than that of telling the historical origins of the Baptist heritage and of philosophically analyzing its significant patterns and its evident continuity of basic tenets. I write with an existential purpose in mind. The book is an active engagement of the roots of truth in the biblical and the historic Baptist soul so as not only to preserve but to restore and to appropriate the personal truth that is the essence and the dynamic of Baptist identity.

Discussions of Baptist identity ordinarily, and rightly, focus upon such core values as those of believer's baptism, religious liberty, confessionalism, the gathered church, soul-competency, separation of church and state, local church autonomy, scriptural authority, and diversity. But something new and out of the ordinary must be said. This does not mean that we are to abandon the historic ways of expressing Baptist identity, but only that we must enlarge our analysis and make it complete.

The facts uncovered by the book show that the identity of Baptists, in the soul of it, is a pilgrimage to personal truth, a persistent effort to enter into a face-to-face fellowship with truth as it really is. The facts further show that the passion for personal truth is not only the essence of Baptist identity but the dynamic that establishes what Baptists do, what they believe, and what they think. It is the purpose or motive of Baptist life and thought. In fact, all that is uniquely Baptist appears to flow from the attunement to personal truth.

Now is a special moment of history for those of us who are Baptists. It is a moment of uncertainty and doubt, one characterized by conflicting feelings and multiple views of the Baptist way. It is also at once a moment of tragedy and hope. On the one hand, we find ourselves not only in a painful transitional stage, but at a point of history in which we are divided on the issue of Baptist identity and are tragically vulnerable. What is unique about Baptist identity could be permanently injured or even lost. On the other hand, we are entering an age of reconstruction in Baptist life and thought. Fresh beginnings and horizons of hope beckon us into new ways of being Baptist.

Such special moments of history, if they are to avoid oscillation between extremes, must seek truth in its depth. But we Baptists have largely lost or covered over our rich heritage of truth. At best, in matters of truth, we appear to live "on the perfume of an empty vase."

What we need is a fresh exposure of our total life and entire thought—our full being, mark you—to the forgotten heart of the classic Baptist heritage as a point of healing and as a place of beginning. It is only by acting as if our legacy were significant, flinging ourselves upon "the truth as it is in Jesus," in the faith that God keeps the good wine until the last, that we can come to that triumphant assurance that we live in truth everlasting. If we do not earnestly set out to find truth right now, where we are, if we do not begin to find it here, we undoubtedly will not find it hereafter. The mere lapse of time cannot lead us to truth. Truth is not in another world, or in another time, from this. It dwells among us in the present, and our distance from it is measured only in terms of faith or its lack. If we put off truth to a future time, if we have only a nostalgia for the past, or if we put off truth to the hereafter, then truth becomes for us an ideal rather than a reality, which everyone honors, and no one attains.

My hope is that Baptists of all persuasions—of the right, the left, and the middle—will celebrate the Baptist heritage of personal truth and fully restore the original Baptist identity and integrity. If we would but establish the classic paradigm as a basis for the full restoration of the Baptist way, if we would but remember and tell our rich heritage of truth, and in remembering and in telling celebrate the personal heart, as well as the dynamic, of our faith and practice, then we could see individuals and churches transformed, the modern and the postmodern worlds better engaged by the Baptist witness to the gospel, our denominational life renewed, and an increased ecumenical participation in the greater Christian community.

We could see one thing more. We could see the books on Baptists rewritten. Across the decades, if not the centuries, the books on Baptist identity and integrity have centered upon events, persons, and movements, as well as more refined ideas of Baptist faith and practice, usually adopting a model of intellectual and institutional progress showing how Baptist distinctives were progressively refined. But the traditional approach found in these books has failed to understand, or even to recognize, the view of truth that is the soul of the Baptist story.

No moral outrage at the failure of the traditional approach to Baptist identity and integrity can be found in this book. What can be found is rather a presentation of the classic disciplines of truth that have profoundly shaped Baptists, along with the hope that future books on Baptist history and theology be written within a larger perspective than that of a study of the organizations, doctrines, agendas, constituencies, and social contexts of Baptists. If the historic and biblical soul of Baptists is that of an ultimate concern for personal truth, and if a holistic approach to history and theology is to be achieved, it is necessary to make Baptist identity and integrity intelligible by an inclusion of the classic view of truth in books on Baptist history and theology.

This book also argues that a chapter should be added to the philosophy books (and those of intellectual history) on the modern era of thought which omit a study of the Baptist contribution to a discovery of the true nature of things. There is a distinctive view of truth forwarded by Baptists in the modern world. It is that of gospel realism and personalism, an approach to truth radically distinct from that of rationalism, empiricism, phenomenalism, the scientific method, and the objective logics of modern thought, and it ought no longer be ignored.

AN ESTABLISHMENT OF THE ORIGINAL TEXT

If the classic Baptist story of truth is to be told in its fullest sense, the book cannot confine itself to historical narrative and philosophical analysis, or to an existential engagement of the classic soul. Nor can it confine itself to the lines of evidence that converge from these sources. If the classic story is to be told in its fullest sense, the book must establish the original text of truth used by English and American Baptists in the seventeenth and eighteenth centuries. After all, the classic Baptist heritage of personal truth stands or falls with the tie that binds it to its unique documentary origin. And, when everything is considered, the duty of those of us who would understand the classic Baptist way of truth is to give an active ear to the Baptists themselves, to their script of truth, not to our script, but to the body of literature current in the formative centuries of the Baptist way of truth. We are required to listen, just listen, to the actual voices of the faces covered with grayish hair, hoary voices that tell of a personal kind of truth that can be held in our hands.

As a first step in creating, or recreating, the original text of truth, and in listening to that text, the book presents a comprehensive set of footnotes. The heavy documentation should enable the reader to trace accurately the sources of hard evidence and the flow of the arguments upon which the construction of the text is based. It should also facilitate a radical hearing of the full text and a refusal to go beyond the only data available.

The second step in creating the original text is a bibliographic one. The bibliographic information in the footnotes at the end of the book provides readers with ready access to all the sources used in the book, and a select bibliography found at the end of the book offers a strategic window into those key documents in which Baptists most rigorously composed the original score of truth. Where a proper hearing of this score takes place, understanding becomes possible.

The third step in creating the original text of truth is that of analysis and commentary. The book delineates the ideas and the meanings, it crafts the systems and the inherent order, and it traces the stages of development that distinctively shape the classic text.

The fourth step in creating the original text is that of the use of quotations. The quotations in the book actually serve a twofold purpose. They objectively create the original factual base of the classic Baptist approach to personal truth. They also create understanding. They enable us to come into contact with the actual thinking of the Baptists and to feel their heartbeats. By listening, by simply listening, to the lost and the neglected words and meanings that constitute the original text of truth, the ancient Baptists can be heard to speak, and in their speaking we are led back to the center of the classic heritage, to the historical drama of personal truth, and we understand.

A CONFESSIONAL RECITAL

These four steps, taken together with a fifth step, that of the use of the historical present tense, should help us construct the text of truth current among English and American Baptists in the seventeenth and eighteenth centuries. The reader will note that in the book the past tense is used to refer to completed events in Baptist history, but, when references are made to the historic positions found within the extant writings of the classic Baptist heritage, then use is made of the historical present. The historical present, in fact, is the verb tense most often used in the book.

Five reasons require the use of the historical present, all of them tied to the creation of the original text of truth, and, in addition, absolutely vital for a confessional recital of the classic Baptist heritage in the present.

First, the book tells a story and expounds its meaning, ever mindful that the classic heritage derives from a definite historical past and therefore stands in historical relation to that past. Second, the book is much more than the establishing of how things once were. It is a living, personal encounter with the original text. It is an act of fellowship or an act of personal communion with our Baptist forbearers who, as our friends and fellow pilgrims, speak to us even now of the historic origin of their encounter with personal truth and who reach out to us in dialogue in the present. Third, the book recognizes that the past and the present character of the classic Baptist heritage are necessarily connected. The present presupposes the past and is known in it; but the past is fulfilled and communicates itself only in the present. Perhaps it would be more accurate to say that, in the living Baptist legacy, the past and the present are a single process.

Fourth, to speak of a causal and chronological sequence of events requires the use of the past tense—"A caused B" or "B was caused by A." But to speak of acts of reasoning, of implication and inference, to speak of ideas and their relations, in the original text requires the use of the present tense—"A causes B" or "B follows from A." And, if "B follows from A" in the logical or rational sense, even though first happening in the past, it follows always and is always present, a fact that demands the use of the historical present. The historical present, indeed, is peculiarly suited to express the ideas that constitute the Baptist heritage of truth. Fifth, the interpretive task of the book includes an account of that matchless truth which is a series of concrete events that have faces, names, and stories—human and divine—events leading backward to the biblical and the historical origins of the classic Baptist heritage and forward to its personal understanding in the contemporary world, a truth that in matters of Baptist identity and integrity is wrought for all time and therefore always present.

In summary, to conceive of the book as primarily a series of ideas arranged systematically and according to their historical development is to miss the point of it all. The historical present should help us get the point. The book is a confessional recital of the classic text of truth and of the living Baptist heritage of personal truth in the present time.

Preface and Acknowledgments

A PERSONAL PILGRIMAGE

Finally, there is a personal element to my writing of this book. In the telling of the classic Baptist story of truth, the lines of my Baptist heritage have fallen to me in pleasant places; my heritage is beautiful to me—to this fact the book witnesses. The book is, as it were, my confession that I am by conviction and by choice a Baptist. It is my affirmation of the classic heritage in which I stand together with other Baptists in the family of God and with our forbearers. The Baptist heritage faithfully holds a concretely personal truth in trust for us. This book is an acceptance of that trust, a promise made to secure against the loss of the Baptist legacy, a guarantee to retell the sacred story once told, a surety to free the Baptist tradition to preach its own sermon, an invitation to Baptists of all persuasions to celebrate together our historic roots, unique identity, and precious integrity in the churches and in the contemporary world.

Often I think that the book is my thinking and my "faithing" aloud with persons in the world I dearly love. Biff Mauldin, my life companion and the wind beneath my wings, is love, grace, and truth incarnate. In life and in language, with the telling of our shared story, she knows instinctively that truth is concretely personal. She is one of the best embodiments of the classic Baptist spirit and story of personal truth that I know.

Linda (Mauldin), Greg, Matthew, and Michael Burks have contributed to the writing of this book, not by their support alone, though such has been considerable, but by their lives which mingle truth, love, and grace in a way understood by classic Baptists. They have been crucial partners who stood by me in my pilgrimage to truth and who encouraged me in those moments of doubt understood only by someone who has undertaken a task of this type. Robert, Barbara, and Anthony Mauldin have played a substantial role in the writing of this book. In act and in thought they have blended together faith and scientific inquiry, tempered it all with love, and offered help of a personalistic nature. Other members of my family—Frank and Louise Mauldin, Susie Elizabeth Rector, Thomas John and Pearl Ethel Wilson, and Patricia, Gary, Kent, Paula, and Austin Middleton—have also assisted me and shared abundant love throughout the course of my pilgrimage to truth.

Clyde Majors and Wallace Roark of Howard Payne University and Dan Cochran of Southwest Baptist University (Missouri), faithful friends, classic Baptists, and professors of Philosophy and Religion, carefully criticized the manuscript, expanded my understanding of truth, and offered heartfelt support throughout the whole of my pilgrimage to truth. Clyde, my brother, assisted me in understanding the dynamic, transformative qualities of truth. Dan, whose game is the unreasonable sport of golf, introduced me to reasonableness as a category in seventeenth-century thought and initially defined it for me. Wallace, a fellow Oklahoman, deepened my comprehension of uniqueness by his reflection on the topic, but most of all by his singular way of being-in-the-world. Dock Adams of The University of Tennessee at Martin and John Newport of Southwestern Baptist Theological Seminary, longtime friends and professors of Philosophy of Religion and Literature, have often dialogued with me on the notion of truth. Their insights have been essential to the writing of this book.

The staffs of three libraries assisted in the research for this study. Appreciation is expressed to the outstanding people in the former Historical Commission of the Southern Baptist Convention, particularly Bill Summers and Pat Brown, in Regent's Park College, Oxford University, and in Southwestern Baptist Theological Seminary, especially Myrta Garrett. A faculty research grant from The University of Tennessee at Martin, Phil Miller (director of research) and A. L. Addington (academic vice-chancellor), greatly helped at one point of my research. Choong Kim, Professor of Anthropology at The University of Tennessee at Martin, gave timely advice and encouragement.

Appreciation is expressed for the excellent editorial assistance of the staff of Providence House Publishers. Of particular help was Charles W. Deweese, Director of Denominational and Academic Publishing, who expedited the completion of this volume by painstakingly editing the manuscript, ever attentive to subject matter and sensitive to style. Thanks are also due Andrew B. Miller, President and Publisher of Providence House Publishers, for founding a press dedicated to the preservation and the enrichment of the biblical and the historic heritage of Baptist life and thought.

Gratitude is expressed as well to the editors of the journals who published my early writings on Baptists and truth—Watson E. Mills, John Briggs, and William R. Millar: "A Notion of Truth among Seventeenth-Century English Baptists," *Perspectives in Religious Studies* 18 (spring, 1991): 39–57; "Truth, Heritage, and Eighteenth-Century English Baptists," *The Baptist Quarterly* 35 (January 1994): 211–28; "A Notion of Truth among Seventeenth-Century Baptists in America," *The American Baptist Quarterly* 14 (September 1995): 270–87; and *The Wicket-Gate* (1993–1995).

Part One

THE SHAPE OF TRUTH

AN OVERVIEW

Part One—"The Shape of Truth"—identifies two essentials that constitute the classic heritage of personal truth fashioned by English and American Baptists in the seventeenth and eighteenth centuries: first, it identifies the given of personal truth upon which the classic truth-theory operates; second, it identifies the dynamics used in the exposition of the meaning of the given. Both essentials coalesce in the determination of the shape of truth.

Chapter One—"The Texture of Truth"—introduces the fundamentals, the categories, and the relations that make up the texture of the given and the dynamics of truth. It argues that English and American Baptists in the classic heritage think of truth as incredibly concrete and personal—as "the truth as it is in Jesus." Truth, which has a face, a name, a story, classic Baptists think, is the person of the Living God—Father, Son, Spirit—and of Jesus Christ, who together fellowship with persons face-to-face, name-to-name, story-to-story within the realism of the gospel of grace. It is the simple good story of characters and events moving within time and place, through conflict toward resolution, in the chapters of the biography of the Living God, a story constituted by the scriptures, abundant life, liberty, and reasonableness, a story told locally in terms of the happenings of contemporary life and language, which are not just vehicles that carry and communicate truths but necessary parts of truth itself.

Chapter One

THE TEXTURE OF TRUTH

That which first moved me to entreat and beseech sinners to be recon-
ciled with God was the consideration of God's mercy to my poor soul. I
have learned by the scriptures and experience, by an experimental
knowledge in my self, by a way that appeals to a good understanding and
good evidence, and by the Spirit of God with my own spirit according to
the Scriptures.

Obadiah Holmes, *"On My Life,"* 1675

A CONSIDERABLE REVOLUTION

A historical revolt of considerable proportions shaped the classic heritage of personal truth among English and American Baptists in the seventeenth and eighteenth centuries. At the center of the revolt was a hunger for a new thing, an eager outreaching of the soul for roots or origins, a longing for something real, basic, substantial, primordial. At the center of the revolt was a passion for truth itself.

Baptists sought to satisfy their passion for truth itself with the reform of the truths of Christianity. In this assumption, as well as in history, they carried forward "the idea of the Reformation to the furtherest issue," and are not unfairly described by H. Wheeler Robinson of Oxford University as "the Protestant of the Protestants."[1] Christopher Blackwood, a pastor of the Baptist congregation at Kent in the seventeenth century, characterizes the quest of the Baptists as a desire for "a thorow Reformation, having formerly seen the mischiefs of half Reformation."[2]

Baptists also sought to satisfy their passion for truth itself with the restoration of the truths in the primitive pattern of the New Testament. Without tarrying for any, they championed such views as believer's baptism and religious liberty for all, formed gathered churches, and in many points of faith, order, and worship restored the purity of the early Christian churches.

But the reformation of the truths of the present day and the restoration of the truths of a past age could not satisfy the deeply disquieting passion of English and American Baptists for truth itself. Truths, after all, are not truth. A body of truths of which a person might otherwise be ignorant is not the same as the living tissue of reality.

The only thing that could satisfy the passion of English and American Baptists was a revolutionary encounter with the primary reality which produces Christianity but is not produced by it. The only thing that could satisfy their passion was that bedrock truth which undergirds not only the New Testament churches but the reformed and the restored churches at all times and in all stages of reformation and restoration. That is to say, the only thing that could satisfy their passion was a radical exposure of their total life and thought to the "grace and truth [that] came through Jesus Christ."[3]

AN INCREDIBLY PERSONAL AND CONCRETE TRUTH

In their revolutionary engagement of the original "truth as it is in Jesus," the Baptists of England and America discovered an extraordinary thing: an incredibly personal and concrete truth fellowshiped with them. They could reach out and touch it, and hold the definite, dynamic, energetic truth in their hands. Truth itself, classic Baptists found, is the tangibly real, substantial good story of particular characters and specific events moving within time and place and through conflict to resolution. It is someone real, not something true. It is composed of faces, human and divine, that have names and that act and speak within the intimacy of personal relationships fashioned by the historical fabric of the gospel story.

What classic Baptists discovered and declared in their considerable revolution was that truth, which has a name, a face, a story, is the person of the Living God—Father, Son, Spirit—and of Jesus Christ, who together fellowship with persons face-to-face, name-to-name, story-to-story within the realism of the gospel.

The essential core, the deep-down bone marrow, of truth is there, just there, in a holy fellowship in which Jesus Christ and the Living God surround faithful persons behind and before, and lay holy hands upon them,[4] and there too the relation of persons of faith to truth, their participation in it, finally their unity with it, when in the grace and the wonder of being made whole by the gospel of the twiceborn they lay their hands upon the person of Jesus Christ and the person of the Living God. All understanding of truth begins and ends with persons and presence, with meeting and mutuality, with grace and truth—all sound understanding, that is.

The earthy texture of the personal truth found by Baptists is astonishing. Truth begins and unfolds at those points in time where "truth and grace meet, and kiss each other."[5] It occurs at the special places in the world set by the "simplicity of the gospel."[6] It takes place in the lives of singular people and forms the unique events in the chapters in the biography of God.[7] In the words of The Geneva Bible, the scriptures used by the earliest Baptists, truth is the drama of John 3:16, the truth in miniature: "For God so loved the world, that he hath given his only begotten Sonne, that whosoever believeth in him, should not perish, but have everlasting life."[8]

In matters of truth, the datum for understanding is the actual world, including persons and their relationships in the life-world. But in the history of western thought, be it theological, philosophical, or scientific, thinkers have often found it difficult to present a general evaluation of truth which does include the personal in its historical and localized character, in its singularity that cannot be universalized, nor grasped in abstractions. Frequently, the concretely personal is completely omitted or else the personal dimension is reduced to another essence which appears to be more basic—the implication being that it cannot be known.

The Baptists of the classic heritage argue the counterthesis, namely, that the personal cannot be omitted or understood as derivative from something more basic. In fact, they opt, truth is best understood in terms of real persons and actual relationships.

The long history of thinking about truth in the western tradition contains general agreement on five essentials which characterize the nature of truth, five essentials far off the mark according to classic Baptists. First, western thinkers have agreed that truth is about something mental. It is about ideas. Second, they have rejected the claim that the localized historical event—the singular or the unique individual—is the subject or the object of truth. Only universal truths count. "Why only here, why not also there, why not in all history?" has been their byword.

Third, western thinkers have agreed that truth is about ideas expressed in statement form—in a sentence in which the subject is affirmed or denied by the predicate. Fourth, whether a universal idea in statement form is thought to correspond to reality, to cohere with it, or to participate in reality, western thinkers have traditionally concurred that the truth of an idea depends on its conformity to what is actually the case. So, whenever they ask about the truth of an assertion, they ask whether or not the statement that makes a truth-claim conforms to reality. In other words, they ask about how thinking or knowing is related to being.

Fifth, western thinkers have commonly asserted that truth-claims must be tested, although bitter battles have been fought between rival tests of truth. Sometimes it has been a three-sided contest among the correspondence, coherence, and pragmatic tests, but more commonly it settles down to a conflict between the traditional tests of correspondence and coherence. The correspondence test holds that a statement is true if it agrees (corresponds) with the fact, reality, object, or state of affairs described in the statement. A whole class of truth-claims are easily checked in this way. "The apple is sweet." Taste it. "Oklahoma is south of Kansas." Locate its geographical position. "Rolston's life has been changed." Look and see.

The test of coherence affirms that a statement is true if it is logically consistent as well as ties in with other true statements—true statements stick together or relate to each other in a synoptic way (each implies the other). This is a test used every day. "Wray has been telling lies about you." Harmonize the report with your friend's life of total honesty. "Christianity is superior to other religions." Ask if its principles make the most sense of life by providing the best synoptic vision of persons, the world, and God.

The Baptists of the classic heritage reject these five traditional ways of thinking about truth. They deny that truth is the conformity of well-verified statements to reality, whether the statements be demonstrated by the correspondence or the coherence test. Truth is not something people know or some universal truths they think about. It is rather the person of Jesus Christ and the person of the Living God—Father, Son, Spirit—in whom persons live, move, and have their being, and the only persons "fit to declare truth" are those "crucified by the power of truth."[9] Truth isn't true statements or universal truths about what's real. Truth is what's real, and what's real is singular persons, human and divine, in relation within the life-world of the gospel story of redemption, a concretely personal truth—"the truth as it is in Jesus."

THE FUNDAMENTALS OF TRUTH

In their equation of truth with the concretely personal "truth as it is in Jesus," classic Baptists identify two fundamentals of truth which make up the given structure of truth itself. The fundamentals always appear together as two foci in an ellipse, or as two partners in a conversation, together forming the essence of personal truth.

In their first fundamental of truth, classic Baptists equate truth with God. They affirm with their usual gospel simplicity and realism that truth is God—truth is what God is and does.

While classic Baptists may speak of truths and may be said to have or to know doctrinal truths, they witness that all truths are second-order phenomena, even pale abstractions, when seen against the primary given of truth, the historical evidence deposited in front of them, which is the person of God present and active in the gospel.

The second fundamental of truth centers upon a given state of character or a kind of life that has content and models reality, and does so more ably than a true statement. Classic Baptists claim that persons bear the original image of God and the recreated image of Jesus Christ, hence, the second fundamental of truth: persons can be and do the truth—persons model or participate in the truth that God is and does.

Classic Baptists variously unpack the meaning of the fundamentals of truth, but note three common ways of spelling out their meaning: (1) the Christological expressions of the fundamentals by the English Baptist Paul Hobson; (2) the experimental orientation of Isaac Backus, Jonathan Maxcy, and other American Baptists; and (3) the trinitarian formulations of the gathered church of English-speaking people in Amsterdam.

The Enjoyment of the Living Christ

In the classic Baptist heritage of truth, the two fundamentals of personal truth, one a primary truth and the other a derived truth, are often expressed in a Christological way. For instance, heeding the kind of advice offered by the English Baptist Henry Haggar that "the saints ought to build

[upon] the Foundation of Christ,"[10] John Tombes of Leominster[11] gives a Christ-centered expression to the two fundamentals. Jesus Christ is "the personal truth," he says, and every believer is "a Microchristus, the Epitome of Christ Mystical."[12]

Another instance, one of the best in the Baptist heritage, is that of Paul Hobson, who founded an English Baptist church in Newcastle and who wrote *A Discoverie of Truth* (1647). Hobson turns the noun "Christ" into the verb "christed"—a move which enables him to speak of the two fundamentals in a verbal sense as "being christed with Christ." A spectator, he argues, knows the object at a distance or from without, but the Christian participates in an intimate approach of "the truth" to the soul. The Christian is literally "christed with Christ," and enjoys the Living Christ, Hobson insists, receiving not a Christ idea or a belief in Christ but rather the Real, Contemporary Christ, not second, but firsthand, which is the privilege of the saints, who know truth from falsehood, and that by living in "the truth."[13]

The modern mind often thinks of understanding and worship as two different things and of two worlds, one of reality and the other of a knowledge of reality. But Hobson, who typifies the approach of all the ancient Baptists, collapses the distinction between them, thinking instead of an existential unity in which there is no possible distinction.

"The truth is one," Hobson declares, "and never truly understood by any, till they be one with it."[14] He does not here suggest that truth is a set of true statements which possess a rational oneness and are known. He rather suggests that truth is primarily the substantially real person of Christ. It is derivatively a warm, personal communion with Christ, a deep familiarity with "the truth" who clutches the believer in truth to the divine bosom. The believer, Hobson witnesses, is made one with Christ, transformed into the very nature and glory of Christ, so that the "old creature is annihilated, and all turned into Christ." In this way the believer not only understands but has Christ, who works in the believer a life. With these words Hobson startles the modern mind and dislodges its separation of understanding and worship, as well as its dualism of reality and knowledge. For he holds that the believer "hath Christ," enjoying none other than the actual person of Christ, and in Christ has a true life.[15]

With a simplicity that befits the gospel, Hobson summarizes the two fundamentals of personal truth. Hobson says of the first fundamental: persons find Jesus Christ deposited in front of them, someone real set as the matchless truth, who is truth in three ways—"First, in that he is the cause declaring truth. Secondly, he is the object, or matter declared by truth. Thirdly, he is truth essentially."

Hobson says of the second fundamental: persons who are "christed with Christ" enjoy the truth in Christ who is all in all to them—"For we are by Christ, in Christ, carried out to Christ; he being the way to God; and the truth that discovers God; and also the life that carries you on, according to the truth discovered to God in that way."16

Paul Hobson's insights into truth reveal a universally telling trait among English and American Baptists in matters of truth. Classic Baptists are committed to gospel realism and display a genius for keeping their notion of truth subordinate to their gospel.

Whereas most systems of truth have to do with the verification of the contents of knowledge, the classic Baptist system addresses the historically localized meeting of truth and grace. Classic Baptists do not ask, "How can we know or verify what we believe?" They rather ask, "How can we be saved?" and "What are we to do, Lord?" They do not ask, "What is truth?" Instead they inquire, "Who is truth?"

Verified truths can be possessed and manipulated, for they are qualities of statements set by tests. But the truth that concerns classic Baptists is not of this abstract, fragmentary character. For them the Word is the true light that shines in the darkness, the Word that becomes flesh, full of grace and full of truth. In this light they are children of God, born not of man but of God, dwelling in the bosom of God, seeing the Father by the Son and through the Spirit, actually participating in the truth that is grace, modeling the truth that God is in their lives at this time and at this place. It's all so earthy and so characteristically Baptist!

Howsoever many the true statements, and all well verified, classic Baptists confess, they are all shams, perhaps lies, apart from Christ and Christlikeness. If persons are the children of God, nothing but the person of Christ satisfies them; no amount of truths, or no lack of errors, gives them truth. If they own a cup full of truths, and could drink it all, they should remain thirsty if they are not "christed with Christ." If persons fellowship with Christ, they are truth derivatively. If they break that fellowship, they are false, and the enemy, no matter how much they pretend to be the friends of truth by holding to truths. Persons need not run to this belief or that experience, to an idea there or a fact here, expecting to find truth in truths. Christ is present, a passionately pursuing love, the companion who walks them through in this world, the parent who welcomes them home—into the kitchen where the feast awaits, and who speaks to them at the kitchen table as beloved children.

Experimental Knowledge

A second way of understanding the two fundamentals of personal truth runs throughout the whole of the classic heritage but is best expressed by eighteenth-century American Baptists, who hold that truth is experimental knowledge.

Truth is not experiential, American Baptists say. It is not a subjective experience, one in a shell, so to speak, a private shell inside a person in which takes place a variety of experiences, all his or hers, even when the terms "spiritual" and "experience" are coupled together as "spiritual experience." American Baptists know that the reality of truth is too scandalously concrete and personal to be contained in experience. Truth, they witness, is rather an experimental acquaintance with a series of salvation events in life. It is participation in the historic, eventful gospel story that reveals itself, encompasses the person, and lifts him or her up into its grace.

Isaac Backus of Rhode Island, who long served a Separate Baptist church in Massachusetts, writes of the experimental quality of truth with these words: "Much of what I have written I knew experimentally before I did doctrinally. [I seek] the highest wisdom which is to know Jesus Christ and him crucified; and wherein things are taught in an experimental way."[17]

In a similar way, Abel Morgan of New Jersey, "not a custom divine, nor a leading-string divine, but a Bible divine," entreats Baptists not to look inside themselves for truth but to "have an experimental acquaintance with the operations of Divine truth upon [the heart]."[18] Likewise, William Straughton, pastor in South Carolina and New Jersey, exhorts Baptists to forsake their fascination "with systems which are at an infinite remove from the holiness of truth, [and] labor instead after an enlarged acquaintance with divine truth." Straughton does not counsel a subjective experience of Christ but urges an acquaintance with "the truth as it is in Jesus," a truth that is a localized historical event "of infinite moment,"[19] a decidedly incarnational kind of truth.

The meaning of the term "experimental knowledge" most often must be inferred from its uses in the writings of American Baptists, but Jonathan Maxcy, pastor of the First Baptist Church of Providence, as well as president of Rhode Island and South Carolina Colleges, sets forth an explicit, stipulative definition of its meaning. In a sermon preached at the dedication of a meetinghouse, Maxcy contends that the true believer does not base religion on conjecture and reason, or upon experience, but rather upon "a truth, a substance, a heart-felt reality, a heaven on earth." Believers, he thinks, "assent because they realize. They believe, because they feel. They rest assured, because they have the evidence of the internal senses."

Maxcy does not mean that religion begins subjectively with experiences, feelings, ideas, or beliefs. Truth's evidence, on the contrary, flows from particular happenings or localized events participated in or lived through, actual occurrences sensed in the world at this time and that place, such as those of the reality of vital piety, significant communion with God, and the operations of the Living God in regeneration, repentance, faith, and sanctification.

In other words, Maxcy thinks, truth emerges from "a cordial reception of the gospel," something realized, a reception wrought in the heart by the persuasion of God's Spirit, an acceptance of reality so evident that the believer "can no more doubt the reality of religion, than he can the existence of the material world," resting assured in "that ineffable resistless glory which beams from an uncorrupted heart." The believer, a new creation who appropriates the salvation events, is infused with action and virtue, with a constant obedience of all the affections to the will of God, and thereby is brought to "a particular knowledge of God, [being] formed into his likeness."[20]

Singularity has the highest truth credentials in the classic heritage. So Maxcy and American Baptists leave the abstractions and the universal statements to the devil. They reach out to an experimental knowledge of God's life embodied in the singular events of salvation. They measure truth by the reasons of the saved heart, by the happenings of redemption, by a life changed by Jesus Christ, not by the standards of a knowledge of true beliefs or by the presence of authentic experiences.

Undoubtedly, if salvation by grace through faith means anything, it means that an experimental knowledge saves persons. And, unless the eventful gospel is squeezed through a rationalistic grid, how can the point be missed that American Baptists consider truth to be the fellowship of persons with God, the Living Center, as well as with each other in the veracity of the primary and dramatic events of salvation?

The Three Witnesses and the New Creature

The first Baptists, the English-speaking people who formed a gathered church in Amsterdam, Holland, under the leadership of John Smyth and Thomas Helwys, dared a radical category shift in the understanding of truth when they protested the authority of the king and the Church of England and sought truth, not in civil or ecclesiastical traditions, but in the relationships of the three witnesses with the new creature.

Of the four confessions of faith[21] written by the first Baptists, the 1612–1614 confession states the two fundamentals of personal truth most succinctly and directly. The first draft, likely written by Smyth before his death in 1612, then revised by the Smyth party, uses trinitarian language in its bold assertion of the fundamentals.

It states: "the new creature which is begotten of God, needeth not the outward scriptures, creatures, or ordinances of the Church, to support or help them, seeing he hath three witnesses in himself, the Father, the Word, and the Holy Ghost: which are better than all scriptures or creatures whatsoever."

This most classic statement makes one point abundantly clear: the Baptists at Amsterdam are not so enchanted with truths that they lose their bearings and become indifferent to the two fundamentals of personal truth. Truth, they affirm, is not the same thing as the truths of the created world, the ordinances of the Church, or even the true statements of the scriptures. With this shrill and clear affirmation, stripped of all consolations and comforts that sustain them, without the support of true statements of any kind, secular or sacred, the first Baptists trust only the competent soul in relation to the Living God. No other kind of truth is accepted. They know that Jesus Christ dwells experimentally with or in relation to the believer. They know too that "the Father dwelleth with the Son, and the Holy Ghost likewise," and through Christ both the Father and the Spirit dwell with the believer as well.

The Baptists in the Smyth party underscore the two fundamentals of truth with great force by distinguishing an intimate acquaintance with Christ from a knowledge about Christ. On the one hand, they observe that a knowledge about or "the knowledge of Christ according to the flesh is of small profit, and the knowledge of Christ's genealogy, and history, is no other but that which the Devil hath as well if not better than any man living." On the other hand, they identify a form of knowledge called "the knowledge of Christ according to the Spirit," an I-thou sort of knowledge of Christ that is effectual for salvation, and one in which the believer models Christ, being grafted into Christ's life, miracles, doings, sufferings, death, burial, resurrection, ascension, and exaltation. In acquaintance with Christ, the Amsterdam Baptists know, "the new creature [who is] led into all truth by the Holy Ghost" participates in the reality of "God manifested in Father, Son, and Holy Ghost [who] is most true."[22]

The 1612–1614 confession of the Smyth party demonstrates several points which apply to the whole of the classic heritage. Classic Baptists are not rationalists who begin with the ideas of reason then end with universal truths in statement form. They are not empiricists, either, for whom knowledge begins with the data of experience then ends with general facts. Furthermore, they do not advocate the view that truth-claims relate to a timelessly mystical experience, or to a subjective experience of any kind, for that matter. Neither do Baptists favor a fideism in which basic assumptions and universal beliefs can be found in the religious belief system. Nor are they objectivists, subjectivists, absolutists, or relativists. They do not ask what is true in the objective and absolute sense, or what is subjectively and relatively certain; therefore, it is not what is in agreement with objective, absolute being that interests them, or what is in agreement with the matters that are subjectively, relatively meaningful for them.

If classic Baptists are to speak of truth at all, they cannot speak on the boundaries but at the center, not in weakness but in strength, and that means one thing only. They must speak of truth itself as the Living God and as an encounter with the Living God.

Classic Baptists satisfy their passion for truth itself, not with abstractions, but with the concretely personal reality of God the Father who is "the one, only living and true God," with God the Son, "full of Grace and Truth," who is "the truth," and with God the Holy Spirit who is "the Spirit of truth," satisfied that the Living God "be worshipped everywhere in Spirit, and in truth," satisfied as well that "the three witnesses, the Father, the Word, and the Holy Ghost are better than all scriptures, or creatures whatsoever."[23] Whoever affirms his or her rightful place in the personal reality of the Holy Trinity thereby models truth, literally participates in its substance, and bears the divine image of the Living God. Whoever negates his or her rightful place does not model the personal truth, and can be said to be false.

THE CATEGORIES OF TRUTH

The English and the American Baptists of the classic heritage are a plain people who passionately embrace "the simplicity of the gospel."[24] The truth they love arises from the common life of a people in fellowship with the Living God who speaks from the bottoms of history, not from the heights, and who acts decisively in the nitty-gritty of life rather than beyond and independent of it.

Classic Baptists, consequently, tease out the meaning of the two fundamentals of truth in five plainly wrapped categories which ultimately divide truth into its essential parts. They are mindful to understand the categories used in the analysis, the exposition, and the organization of truth, not by their own ways of thinking, but by gospel ways discovered in the life-world. Only the realistic personal truth of the gospel of grace sets the domain of truth. Only personal truth reveals the fundamentals and the categories, as well as the relations, of truth. No vacancy is left; no region escapes personal truth's simple embrace and initiative, or gracious disclosure.

When the writings of English and American Baptists in the seventeenth and eighteenth centuries are laid out systematically, basic categories of understanding appear, and continuity of tenets is evident. Significantly, so close is their agreement that one set of Baptist writings could be substituted for the other without difficulty or without suspicion that they had in fact been switched. When Baptists of the classic heritage divide the fundamentals of truth into their essential parts, they use common categories that recount the realities of the gospel. They say with one voice that, in the drama of the good story, truth is (1) Jesus Christ, (2) the Holy Trinity, (3) the Holy Scriptures, (4) Abundant Life and Liberty, and (5) Reasonableness.

The First Category: Truth Is Jesus Christ

Nowhere do the Baptists of the classic heritage more decidedly lash their categories to the personal domain of the gospel than in the statement of their first category wherein they identify truth with Jesus Christ.

Classic Baptists initially find themselves challenged in the present life-world by the person of Jesus Christ, who is Mediator, Prophet, Priest, and King. Then, in their response to Jesus Christ, they find themselves encountering, again in the life-world, not only their Saviour and Lord, but "the truth." For what is truth, they find, but Jesus Christ and the challenge-and-response movement between Christ and the believer? To speak of this as dialogue would be to confine challenge-and-response to speech and communication. It is important for classic Baptists that they begin not with speech and communication, even that of the good news, but with someone real, namely, with the infinite riches of the person of Jesus Christ in the good story.

In the classic heritage, English and American Baptists begin where the gospel begins—with their Saviour and Lord, hence, their first and primary category: truth is Jesus Christ, the truth, the truth exalted by God, the Truth of all truth, the truth who is in union with the Father and through the Spirit with the believer.

So firmly do classic Baptists hold to this first category of truth that they heartily accept Roger William's view that Christians may be utterly wrong in basic beliefs and may hold to error, yet no one should "imagine that they are not saved, [because] the Foundation of all foundations, the Cornerstone itselfe is the Lord Jesus alone, on whom all depends, persons, doctrines, practices."[25]

The Second Category: Truth Is the Holy Trinity

Among the categories that define what truth is and describe the texture of the fundamentals of truth, the category that equates truth with the Holy Trinity is pivotal. For this category not only establishes truth as concretely personal but saves classic Baptists from unfruitful views which picture truth as above the world or as identical with it. Classic Baptists know that truth is the person of the Living God who acts (who creates, redeems, reveals, guides, etc.) in the life-world. They know too that truth is the person of faith who personally encounters the Living God manifested as a Holy Trinity, the Son dwelling in the heart by faith, and the Father dwelling in the Son, and likewise the Holy Spirit. Truth's essence remains a mystery for classic Baptists, yet a mystery that reveals its meaning. Truth is known by them as the Triune God come near the person, shaping the person in the image of truth itself.

As a result of the gospel reality of God come near, classic Baptists word a second category of truth thusly: truth is the Holy Trinity—God the Father is the one only living and true God, God the Son is full of truth and grace, and God the Holy Spirit is the Spirit of truth, all in union with each other, related severally and together to those persons who voluntarily participate in the truth the Living God is and does.

The Third Category: Truth Is the Holy Scriptures

In the Baptist debate of 1668 on the American frontier, William Turner, a member of the church at Boston, speaks of his desire "to lie under the truth of God," that is, to abide by the truth of the scriptures.[26] Classic Baptists universally agree. They embrace the authority of the scriptures, for they think that truth is the Holy Scriptures.

Truth may be learned from reason and nature, classic Baptists hold, even a truth that subserves the knowledge of God, but an authentic participation in truth and a vital understanding of it in the life-world necessarily require that believers live and act within the personal framework of the words and the worlds of the divinely inspired scriptures. For, classic Baptists claim, the scriptures are God's actual address, the self-revealing thought and will of the Living God, not merely words about God, but the personal, real Word of the Living God established in the person of faith who existentially appropriates or lives under "the Holie Word off God" in the life-world.

Thus, the third category of truth: truth is the Holy Scriptures, the God-breathed scriptures of truth, the will and mind of God, already but not yet, in the process of becoming, ingrafted in the heart of the believer by the Living God.[27]

The Fourth Category: Truth Is Abundant Life and Liberty

In the gospel that sets their truth-theory, classic Baptists discover that truth is thoroughly practical by turn. Truth is who a person is and what a person does. It is how a person lives. It is a person's attunement or way of being-in-the-world. But truth is not just any way of being-in-the-world. Classic Baptists find that it is a particular kind of life, an eternal one.

Jesus Christ creates, and recreates, the person of faith as a new creature, whose interaction with "the truth," and thereby with the Holy Trinity, classic Baptists discover, shapes all subsequent actions and states of being. In the eternal life lodged only in the reality of the person of Jesus Christ, they find, truth appears in the person of faith as a lifework of faithfulness, hope, love, obedience, holiness, and freedom.

The person of faith does not first know truths and then apply them to life. Truth is not something a person knows or has. On the contrary, classic Baptists affirm, truth is an overflow of divine blessedness in life.[28] The person of faith is permeated and energized by the presence of Jesus Christ, enjoys an abundant life and liberty in union with the Holy Trinity, and in this overflow of divine blessedness in life is enabled to be and to do the truth—to practice the truth.

Without this practical attunement, personal truth remains incomplete. But when the believer is and does the truth, when he or she exists truthfully in the overflow of divine blessedness, building upon the foundation of Jesus Christ, the fruit of eternal life leaves behind the unmistakable taste of personal truth.

Classic Baptists, therefore, word a fourth category of truth this way: truth is abundant life and liberty, a walk in love with the Living God in the life-world, the practice of eternal life which enables a person of faith to be and to do the truth.

The Fifth Category: Truth Is Reasonableness

Classic Baptists, who hold that the personal structure of truth carries with it necessary outworkings in the understanding, forward the thesis that truth has a reasonable texture. When the person of faith is transformed, they argue, the whole person is transformed, including reason. God, not man, is the supreme rational agent. If human reason is to know truth, it must first be redeemed and sanctified then disciplined by the rationality of God, a divine process which enables sanctified reason to weigh evidence, to steadily increase in knowledge, and, most significantly, to think the mind of Christ and the mind of God. Sanctified reason initiates nothing. If the new being in Christ is to think the truth, he or she must participate in the rationality of the Living God who "persuades and satisfies the understanding."[29]

All human reasoning, classic Baptists witness, arises out of this participation in God's rationality, so they word a fifth category accordingly: truth is reasonableness, a truth that moves without violence, with a rational force in the reasonable soul enlightened by the Living God.[30]

THE RELATIONS OF TRUTH

In their classic reflections upon personal truth, Baptists do not think of truth as if it were horizontal, but spiral; it mounts and gathers within itself the multiplicity of fundamentals and categories into relations or bonds of truth. Personal truth, after all, is a highly textured, situated reality; there is one truth, which is manifold. Each of the fundamentals and the categories of personal truth is unique and has its own integrity, yet each is related to the other. Each relation also has its own integrity and definition, set by its own uniqueness; still, its meaning is linked to the fundamentals and the categories that comprise the relation. The unifying relations find their meaning in the diversity of the parts, and the diverse parts find their meaning in the unifying relations.

Since all things within the living, personal truth stand individually yet together, truth cannot be reduced to but one fundamental or single category which is separated from the others and elevated to the place of preeminence. For example, classic Baptists do not hold to biblicism, which elevates the scriptures to the place of final authority. Nor do they reduce truth to but one of the unifying relations between the categories, such as the relation of the Holy Spirit and the free, competent soul, that is, not without damage to the parts or the whole of truth, or their demise.

Classic Baptists rather think of truth holistically or contextually. They (1) fasten upon each unique fundamental and category in the fabric of truth, (2) identify the unifying relations which link one to another, (3) understand the ways in which the unifying relations interact, (4) relate all things to the personal, (5) and secure everything in the gospel.

In a discussion of the resolution of controversies, for instance, Thomas Grantham, a General Baptist from Lincolnshire, contends in 1663 that "amongst all men who pretend to own Christ, the only infallible and authoritative Judge of their Controversies about Religion is the LORD Himself, as he speaketh by his Spirit in the holy Scriptures; together with right Reason."[31] The same contextual approach to truth is illustrated by the 1675 testimonies of Obadiah Holmes, pastor at Newport, Rhode Island. Holmes writes of truth's essentials: "That which first moved me to entreat and beseech [sinners] to be reconciled to God was the consideration of God's mercy showed to my poor soul. I have learned by the scriptures and experience, by an experimental knowledge in my self, by a way that appeals to a good understanding and good evidence, and by the Spirit of God with my own spirit according to the Scriptures."[32]

A PASSION FOR TRUTH ITSELF

A consuming passion animates English and American Baptists of the classic heritage. There is a burning fire in their souls, and they are weary with holding it in, and they cannot. It is necessary, vital, an ardor for an end to falsehood, a fierce desire for the sole presence of the original truth itself. It is a passion for basic gospel reality.

In every feature of Baptist life, in speech and in bearing, the passionate desire for truth itself is not a longing for truths. It is an intense desire for the person and the presence of the Living God, for meeting and mutuality in the gospel story of Jesus Christ, for "the foundation of the apostles and prophets."[33] It is a craving for something basic, something originally understood at the frontier of what can be said, a yearning for the roots of veracity, simple integrity and honesty, for the primordial truth itself.

Let there be no mistake about the fact that classic Baptists are concerned with truths. Their care for truths runs deep, for they do not think of personal truth as a diffuse appreciation of revealed truth but as the concrete stance of the whole person before God. This necessarily includes doctrinal expressions and a study aimed at gaining truths. In point of fact, the Baptists, who form a significant part of the Protestant Reformation, strengthen the protest of evangelical Protestantism by their constant witness to such truths as believer's baptism, the gathered church, soul-competency, the autonomy of the local congregation, and the principle of religious liberty.

But, it must be asked, why is it that the deeper, more complete under-standing of these truths by classic Baptists does nothing to lessen their passion for truth or to dissolve their questions about truth? Why does their understanding of truths set them on a course to truth more madly ener-getic than before?

The answer of Baptists in the classic heritage is this: because truths cannot be identified with truth itself. Truths about Jesus Christ are not the same thing as the actual person of Jesus Christ. An intellectual assent to the truths of the scriptures does not measure up to the matchless glory of "the word of truth" living richly in the heart. The sweet savor of salvation is no true doctrine, but the lived reality of the new birth and eternal life.

True statements of faith and practice have their place in the pilgrimage to truth, of course. Classic Baptists, however, do not confuse true state-ments with their primal source, meaning, and value in gospel reality. They know that true statements terminate the search for truth, the very search for truth appearing as little more than an invitation to find true state-ments. Classic Baptists acknowledge a number of true statements. Still, this fact in no way keeps them from a pilgrimage to truth itself, to secure its meaning, to gain an approach to it, finally to open up truth itself. The personal truth of the gospel counts supremely. Only it is ultimate. Only it is finally real. Truth is a singular kind of truth, a reality set against all truths as their ultimate ground, for the claim to truth which is made here by the Baptists means truth primordially.

Classic Baptists display a particular genius in matters of truth. They are gospel realists who think of truth as concretely personal. For them truth does not arise from ways of knowing, out of epistemic starting-points, or from a cognitive grasping of truths. Baptists do not defend the thesis that the locus of truth is the statement, an experience, a belief, a doctrine, a judgment (whether objective or subjective), or a principle (whether absolute or relative). Truth is a concretely personal reality, not a mode of knowing. In fact, it is so real, so personal, and so concrete that it can only be described as "the truth as it is in Jesus."

Truth, which has a name, a face, a story, is the person of the Living God—Father, Son, Spirit—and of Jesus Christ, who together fellowship with persons face-to-face, name-to-name, story-to-story within the realism of the gospel of grace. It is the simple good story of characters and events moving within time and place, through conflict toward resolution, in the chapters of the Living God's biography, a story constituted by the scriptures, abundant life, liberty, and reasonableness, a story told locally in terms of the happenings of contemporary life and language, which are not just vehicles that carry and communicate truths but necessary parts of truth itself.

No truth but the concretely personal can be recognized, no other can be endured, lest classic Baptists deny the truth grasped in their hands, and justly hear the words of condemnation from their Saviour and Lord, "He who has seen me has seen the Father; how can you say, 'Show us the Father?'"[34]

A TIME OF AFFIRMATION
THE SEVENTEENTH CENTURY

AN OVERVIEW

Part Two—"A Time of Affirmation: The Seventeenth Century"—is a philosophical and a historical analysis, as well as a confessional recital of the original text, of the classic Baptist heritage of personal truth as it appears in the documents of the English and the American Baptists of the seventeenth century. In particular, it is an analysis of the fundamentals, categories, and relations of personal truth.

Chapter Two—"Christed with Christ: English Baptists I"—analyzes the manner in which English Baptists equate truth with Jesus Christ and the Living God. This chapter, just as the third one, draws materials from the writings of Particular and General Baptists, who at times disagree theologically about truths but agree concerning the nature of personal truth.

Chapter Three—"A Life Worthy of God: English Baptists II"—examines the ways in which English Baptists identify personal truth with the Holy Scriptures, abundant life, liberty, and reasonableness.

Chapter Four—"Experimental Acquaintance: American Baptists I"—traces the understanding of personal truth among Baptists in the American colonies, who hold that truth is Jesus Christ, the Holy Trinity, and the communion of the Living God and believers.

Chapter Five—"Walk According to Truth: American Baptists II"—explores the claim of American Baptists that personal truth is a practical way of existing: a walk in the truth of the Holy Scriptures, abundant life, liberty, and reasonableness.

Chapter Two

CHRISTED WITH CHRIST
ENGLISH BAPTISTS I

For the Scripture, which is the word of God, none can understand but
such that live in God, and so receive the knowledge of his mind, not from
the second, but first hand, which is the privilege of the saints, who know
truth from falsehood, and that by living in the truth.

Paul Hobson, *A Discoverie of Truth*, 1647

ALL WHO WOULD TRAVEL TOGETHER TO HEAVEN

In a sense, no doubt, the discovery of truth and its distinction from error have been the tasks of life and thought at all times. But this winnowing process is carried on more actively at certain times than at others. The periods of classical Greek philosophy, the Hebrew prophets, and the New Testament are cases in point. Another period of active winnowing is the seventeenth century.

The books on the seventeenth century say little, if anything, about the role of English (or American) Baptists in the separation of truth from error. The philosophy books rather speak of Rene Descartes and John Locke. The theology and the history books tell only of Baptist faith and practice. Yet, despite the silence of these books, English Baptists played a substantial part in the discovery and the declaration, according to their lights, of the nature of truth.

The substantial part played by English Baptists in the discovery and the declaration of truth lay in their equation of truth with the personal reality of the gospel. In the seventeenth century, the empiricists turned to experience for knowledge; the rationalists sought truths amidst ideas and by means of intuition and deduction, while the new science turned to experimentation. The General and the Particular Baptists in England, however, were enchanted with neither experiences nor ideas, and they didn't ply their course with scientific facts. Nothing can be true in any ultimate sense, for them, unless its meaning arises from an encounter with the personal truth of the Redeemer's kingdom, where "all who would travel together to heaven" shall come into the unity of the knowledge of Jesus Christ, unto the full stature of personal truth itself.

The confidence of English Baptists in personal truth was not born out of any conviction that they owned an absolute, objective knowledge of truth or a subjective certitude, albeit a relative one. They distinguished between knowing better and knowing worse, not between knowing absolutely and relatively, or between knowing objectively and subjectively, as did their modern counterparts. In pursuing the knowledge of truth they began, not with the utter ignorance of truth, but with a partial knowledge born of encounter. They began with a knowledge born of the vital fellowship of God and persons, a knowledge found only in Jesus Christ.

In the process of bringing their partial knowledge of personal truth to maturity, English Baptists understood that "the more dark and dangerous the ways be, the more necessary and needful will light be found of all that travel; so the more dark and dangerous the errors be, the more needful and profitable will truth be found of all who would travel together to heaven." They saw that dark and dangerous ways of error butted down upon their knowledge of truth, arresting its increased clarity and completeness. Still they remained confident that "those that have the truth, and those that would have the truth [should not] be afraid of error: seeing truth discovereth dark and dangerous ways of error, though abroad in open books, even as light discovereth dark and dangerous places, though abroad in open highways?"[1]

The confidence of English Baptists did not arise from some hitherto unsuspected reality. They knew that truth which had been with them from the beginning—the truth that is (1) the person of Jesus Christ and (2) the person of the Living God.

TRUTH IS IN JESUS CHRIST

English Baptists support the principle that nothing is understood "as it is in its selfe, unlesse it be apprehended by a light suitable to its selfe." If a white object is seen through a red tinted glass, Paul Hobson illustrates the principle, then the object appears as red and not as white, and that because of the light through which it is perceived. Likewise, when the Old Testament law is judged by the bare expressions of justice, "and not in the light of love, [it] appears rough and not lovely." But when the law is gathered up in Christ, it is seen as lovely.

When English Baptists apply this principle to the discernment of truth, they find two conditions to be essential for a proper understanding. First, they find that they do not see truth by a light other than that of truth itself. They "see truth in truth."[2] Second, English Baptists find that the only light suitable to truth, the only one that reveals and exalts truth, is that of Jesus Christ who is "the personal truth."[3] Believers know Christ, from Christ, who is the primary given and the light of truth, the Baptists discover, just as they "know God, from God, [and] live upon their being knowne" of Christ who is the true light that enlightens them, rather than living upon their knowing of Christ.[4]

With their minds fastened upon this cardinal yet scandalous trust in the singular light of Jesus Christ, who is both "the truth [and] the Word of truth," English Baptists first intend to build only upon Jesus Christ as the cornerstone of personal truth. Their prayer is that of Anselm: "I do not endeavor, O Lord, to penetrate Thy sublimity, for in no way do I compare my understanding with that; but I long to understand in some degree Thy truth."[5]

A second intention flows from the first. English Baptists fervently pray that God show them "how the Saints may build upon this Rock, Christ."[6] They long to know how the saints may enter into union with Jesus Christ and become Christlike:

> We speak now of a righteous spirit, a freed spirit, a spirit made one with Christ, a spirit overcome in the enjoyment of Christ's spirit, a spirit rapt up, overwhelmed by the sweet inflowings, so that by the very coming in and enjoyment of Christ, they are made one with Christ, transformed into the very nature and glory of Christ. So that all selfe is annihilated, and all

turned into Christ; Hee is removed from his former center, his owne bottom; there is a new ingrafting and being carried up into Christ, so that he is transformed unto the hidden, divine, superexcellent glory and riches and life of Christ, so as he is (as I may say) christed with Christ, made glory with the very glory of God and Christ, so that they not onely know in their understandings, but have, feel, and enjoy it, and it works in them a life, and fruit sutable to this glory and transformation.[7]

Three specific images of the meaning of the claim that truth is Jesus Christ and union with Christ surface in the documents of English Baptists in the seventeenth century. The images are those of (1) the resurrected Christ, (2) the actual rule of Christ, and (3) life in Christ.

The Resurrected Christ

The image of truth as the Resurrected or the Contemporary Christ appears scattered throughout the writings of English Baptists, but it appears with greatest force in the writings of John Smyth, 1607–1612. Smyth may even consciously make this image the center of his theology.[8] From his defense in 1609 of his Anabaptist convictions[9] to the 1612–1614 confession, the first draft likely that of Smyth, in which clearly one-fourth of the articles concern the work of the resurrected Christ,[10] Smyth acknowledges that Jesus Christ is "the truth and the true Son of the living God," who even now in this time and at that place reveals the nature of God and establishes the truthful relation of the Living God and believers.[11]

Smyth does not think of the resurrection of Christ as a relic of history locked in the past. He thinks that the real Christ is the risen Christ. He thinks too that the risen Christ is the indispensable center of personal truth. Indeed, the risen Christ, he maintains, is more indispensable than the incarnate and crucified Christ. He writes, "Christ Jesus, in His resurrection, ascension, and exaltation, is more and rather Lord and Christ, Saviour, annointed, and King, than in His humiliation, sufferings and death."

One reason for the preeminence of the resurrected Christ, Smyth argues, can be found in the fact that the end is more excellent than the means. In the case of Christ, it is demonstrably certain that Christ's sufferings were the means by which Christ entered into glory, the intended end. Another reason for the priority of the resurrected Christ is that the efficacy of Christ's resurrection in the new creature is more noble and excellent than the efficacy of Christ's death in the victory over sin, suffering, and death.[12] Furthermore, what is said of efficacy may be said of Christ's authority.

In the 1612–1614 confession, Smyth and the signatories repeatedly call attention to the risen Christ and to the hallowing of the resurrected life in the believer. They assert that Jesus Christ mediates the New Covenant and is the King, Priest, and Prophet. Furthermore, they claim, in the resurrected Christ believers are "made spiritual Kings, Priests, and Prophets, while in their preaching and ministry [believers] represent the ministry of Christ; who teacheth, baptiseth, and feedeth the regenerate, by the Spirit inwardly and invisibly." In other words, believers model the truth that the resurrected Christ is. So intimate the relationship of the resurrected Christ and believers that Smyth and the signatories of the 1612–1614 confession audaciously perceive that "the regenerate do sit together with Christ in heavenly places." They boldly think too that the relation of Christ and believers is like unto that of Christ and the Father—"they sit with Him in His throne as He sitteth with the Father in His throne."[13]

Smyth's image of the intimate relation between believers and the resurrected truth is one thing, the depths of intimacy imaged by him another, and it is his image of deep intimacy that is astonishing. Smyth does not advocate an experience of Christ, a Christ-mysticism, or an assent to truths about Christ, scriptural or doctrinal. Believers, he avers, encounter the Contemporary Christ, participate here and now in the person and the work of the Living Christ, and gain the knowledge of Christ according to the Spirit, which is to be actually, not figuratively, grafted to Christ's birth, life, miracles, doings, sufferings, death, burial, resurrection, ascension, and exaltation.[14] The gospel realism of the classic view could not be more evident. Truth is the Contemporary Christ, and believers model that truth.

The Actual Rule of Christ

Thomas Helwys agrees with John Smyth's understanding of truth as the person of Jesus Christ, but he describes the "truth as it is in Jesus" with the image of the actual rule of Christ in the Kingdom of God rather than with the image of the resurrected Christ. Jesus Christ, he observes, occupies a kingly office, along with the offices of prophet and priest. Christ, who is "the truth," is universally sovereign, actually rules in the hearts of persons of faith, who are heavenly citizens in the Kingdom of God, directly encountering "the truth" and possessing the competency to deal with "the truth" for themselves.

Upon his return from Amsterdam to England in 1612, Thomas Helwys published *A Short Declaration of the Mistery of Iniquity*. This polemical attack on the Anglican Church, and the book's defense of religious liberty for all, soon got Helwys into trouble. He wrote King James a note on the flyleaf and sent the book to him. Helwys was shortly in Newgate prison, where apparently he died in 1616. The note challenges,

> Heare O King, and dispise not ye counsell of ye poore, and let their complaints come before thee. The King is a mortall man, e not God therefore hath no power over ye immortal soules of his subjects, to make lawes e ordinances for them, and to set spiritual Lords over them. If the King have authority to make spiritual Lawes, then he is an immortal God and not a mortall man. O King, be not seduced by deceivers to sin so against God whome thou oughtest to obey.[15]

This personal word to the king dramatically rejects all interference in soulish decisions by the orthodoxies and the hierarchical structures centered in civil and church authorities, as well as summarizes Helwys' position in the 1612 book. But, more importantly for an analysis of his truth-theory, it supports the view that the radical heart of truth is found in the actual rule of Jesus Christ.

The king, Helwys opts, "hath no authority as a King but in earthly causes." Although the citizens of God's kingdom live in the world, only God in Christ has the right and the power to rule in heavenly concerns. John Smyth agrees. He thinks that the magistrate is not to interfere with religion or matters of conscience, to force individuals to this or that form of religion or doctrine, "but to leave Christian religion free to every man's conscience, for Christ only is the king, and lawgiver of the church and conscience."[16]

Jesus Christ is not only understood by Helwys to have the right and the power to rule, but to exercise in the present world the right and the power to rule. Helwys, along with the English people at Amsterdam in 1611, and Thomas Collier, the "Baptist apostle to the West," together argue that the only true kingdom is by nature a spiritual one, a kingdom founded upon the rule of Jesus Christ who is "TRUE GOD, and TRUE MAN," the Mediator, the Priest, the Prophet, and the King of all the saints. Thus, the saints in the spiritual kingdom, they infer, are beholden to no external authority, for they have "the truth." The saints "have CHRIST given them, with all the meanes off their salvation." The churches too have Christ given them, for every particular Church, and all the world, has Christ acting in the present, as a fact, genuinely and veritably given.[17] The conclusion is inescapable. Truth is Christ, and it is Christ's rule exercised among the saints in God's Kingdom.

Sometimes Christ rules in extraordinary ways, John Turner says, such as when God calls persons in their "misery and rudeness [commonness] by himselfe in a field alone, or a Vision in the night." At other times Christ rules in ordinary ways through the good times and the bad, and upon occasions of reading, study, prayer, preaching, and teaching.[18] But, whether in extraordinary or ordinary ways, Christ actually rules as the sovereign Lord in individuals and in the body of Christ. This rule, a most tangible reality, say Turner and Helwys, and English Baptists in general, is the personal truth.

In Christ

The most delightful of all English Baptist images which equate truth with Jesus Christ and with union with Christ is presented by Paul Hobson. In his exposition of John 14:6 ("I am the Truth"), Hobson advances the view that truth cannot be understood as general or universal, but only as singular and relational. Truth is the singular Jesus Christ in relation with singular persons in the life-world.

Hobson, a Christocentric thinker, as well as a personalist and a gospel realist, grounds his description of truth in its Christological modes, which are three in number.

First, Christ is "the cause declaring truth." Christ is "the way to walk in, a light of truth to discover the way, and a power to carry us on in the way." In fact, Christ alone "brings down life from God, and carries up the soule again to God."

Second, Christ is "the object, or matter declared by truth." The gospel offers "a full Christ, from a free God, to a nothing creature: in which tender, God is pleased to give downe life from himself, not onely to be held out to us but also to be revealed in us, really becomes life for us, to produce in us what in the Law is required of us."

Third, Christ is the indispensable quality of truth, that is, "truth essentially: For God was the Word and the Word was God."[19]

Building upon this Christocentric foundation, Hobson worries the question as to how believers can relate to the Christ who is the personal cause, object, and essence of truth. One way, he thinks, is for persons to live in Christ. Persons receive the knowledge of God's mind, not in a secondhand way, he observes, but firsthand, and that by living in truth. This enables them to distinguish truth from falsehood by means of an intimate acquaintance with Christ. Hobson doesn't equate firsthand truth with comprehension, or with an intellectual assent to the truths of God. He also explicitly says that truth cannot be equated with the natural light grasped by reason, with a knowledge gained from properly understanding the law, or with a notionary—a speculative and an imaginary—rather than a factual way of thinking. On the contrary, firsthand knowledge requires that persons initially be grasped or caught up in the bosom of God and thereby become intimately acquainted with God, living as friends of God.

With this idea of an appreciative form of knowledge squarely in mind, Hobson describes true knowledge as "a supernatural light set up in the soule by God; the life of which light hath his residence in God." True knowledge is not resident subjectively in the believer, or objectively outside, for that matter. It resides in a singular, relational way of being or existing in Christ. For it is the "DISCOVERIE OF CHRIST IN US."[20]

Hobson here pictures the relation of Christ and the Christian as that of an internal relationship, i.e., as a relation in which the terms related are affected or changed by the relation.[21] In Christ, the believer is transformed into the very nature and glory of Christ. Hobson does not use figurative or metaphorical language in making this assertion. He speaks descriptively. In the internal relation to Christ, the old self is "annihilated, and all turned into Christ; Hee is removed from his former center, his owne bottom; there is a new engrafting and being carried up into Christ, so that he is transformed into the hidden, divine, superexcellent glory and riches and life of Christ." The believer is in actuality made one with "the truth."[22]

The Contemporary Christ and Encounter

In the three images of truth, those of the resurrected Christ, the actual rule of Christ, and life in Christ, just as throughout the whole of their writings, English Baptists affirm that truth is the Contemporary Christ who encounters, rules, and indwells persons of faith. At the core of this affirmation is the profound conviction that the words of Jesus, recorded in the fourteenth chapter of John, reveal the heart of truth: "I [and none other] am the way, and the truth, and the life; I am in my Father, and you in me, and I in you." It is this radical affirmation of personalism coupled with gospel realism that establishes the only truth with which English Baptists deal—a truth unconditionally and necessarily that of an I-thou relationship.

WERE THAT TRUTH WERE UNDERSTOOD IN ITS CENTER

In the classic heritage, English Baptists plead with "all who would travel together to heaven" to respect the unique integrity of personal truth. Lawrence Clarkson, introduced to Baptist ways by Paul Hobson, voices the plea, "Were that Truth were understood in its Center, that Truth were apprehended in its Eliment."[23]

Something of truth's center and element is understood by English Baptists. And what they understand makes them not mere dissenters but mavericks. For they maintain that persons not only directly encounter the truth that is Jesus Christ but that they directly encounter the truth that is the Holy Trinity as well. "One of the glories of the Christian Religion," Baptists proclaim, is that "it came upon its own Piety and Wisdom; with no other force, but a Torrent of Arguments and Demonstrations of the Spirit,"[24] which establish that truth itself[25] is God, and that those persons who live in the Father, Son, and Spirit participate in "the one, only living and true God."[26]

A single world, not two worlds—one of the reality of God and the other of a knowledge of that reality—is engaged by English Baptists. They claim to encounter directly the reality of the Father through the Son and by the Spirit, and in this encounter they collapse the distinction between reality and knowledge. Truth, they opt, is encounter. English Baptists understand themselves to be children of God, already but not yet recreated in God's likeness. And as children, they understand that they share at present in the reality of the Father, Son, and Spirit, and shall in the future grow even more into that reality.[27]

English Baptists characteristically word their radical contention this way: "every person that is regenerate and risen again with Christ hath these witnesses in himself; for Christ doth dwell in his heart by faith; and the Father dwelleth with the Son; and the Holy Ghost likewise; and that the grace of our Lord Jesus Christ, and the love of God, and the fellowship of the Holy Ghost is with them."[28]

Clearly, for English Baptists, the personal characterizes truth. They think that truth is the Holy Trinity. They think too that truth is the direct access of persons of faith to the Father, the Son, and the Spirit. Truth is Immanuel—God with us—who is revealed in personal presence, in gracious communion with persons in the life-world of the gospel, as the Living God come near in person.

The particulars of this profoundly personal truth are variously expressed by English Baptists. Sometimes (1) they speak of truth with precepts about the being and the actions of God and persons. At other times (2) they note that truth has a revelatory essence and uncovers itself in nature, law, and redemption. At all times (3) they depict the truth of God as the reality of God.

The Being and the Actions of God and Persons

The English speaking people gathered at Amsterdam, who address their confessions[29] "to Al The Humble mynded which love the truth in simplicitie," defend the truth of God.[30] Their defense centers in several precepts or standard rules which define personal truth in terms of the being and the actions of God and persons.

"In the beginning God"—with this precept the Amsterdam Baptists begin their confessions both logically and chronologically, and with it in place they present systematically the story of faith in its particulars.[31] They do not begin with a creedal affirmation of true beliefs about God, but with a confessional witness to the primordial being (the existence) of the Triune God.

With the very first article of their very first confession (1609), they witness to the first and foundational precept of truth this way: "there is one God, the best, the highest, and the most glorious Creator and Preserver of all, Father, Son, and Holy Spirit,"[32] who is "most true"—the Father is the only true God, the Word is "the true Son of the living God," while the Holy Ghost is "the Spirit of truth [who] leadeth into all truth." Nowhere in the Amsterdam confessions, or throughout the whole of their writings, do English Baptists abrogate their witness to this precept and its strategic importance as the beginning-point of an understanding of truth. Everything begins, as well as ends, unfolds, and finds its meaning too, with the witness of Baptists to the being of the Living God, or not at all.

"In the beginning God created"—if truth is the being of the Holy Trinity, as the first precept holds, truth's expression (modality), and thus the basis for living and knowing the truth, is that of action—the second precept.

God's essence is incomprehensible and ineffable, a mystery, the Amsterdam Baptists insist. Yet, the saints are not without a witness to truth, for the mystery has a meaning. The hinder parts of God can be engaged in the titles, properties, and effects of God imprinted in the natural creature, and expressed in the Holy Scriptures.[33]

The chief expressions by which God is engaged, however, are the "THREE which beare record in heaven, the FATHER, the WORD, and the SPIRIT; and these THREE are one God" who acts in the events of creation, redemption, and providence. Because truth is seen in truth, the Amsterdam Baptists counsel, the only light finally suitable to the truth of God is that of the full range of actions performed by the Holy Trinity who creates all things, responds to the falling away from truth, makes persons "come to the knowledg off the truth," recreates them alive in Christ, guides them by the Spirit, and forms the saints into Godlikeness.[34]

If the truth of the three witnesses is to be encountered in actions, God must not only act, but persons too must act. Persons must embrace the actions of the Holy Trinity by "an assured understanding and knowledge of the heart, [one] obtained out of the Word of God, together with a hearty confidence in the only God," a faith that is a true, living, working faith through which persons come to a saving knowledge of God.[35]

"In the beginning God created the heavens and the earth"—the third precept of truth which informs the Amsterdam confessions speaks of the purpose of God's actions and establishes the verity of persons in that purpose. Baptists think that God acts with the intent that persons be formed in the image of truth itself or made in the likeness of God's attributes. The first Baptist confession (1609) states the third precept succinctly: "God has created and redeemed the human race to his own image, and has ordained all men to life."[36]

The affirmation of a privileged access to the truth of God—of a personal encounter of believers with the being and the actions of the Living God—inspired English Baptists throughout the passage of the seventeenth century. But, like many ideas of comparable historical influence, it is subject to variant interpretations. For instance, one twentieth-century commentator argues that, when the 1612–1614 confession speaks of the encounter of the new creature with the Holy Trinity, apart from any reliance upon the scriptures, ordinances, or creatures, it "endorses a subjectivity that later was harmful to General Baptists in England."[37] Another contends that the confession refers to an inner revelation which was unsuccessfully blended by the early Baptists with the written revelation.[38] Other commentators suggest that, when Smyth and his followers renounced their baptism and disbanded their church for over a year, they found that they were no worse off without the ordinances, creatures, or scriptures, while Smyth depended on the inner witness of the Spirit, being one step shy of Quakerism.

But, the question must be asked, do not these commentators confuse the personal with the subjective? Do not they also fail to distinguish the classic approach of Baptists from the dualism of the subject and the object (subjectivity and objectivity) found in seventeenth-century rationalism? Amsterdam Baptists conceive of personal truth as essentially relational, not as an inner witness, an inner light, a trinitarian mysticism, a spiritual experience, or any other form of subjectivism.

The Amsterdam Baptists, just as all classic Baptists, are gospel realists not dualists. They agree with the statement of Thomas Helwys that "Mens religion to God is betwixt God and themselves."[39] True religion, they discern, wears neither the face of a subjective happening in the believer nor that of an objective phenomenon occurring outside the believer. The Amsterdam Baptists know that true religion happens between God and persons, it being relational in essence, its existence that of a substantial divine-human fellowship, as is suitable to personal truth.

That Amsterdam Baptists conceive of truth as having a relational character is readily seen in their frequent use of narrative terms. In their four confessions (including that of 1612–1614) they tell a story with multiple references to characters, incidents, and plots, all of which serve to define the relationships at the heart of truth. They tell of real characters, those of God and Satan, of sinners and saints, and of Jesus, the Spirit, and the faithful. The Amsterdam Baptists relate these characters to a host of actual incidents: to the creation, the fall, the covenant, the Kingdom, providence, the cross, the resurrection, the ascension, Pentecost, the people of God, and the second coming. They are also mindful not to ignore the historic plots which integrate the story and give substance to its characters and incidents, and hence to its relationships. They tell of the conflict of good and evil and of the interplay of sin, salvation, and sanctification; they convey a sense of beginnings and endings, of key events too—the whole of redemptive history.[40]

Through their use of narrative terms, in their confessional telling of the old, old story of salvation, the point cannot be missed that the Amsterdam Baptists know only that truth which is the good story of God and persons in relation.

In their confessional statements, Amsterdam Baptists are not subjectivists (just as they are not objectivists). Subjectivism first splits asunder the subject and the object, the knower and the known. Then it begins the search for truth with the subject—with either the subject of the "I think" or of the "I experience." The locus of truth for subjectivism is thus the inner world of the thinker or the perceptions of the experiencer isolated from the world. Truth arises within the subject, as a subjective state, in assemblages of experiences or ideas, which somehow mirror or represent the world.

Unfortunately, subjectivism is forever strapped with an egocentric starting-point and the insurmountable difficulty of reconciling ideas and experiences with the actual world, which not so politely refuses to become either an idea or an experience. The world remains remote, unknown, and unknowable unless one collapses the distinction between ideas or experiences and the actual world.

But such a collapse is tantamount to idolatry, reducing the truth of God—the reality of the being and actions of God and persons—to ideas or experiences, abstractions all, a move the Amsterdam Baptists do not make. Truth is the concrete story of grace; the story of grace is the tangible truth—something real betwixt persons and the Living God, that says it all for the first Baptists at Amsterdam, and well too!

Revelation, Nature, Law, and Redemption

While the Amsterdam Baptists depict truth and its encounter with precepts about the being and the actions of the Living God, General Baptists, in their first confession representing more than one church, The Faith and Practice of Thirty Congregations (1651), use the language of revelation to describe truth and its encounter. Truth, the General Baptists assembled in the Midlands picture, uncovers itself to persons, enters into fellowship with them, both in the general revelation of nature and the moral law and in the redemptive events of special revelation.

English General Baptists invite all people to respond to the gracious revelation of God in nature and in redemption, and to be in God, for this is "the truth of the gospel [and] the knowledge of the truth [to which] the Father, the Word, and the holy Spirit bear record." They extend this invitation in their 1651 confession with the same spirit of humility which informs the whole of the classic Baptist heritage of truth:

> Loving Brethren, if we could have conveniently convayed this Copie unto your hands, before it went to the Press, doubtless we might have gained your Christian Advice and Assistance herein, which might have been very Beneficial to the Truth, wherein you are with us alike concerned and engaged; but by reason of the distance of place, and also

being unacquainted, hath hindred our sending; but we hope our forwardness herein will not be any hinderance to you for the future, to manifest your concurrence with us, so far as we own the Truth; for the preserving of our Union with God, and our Joy and Peace with each other, but the rather to give you occasion to make use of the Ability and Power God hath betrusted you with, for our Informations in what you judge is wanting, and for our further Confirmation and Encouragement in those things you approve of with us, have we published this ensuing Treatise; That so we may agree with love in peace and truth, by the Assistance of our blessed Lord and Saviour Jesus Christ.[41]

It is in the spirit of these words of modest invitation that General Baptists speak in their 1651 confession of the general and the special revelation of "the Truth," which is the Living God, infinite in power and wisdom, universal, invisible, eternal.[42]

On the one hand, General Baptists say, persons engage truth in general revelation.[43] God calls all persons to a serious consideration of the natural works of creation, which reflect God's handiwork. God calls them as well to reflection upon the moral law that declares the will of God to the conscience (e.g., the awareness that the consequences of sin are sorrow and death or that persons cannot save themselves). When persons search for truth in this general revelation, General Baptists hold, they come to a definite knowledge of God's attributes of wisdom and power, and of themselves, and thereby come into an engagement of the order of personal truth.

On the other hand, General Baptists attest that truth is encountered in the redemptive events of special revelation, in particular, those of Jesus Christ, the Holy Scriptures, and the gifts of the Spirit. Among these events, Jesus Christ plays a key role. For Christ, who is the "Apostle or Prophet of the Truth professed, or the true profession of Saints," is not only "the Lawmaker, but the Law giver to every man that liveth in the world, in that he giveth every man therein some measure of light."[44] Christ has this right to witness to truth, General Baptists reason, for Christ is the "Word of truth" who not only gives light to every person but is both the message and the matter or object illuminated, a personal reality who gives meaning and structure to the truth.[45]

In their analysis of the events of special revelation and their truth quotient, General Baptists, in the 1651 confession, introduce a time-factor. They contend that a serious consideration of truth involves truth now known and yet to be known.

Faithful persons know some truth now, in the present, where they are, their knowledge predicated upon a direct connection with God. General Baptists hold that the saints are in God, and participate in "the truth," which allows them to cultivate the infinite riches of an eternal life found in Jesus Christ. These treasures, given as gifts of God to individuals and to churches, empower the saints here and now to obey or believe in God's name. They also provide motives to help the saints live in a holy and a righteous way in this present world, to act out of love, and to do all to God's glory.[46]

Other truth is future. It is yet to be known, although the saints do know that when it occurs it too will be predicated upon the immediate relationship of the Living God and believers. The General Baptists declare that those believers who "serve the Lord with integrity of mind and spirit, improving their abilities and power, are not only called faithful Servants of the living God, but they have the promise of God to be intrusted with more of the manifestations of himself, which is called the misterie which hath bin hid from many ages, and generations, which the disobedient shall not injoy."[47]

The Reality of God

English Baptists at times witness to a truth that is the being, the actions, and the revelation of God. But their more common witness, which may well be the truth-vocation of English Baptists, is a ringing "Amen" to the reality of God. Truth, they witness in the whole of the rich confessional activity of the seventeenth century, is not truth about something but concerns someone. It cannot be reduced to ideas, to objects of knowledge, to saying "yes" to experiences, to true beliefs, or to statements and doctrines—all of which are mere things. Truth is rather someone real who has a biography or a story. Truth is the reality of God.

In each and every confession, English Baptists begin logically and, with but one exception, chronologically with an affirmation of the reality of God. For instance, the first article of the Midland Association Confession (1655) affirms: "We believe and profess, that there is only one true God, who is our God." While the initial witness of the Orthodox Creed (1679) is that "there is but one, only living and true God."

The one exception to this universal vocation of English Baptists appears to be that of the Second London Confession (1677) of Particular Baptists, which is based on the Westminster Confession of Presbyterians and Congregationalists. It does not begin with an "Amen" to the reality of God.

It rather begins chronologically with a statement on the scriptures: "The Holy Scripture is the only sufficient, certain, and infallible rule of all saving Knowledge, Faith, and Obedience"; it is the revelation committed unto writing.[48] With this statement, the Second London Confession, one of the most important of the Baptist confessions, appears to hold that the scriptures and the truths contained therein serve as truth's starting-point, if not its essence.

Hence, some twentieth-century commentators argue that for Particular Baptists the scriptures are "the only authoritative source of God's revealed truth."[49] But this view cannot be accepted. For it does not take into account the confession's personalism and its gospel realism, which together equate truth with the personal reality of God. Nor does it recognize that Particular Baptists hold to the priority of personal truth in all matters, including the truth of the scriptures. Moreover, it fails to distinguish the classic Baptist starting-point from that of modern rationalism.

With a history-changing move in the seventeenth century, the French philosopher Rene Descartes establishes epistemic maxims as the foundation for all truth-claims in the modern era. He begins the search for truth with first principles, reason, ideas, and the subject as thinker ("I think therefore I am"). Are Particular Baptists in the second of their London confessions making a similar move? Do they shift the logical starting-point of truth away from the primal ground of the reality of God and think of the scriptures as the rational, conceptual, logical, and sole starting-point of a knowledge of revealed truths? Are they substituting truths for truth, epistemology for ontology and theology, knowledge for reality, the text of the scriptures for the God of the scriptures?

The answer to these questions is clearly "no." Although they begin chronologically with a statement on the scriptures, Particular Baptists do not begin logically or in fact with a knowledge of truths, even those of the scriptures, but with the concretely personal truth. Two pieces of hard evidence show this to be the case, as well as demonstrate that the 1677 confession fully accords with the classic Baptist heritage.

First, consider the evidence which serves to establish the fact of an encounter with the reality of the person of God in nature (of a general revelation of God) apart from and prior to an engagement tied to special revelation and the written scriptures.

In the first paragraph of the confession's first chapter, Particular Baptists claim that "the light of Nature, and the works of Creation and

Providence do so far manifest the goodness, wisdom, and power of God," all qualities of the personal, "as to leave men unexcusable." In subsequent sections of the confession, they contend that general revelation requires not a noetic but a personal response to God who is "to be feared, loved, praised, called upon, trusted in, and served, with all the Heart, Soul, and Might."

The Particular Baptists assembled at London in 1677 are careful not to confuse general revelation with direct revelations, such as those claimed by Quakers and radical Anabaptists, or with a reliance upon human traditions, for example, in Roman Catholicism. But the evidence of their own words proves that they do not exclude the possibility of a general revelation decidedly personal in character. They do not claim that a saving knowledge of truth can be found in nature, it being reserved for the events of special revelation. However, they accept a general revelation independent of the scriptures, and it personal in its origin, in its substance, and in its appropriation. General revelation originates in the sovereign grace of a personal God. Its substance is that of personal attributes, such as goodness and wisdom. It requires a personal knowledge that arises from a personal response of the whole being to the initiative of a personal God in the natural world, a response eliciting fear, love, trust, and service, all dynamics distinctive of persons in relation.

The scriptures reveal many things, while nature but a few, but nature's role, though it be minimal, is crucial.[50] What is embraced in general revelation is God's reality, the presence of goodness, wisdom, and power, not a knowledge about God's moral and natural attributes. What is appropriated in a personal way is truth, not truths which speak of truth. What is revealed and appropriated is the reality that is truth, not reality and truth isolated from each other and in need of reconciliation, as if truth somehow must represent or mirror reality.

Second, and the more important piece of evidence, the London confession of 1677 repeatedly and rigorously upholds the priority of the domain of personal truth and that of the reality of God, as well as the primal God-person relationship, over the truth of the scriptures. It offers five specific reasons why personal truth is the absolute heart of truth, having priority in matters of revelation, including the truth of the Holy Scriptures.

Reason One: The Priority of the Sovereign God. The entirety of the Second London Confession supports the view that God's sovereignty extends to all things. So it comes as no surprise when the confession insists that the basis of scriptural truth lies in "the one, only living and true God." It makes the point sharply, "The Authority of the Holy Scripture for which it ought to be believed dependeth not upon the testimony of any man, or Church; but wholly upon God who is truth it self."[51]

Reason Two: The Priority of the Holy Spirit. Particular Baptists witness that the dialogue of the Holy Spirit with the human heart has priority over scriptural truth and is the personal starting-point of truth. Persons may be persuaded reasonably as to the truth of the scriptures, they testify, because of the incomparable excellencies of the contents of the scriptures, the efficacy of the doctrines, the majestic style, the coherence of all the parts, and the discovery of the only way of salvation. However, Particular Baptists confess in 1677, "our full perswasion, and assurance of the infallible truth, and divine authority thereof, is from the inward work of the Holy Spirit bearing witness by and with the Word in our Hearts."[52] John Smyth and Thomas Helwys could not have made the point any more forcefully.

Reason Three: The Priority of Revelation. Particular Baptists understand that revelation grounds the scriptures, not the reverse. They state, it "pleased the Lord to reveal himself [and to declare a] knowledge of God and His will, [then] afterward for the better preserving, and propagating of the Truth to commit the same unto writing, [for] those former ways of Gods revealing his will unto his people being now ceased."[53] Particular Baptists know that the scriptures necessarily preserve and propagate the revelation, but they know too that the scriptures are not intrinsically vital, nor do they establish the reality of God. Truth itself is in and of itself vibrantly alive; the revelation of the Living God precedes and vitalizes the God-breathed scriptures.

Reason Four: The Priority of God's Purpose. According to the Second London Confession, God's purpose gives meaning and definition to the scriptures. This purpose, part of God's intentionality and thus part of the truth of God, is to give that knowledge of God which is necessary for salvation or, in other words, to give "all saving Knowledge, Faith, and Obedience."[54] The scriptures originate in the holy, redemptive purpose of God, centered in Jesus Christ, the confession insists. They are also sustained by it. God's purpose has precedence in all things scriptural.

Reason Five: The Priority of Faith. Faithful relationships insure the truthfulness of scriptures. The second of the London confessions opts, by "faith a Christian believeth to be true, whatsoever is revealed in the Word; and so is enabled to cast his Soul upon the truth thus believed."[55]

Each of the five reasons taken separately has the force of argument, but the reasons taken together have great force. They effectively demonstrate that Particular Baptists, who begin the second of their London confessions chronologically with a statement about the scriptures, begin in fact and logically with the reality of God. With five substantial arguments, they witness that the person of the Holy Trinity in fellowship with persons of faith constitutes the truth that reveals itself and secures the truth of the scriptures. In this sure knowledge they are at one with all Baptists of the classic heritage who think of truth as the reality of God.

The Living God and Encounter

English Baptists witness to the truth that is the person of the Living God and the encounter of persons with the Father, the Son, and the Holy Spirit. In their unwavering affirmations of the being and actions, the revelation (general and special), and the reality of God, they with one voice confess their faith that truth is the Living God manifested in speaking and acting, by divine initiative, within the tangible life-world of persons. Truth is primordially a person addressing a person. As long as truth is about something, as long as it is truths about God, English Baptists know, it is not truth. Truth is the Living God: "I, and none other, am the Lord thy God."

DANDLED UPON THE KNEE OF CHRIST

"Christed with Christ"—these words sum up the whole of the seventeenth-century English Baptist claim that believers not only know the Lord and Saviour, Jesus Christ, and the Living God in the understanding, but have, feel, and enjoy them, and the enjoyment works a life in persons of faith. So intimate is their holy fellowship, that faithful persons can freely and with a childlike spirit and affection ask anything of God and approach into the very heart of God. They have propriety in Christ—in "the truth." They know that they are the children of God—of truth itself—and that as children they have "a principle from God, which qualifies them so, that they can stand for God." That is, they have "the truth of Christ in their hands."[56]

Or, in the words of Paul Hobson, "They are christed with Christ, one with Christ, suckt and drawne up into Christ and become friends of Christ—dandled upon the knee of Christ, hugged in sweet imbracements, refreshed by the kisses of the mouth of Christ, they shall sup with him, they shall lye with him, they shall live with him, they shall dye with him."[57]

Chapter Three

A LIFE WORTHY OF GOD
ENGLISH BAPTISTS II

*The earnest desire of my soule, and willingness of Spirit, [is] to give satis-
faction (so farre as God hath given me Light) to every just demand, both
for the vindicating of that truth wee desire to walke in, as also to satisfy
(if possibly by the Word of God I may) every man's Conscience.*

William Kiffin, *A Brief Demonstrance*, 1645

ON EARTH AS IN HEAVEN

The English Baptist identification of truth with God transforms the effec-
tive meaning of truth. Since truth is God, then it follows that truth for
a person consists in relating to God directly in the approach of God to
the human soul, modeling the truth that God is and does, uniting with God
in a person-to-person encounter in life. And, since the encounter with truth
takes place in life, it follows that truth is thoroughly practical. Truth is, in fact,
a certain kind of practice. It is a way of living that models the truth of God.

Hence, seventeenth-century English Baptists discover, truth is essentially "a life worthy of God,"[1] one that has content and competently models
the truth that God is and does. They do not find truth in the confused
wilderness of cathedrals made by human hands, nor in temples in heaven
above. English Baptists rather find it in a garden where God intimately
abides with the saints in life, where they are here and now, on earth,
making the nitty-gritty and the messiness of ordinary lives the heart of
truth. Paul Hobson depicts God in Christ and through the Spirit enclosing

the garden, filling its houses of living stones with the special love and power of Christ,[2] shaping all persons with sweet refreshings, admitting the saints to eternal life here in this world, empowering them to "live as saints, and trade as saints on earth as in heaven."[3]

The practice of "a life worthy of God," for English Baptists, has the clear shape of the life enjoyed by the twice-born children of God. Three realities, they say, comprise the practice of a worthy life and clearly define it. The modeling of truth is the practice of life in obedience to (1) the Holy Scriptures which are "able to make us wise unto salvation, through Faith in Christ Jesus, and [are] profitable for Doctrine, for reproof, for instruction in righteousness, that we may be perfect, thoroughly furnished unto all good works."[4] English Baptists also think that Jesus Christ lifts up the disciple into a new and a determinate way of being and acting, which can only be described as the practice of (2) abundant life and liberty. A final component which gives definition to the modeling of truth in life is that of (3) reasonableness. English Baptists hold that God persuades the enlightened conscience and satisfies the understanding, thus the attunement of reasonableness must be present in the practice of a worthy life.

BY WHAT WARRANT OF THE WORD OF GOD

"A life worthy of God"—this means first of all that a life which participates in the truth of God must be a life formed by the Holy Scriptures.

William Kiffin, who signed most of the important documents of Particular Baptists for half a century, frequently begins his queries with the phrases "by what warrant of the Word of God" and "by what Scripture warrant." Kiffin's stance before truth mirrors that of all English Baptists who commit themselves to a life of obedience to "the word and revealed mind of God [which is to be used] to try all things whatsoever are brought to us, under the pretence of truth."[5] English Baptists test each and every pronouncement and practice, all persons, actions, and ideas whatsoever, by the standard of the scriptures, particularly by the New Testament, because the scriptures represent "an absolute and perfect rule of direction, for all persons, at all times, to bee observed."[6]

Although the scriptures are truth and have authority, acting as the rule and the unfailing word of God, English Baptists broadly define the meaning of the truth of the scriptures and their authority. The Holy Scriptures do not stand alone but are constituted by their relation to Jesus Christ, the

Holy Spirit, and the Holy Word of God. Their truth is relational, not autonomous, essentially the word spoken by the Living Christ and the Indwelling Spirit, as well as the word related to the sacred, self-revealing thought and will of the Living God in the gospel story.

The Word in Christ's Mouth

The absolute sufficiency of Jesus Christ makes the scriptures sufficient; "the truth" makes the scriptures "the Holy Word of truth." William Dell, a member of Maulden Baptist Church (Bedfordshire), makes the point this way: the scriptures are "the word in [Christ's] mouth."[7] John Smyth agrees. He thinks that Jesus Christ is the Lawgiver, who in the New Testament has set down an absolute and perfect rule of direction, yet the truth of the New Testament is not self-sufficient but rather requires Christ as its mediator.[8] The London Confession of 1644 (1646, Second Edition) similarly contends that Christ daily causes truth to appear.[9] And, John Tombes avers that "the Scriptures themselves are but a sealed book, except Christ by his Spirit speake in them, and by them, to our understandings and hearts."[10]

What do English Baptists mean when they define the truth of the scriptures as that of the word in the mouth of Christ? Daniel King, in 1650, gives an answer, "Because that which is in the mouth is ready to be uttered, in regard of publishing and declaring the truth."[11] King thinks that Christ indwells the preaching and the teaching of the scriptures, gives them immediacy as well as power, and secures their truth. English Baptists are so convinced of the sufficiency of Christ in the grounding of the truth of the scriptures that they affirm with John Tombes: "What matter is it what the forme be, if God fill it? There is no means of any efficacy without Christ, and the smallest means is of absolute sufficiency through Christ, [who is] the interpreter of holy Scriptures, that is, Christ by his word and Spirit."[12] The power to achieve the intended results does not reside in the efficacious thing, such as the scriptures themselves or their proclamation. It rather resides in Jesus Christ who is all-sufficient, for Christ is finally "the truth."

In the Light of the Spirit

The truth of the scriptures is that of "the word in [Christ's] mouth" and, English Baptists quickly add, it is that of the word "in the light of the Spirit."

Thomas Collier, a leader of churches in the West Country, speaks of the necessary role of the Spirit in the determination of scriptural truth with this challenge, "I Query of anyone who knows the Lord, whether the Scripture, without the Spirit of Christ, doth, or can teach any one true and saving knowledge." Collier's uses of the words "doth" and "can" are telling, and characteristic of Baptists. Without the Spirit the scriptures neither do nor even can teach truth. Collier punctuates his contention with this statement, I "hold forth the truth and authority of the Scripture in the light of the Spirit; that so souls by the teaching of the Spirit of Christ may come to a right understanding of them."[13]

The Holy Spirit and the Holy Scriptures, for English Baptists, exist in a mutual relation which defines the truth of the scriptures. John Turner, for instance, identifies two essential keys to saving knowledge. One key is that of the inward testimony of the Spirit who guarantees that the "translated Scripture [is] the true word of God."[14] Thomas Grantham, a General Baptist from Lincolnshire, speaks of the first key's importance and ties it to reasonableness: "The Spirit speaking in the Scripture, together with right reason as truely subservient, is that whereby we are to resolve all differences."[15] The other key to heaven is that of the scriptures themselves. Turner wonders how disciples might know if they are led by "the Spirit of truth." His answer speaks of this second key: "When [they] walketh in the wayes of God's Word."[16]

Both keys of truth have their own integrity. Yet, neither exists apart from the other, the truth of the one dependent upon the truth of the other, the Holy Spirit and the Holy Scriptures mutually enriching both the part and the whole, and together being mutually enriched by the word in the mouth of Jesus Christ, a word permeating the hearts of disciples. English Baptists clearly do not conceive of the scriptures as an isolated textbook of truths but as a source book. This source book, they affirm, takes shape in the interplay of persons in a drama happening here and now, an earthy conversation that reveals all things necessary for salvation, as well as the mind and will of God.

Only the Word of God Is the Rule

The Living Christ and the Indwelling Spirit speak in the present time, and those disciples who heed the voices of the Christ and the Spirit fellowship with truth. However, fellowship with truth allows of no slack, English Baptists witness, for a worthy life is formed by the Holy Scriptures which serve as the only rule.

The Holy Scriptures serve as the rule that teaches, convinces, corrects, and instructs in righteousness. In a few words, they serve to nurture eternal life. The Orthodox Creed (1679) of General Baptists, largely written by the farmer Thomas Monck, testifies of the nurturing role of the scriptures in redemptive affairs. It holds that since the faithful have the scriptures delivered to them now, they ought not to depend upon an objective knowledge derived by natural religion through a study of the works of creation or the moral law, nor ought they to rely upon a subjective knowledge derived from within the person, say by an inner light, immediate inspirations, dreams, or prophetical predictions. Both kinds of knowledge, the objective and the subjective, do not secure saving knowledge, but the scriptures do. They tell of Jesus Christ and instruct in the ways of salvation and eternal life.[17]

The Holy Scriptures not only serve as the rule of eternal life but as the rule of faith and practice. The London Confession represents all Baptists in the classic heritage when it affirms, "Onely the word of God contained in the Canonical Scriptures is the Rule of Knowledge, Faith, and Obedience."[18] Or, in the words of the Baptist catechism of 1693, the scriptures are "the only infallible rule of faith and practice."[19]

The scriptures, which nurture eternal life and guide faith and practice, are depicted by English Baptists as the sole or the only rule. They are depicted in this manner because the scriptures are understood by them to be the revealed mind of God in the particular. And, they know, if the person is to model truth, he or she is required to live under the governing power of the particulars of revelation found in the scriptures

English Baptists characteristically use the term "rule" to refer to something by which persons square their faith and practice and by which they try all things. The Somerset Confession of 1656 links a rule to Christ who directs, informs, and restores. The Standard Confession of 1660 thinks of a rule as a regulation.[20] Thus it is that English Baptists think of the scriptures as the sole guide, standard, or measure.

Albeit the necessary and the sole rule observed, English Baptists do not conceive of the scriptures as producing the truth measured. The Holy Scriptures rather have a mediating authority. God in Christ through the Spirit finally authors truth and can be said to be the ultimate authority. The scriptures mediate or regulate, they govern or measure, the truth that God is. They consequently bear the marks of the truth of "the Lord Himself,"[21] their excellence arising from the authority of Jesus Christ, who is the only Lord, and from the assistance of the Holy Spirit.[22]

The Unfailing Word of God

Although English Baptists universally agree with John Murton of London that the Holy Scriptures were set down by the Holy Spirit,[23] the term "infallible" does not appear in connection with the scriptures until the years 1650 and 1677. Obviously the concept could emerge before its specific designation by a technical term, and this is the case. However, whether the term explicitly appears or implicitly operates in a text, prescribed boundaries of usage condition its meaning. Baptists trust the scriptures to be the unfailing Word of God because of a dependable interpretive framework, an unfailing context, which opens up an otherwise sealed book and establishes its truth.[24]

The unfailing dependability of the scriptures, in the first place, is associated by English Baptists with the context of the revelatory activity of "the Spirit of truth" who "dwelleth in the regenerate and who leadeth them into all truth."[25] Thomas Murton opts that the plainness of the scriptures, which are "the fountayne of all truth,"[26] results from the work of the Holy Spirit.[27] The first of the London confessions observes that faith is a gift of the Spirit, one that enables the believer "to see, know, and beleeve the truth of the Scripture."[28] The second of the London confessions traces the infallibility of the scriptures to "the inward work of the Holy Spirit bearing witness by and with the Word in our hearts." It also traces infallibility to "an infallible assurance of faith" founded on Christ and upon the evidences of the gracious work of the Holy Spirit, an unfailing assurance it specifically denies to the essence of faith.[29]

The truth of the scriptures, in the second place, is related by English Baptists to the unfailing context of the purpose of the scriptures, which English Baptists identify with redemption. Thomas Helwys thinks that the purpose of the scriptures lies in their testimony to Christ and in their containment of the "Holie Word off God." The London Confession identifies the purpose of the scriptures with their presentation of salvation and a knowledge of God's glory and attributes, the person and work of Christ, and the workings of the Holy Spirit.[30] In like manner the Midland Confession says that the purpose that undergirds the scriptures is that of revealing the mind of God, showing the way to salvation, and furnishing the faithful with good works.[31]

English Baptists could not speak more plainly. They speak of the truth of the scriptures as conjoined with redemptive purpose. At no point do they speak in ways other than those set by personal truth. Nothing is more characteristically personal than purpose, and nothing more characteristic of the English Baptist speech about the scriptures than the contention that the redemptive purpose of the gospel serves as the unfailing context that establishes the unfailing truth of the scriptures, not the reverse.

The truth of the scriptures, in the third place, is traced by English Baptists to the unfailing context of the analogy of faith.[32] They maintain that the actuality of the gospel underlies the clear and the unclear passages in the scriptures. Hence, because their source in the reality of the good story is the same, the clear and the unclear bear a similarity which allows an inference to be made from the clear to the unclear, one which reveals the meaning of the unclear and sets its veracity, forming a part of its substance. In this way the clear and the unclear together have the unmistakable taste of unfailing truth, not only for the learned, but the unlearned.[33]

The Scriptures Contain the Holy Word of God

The first Baptist statement on the scriptures, published by Thomas Helwys in 1611, definitively addresses the heart of their relation to truth. It affirms: "That the scriptures are written for our instruction, & that wee ought to search them for they testifie off Christ, And therefore to be used with all reverence, as conteyning the Holie Word off God, which onlie is our direction in all thinges whatsoever."[34]

The use of the phrase "conteyning the Holie Word off God," a use mirrored in the writings of Thomas Murton and The London Confession,[35] appears puzzling, and its interpretation controversial. Russ Bush and Tom Nettles argue that the phrase does not parallel modern views that the scriptures contain, but are not, the word of God. Rather, they say, the phrase holds that the scriptures "contain exclusively the word of God [or] all of its contents are the Holy Word of God." W. R. Estep observes that the phrase refers to the kerygma or to the redemptive story of Christ. Gordon H. James thinks that it resembles the view that the scriptures are the record of or the witness to God's revelation.[36]

Another interpretation presents itself, one in keeping with the notion of personal truth in the classic heritage, and reflective of the ordinary meanings of the words in the phrase, an interpretation closely allied with that of W. R. Estep. To say that the scriptures contain the Word is to say that they have the Word within, enclose or include it, are able to hold or have the Word. It is to say that through the scriptures, which are not self-referential, the believer confronts the Word. There is no textual evidence that the use of "conteyning" by Helwys connotes any meaning but that of this ordinary usage. To say that the scriptures have within themselves the Holy Word of God means that they include the sacred, self-revealing thought and will of the Living God in the good story. Thus, when faithful persons open the scriptures, they do not merely find the words of the good news but the actual Word in their hands. They find the Living God who meets them and enters into fellowship with them here and now.

This interpretation harmonizes with the view of personal truth operative in Helwys' confession. It is also consonant with the classic heritage's
understanding of the scriptures which claims that in, by, and through the
living scriptures persons meet the Holy Word of God. The scriptures reveal
the redemptive purpose of the Father; they are the word in Christ's mouth;
they are the revelatory activity of "the Spirit of truth"; that is, they are the
Holy Word of the God. Helwys and the English Baptists begin where they
are—as children of the Living God, new creatures in relation to the "three
witnesses, which are better than all scriptures or creatures whatsoever." In
the language of the 1611 confession, they start with "the Holie Word off
God." They start with the primary reality of the Holy Trinity in fellowship
with the saints. This claim to truth is starkly personal and realistic, firmly
rooted in a gospel model of truth.

A PRACTICAL OUTWORKING

The contours of "a life worthy of God" are mapped by English Baptists
in terms of their everyday encounter with saving knowledge, first with the
contours of a disciple's walk in communion with the Holy Scriptures, then
with those of the practice of abundant life and liberty, a practice equated
with truth. Their mapping typically combines both sets of contours. "A
visible believer," English Baptists of the Abingdon Association witness, "may
be manifestly discerned and known by these two things: his profession or
confession of Christ and his practise or conversation [life]; and the agreement betweene both these and their suitableness to the rules of Scripture."

"True religion is Scientia affectiva, non speculativa," Richard Claridge
explains of the Baptist equation of truth and practice, "a loving of God, and
our Neighbor as our selves, not the bare theory of the Gospel."[37] Henry
Haggar speaks of the equation of truth and practice with insistent tones.
He urges that the foundation of the Christian life is Christ Jesus, and that
upon this foundation the saints must build, not by hearing the sayings of
Christ, or by believing them, but by doing them, by doing the truth.[38]

When English Baptists clarify what it means to practice or to do the
truth, they do so with reference to the marks emergent in the life of a
twice-born person. They typically refer to such marks as love, obedience,
Godliness, hope, humility, sacrifice, and the like to the full range of the
deeds of regeneration and the fruits of the Spirit.[39] And they just as typically use these marks both to define truth and to test for it.

Love

The prime virtue, the mark most definitive of the practice of a twice-born person, is that of love. Without it "Christianity is an empty Name," English Baptists maintain. Without it truth is a vacuous term. Without it participation in personal truth is nonexistent. Love is greater than the hope of heaven, a most magnificent hope, even greater than faith. It is greater because God, who is truth itself, is love itself, at once truth and love, the two identical in God. It is also greater because God so loves the world that the only begotten Son of God is given, establishing whosoever believes within the gracious love that is truth. This tangible love in the life of the disciple, like no other, defines personal truth.

Love not only defines personal truth but serves as one of its key tests. Richard Claridge says of this test: "Holiness which is against Love, is a Contradiction: it is a deceitful Name which Satan putteth upon Unholiness. All Church Principles, which are against Universal Love, are against God, and Holiness, and the Churche." Again, he identifies love and truth and applies the test of love with these words, "to hate our Brethren, by rendering their Doctrine odious, and branding their persons with such black Characters as our own Pride and Passion suggest, is to tell the World we have not learnt Christ in the Truth and Love of him. 'Tis a manifest Argument we have lost our first Love, when we thus inveigh against those that dissent from us."[40]

Richard Claridge and Paul Hobson summarize what English Baptists mean when they claim that love is both the definition and the test of truth. Their words are quoted in full, without comment, for they need none, first the words of Claridge, then those of Hobson.

> The Disciples of Christ should be known by imitating their Master, namely, by an extraordinary and reciprocal affection. The Primitive Believers were famous for this Divine Quality, being of one Heart and one Soul. Love is a Fruit of the Holy Spirit, the special Livery of the Children of God; tis impossible to be a true Believer without it, for the right Faith worketh by Love. But Hatred, Variance, Wrath, Strife, Envyings, are works of the Flesh. Where Love is, God is, for God is love. But where Strife and Division are, God is not; for he is not the Author of Contention, but of Peace. Love is not an Appurtenence of my Religion, but my Religion it self; Love is the End of Faith, and Faith is but the Bellows to kindle Love; Love is the fulfilling of the Law; the End of the Gospel; the Nature and Mark of Christs Disciples; the Divine Nature; the Summe of Holiness to the Lord;

the proper Note by which to know what is the Man, and what is his State, and how far any other of his Acts are acceptable to God.[41]

Those that lie in the heart of Christ, that have found themselves transplanted from themselves, transformed into Christ, by Christ, they finde their heart transformed with loves & ravishments towards him, to him, and none else, but as they see them, and enjoy them in him, and him in them; there are intercourses & returnes of love to each other. This is not the righteousnesse of Justification, but this is Christ himselfe; his hand taking hold of thee, bringing thee over from thy selfe into himselfe, so that Christ in loving thee, he loves himself; and thou in loving him lovest thy selfe, in one and the same act; and in all your acts Christ acts, and in all Christ acts within you, you are swallowed up in Christ. He is bold with God, he is free and familiar with God; there is such intimate communion between Christ and him, that he can freely and with a Sonlike spirit and affection, ask any thing of God, he approaches unto his very Bosome, to his very Heart.[42]

Obedience

A tangible love defines the practical outworking of truth in the life of the disciple, and so too does the visible mark of obedience. To do the truth, for English Baptists, is to act obediently. In his discussion of the constitution of a church, the evangelist Thomas Collier well represents the view of English Baptists when he characterizes "the household of Faith, born from above of the Spirit and Truth," as composed of those persons yielded in obedience to the will of Christ. The community of believers, he also notes, must exhibit a corporate obedience to Christ's will in the acts of baptism, prayer, praise, preaching, common assembly, forgiveness, fellowship, care for the needy, and piety—all social and necessary activities in the practical essence of truth.[43]

Godliness, Hope, Humility, and Other Marks of Truth

Other tangible marks of a practical outworking of personal truth are championed by English Baptists. The 1612–1614 confession, for example, affirms that Christ is the King, Priest, and Prophet, and that believers through Christ are made spiritual Kings, Priests, and Prophets. Therefore, they "cannot lie, nor steal, nor commit adultery, nor kill, nor hate any man, or do any other fleshly action."[44] The requisite marks of truth also include the holy duties of Godliness, hope, faith, unity, humility, and peace. Moreover, truth is naturally considerate, plain, and careful in speech.

These practical marks of truth, and others of similar ilk, English Baptists believe, do not result from holding correct truths. They are the very fabric of the truth formed in Christ and given by the Spirit to the disciple, and by this fabric Baptists test for truth. Their test is this: whenever the marks are present, truth is present; conversely, pride and vain glory, just as tyranny and hatred, contradict truth and count as error—so too other high conceits, such as hypocrisy, covetousness, envy, boasting, and division.

Liberty

English Baptists concern themselves with the marks of truth that correspond to the complete list of Christian virtues. But there can be no question that the genius of their understanding of the practical outworking of truth is a focus upon liberty. Baptists are of one voice about the centrality of liberty: "Christ's people are a willing people, therefore not forced."[45] Leonard Busher, about whom little is known, except that he gives the idea of liberty a full and critical evaluation, says that people can only attain the "one true religion of the gospel by a personal, voluntary response to God."[46] Edward Barber, a London tailor, agrees: a spiritual gospel requires spiritual worshipers, and that means free worshipers.[47]

Truth's condition, English Baptists avow, is that of liberty, and they fear no cause of truth when it has the freedom to plead for itself. Samuel Richardson, a member of the original Particular Baptist congregation in London, asks if errors will prevail in a climate of freedom. His answer is that of all English Baptists: "if truth may be suffered, it will prevail against errors. If truth may have liberty, it can maintain itself."[48]

So convinced are English Baptists that liberty is the basic condition of truth that they agree with the most inclusive statement of freedom in the seventeenth century, that of Thomas Helwys, who writes these immortal words, "Let them be heretikes, Turcks, Jewes, or whatsoever it apperteynes not to earthly power to punish them in the least measure" in matters of spiritual truth.[49] Force, Baptists universally espouse, is unbeseeming a gospel of love and peace, a gospel full of toleration.[50]

Liberty not only serves as the condition for truth's appearance but is a necessary ingredient in the definition and the test of truth. English Baptists hold that "to understand and conceive of God in the mind is not the saving knowledge of God, but to be like God in His effect and properties; and to be made conformable to His divine and heavenly attributes." The early Baptists and the General Baptists think that God, who is liberty itself, created persons with a freedom retained to the present day by all people, despite the advent of sin. Thomas Helwys thinks that the retention of freedom signals the fact that it is an inalienable right. Particular Baptists deny this view, asserting the loss of freedom in the fall. However, they agree that God created persons in the image of God, and so has redeemed them to the same end.[51]

Whether they think that persons are stripped of liberty by sin, or not, English Baptists agree that faithful persons participate in "the truth" who is the essence of liberty, made originally in the image of "the only true God," redeemed unto the image—free in origin and in new birth, a God-given grace and a spiritual essential, free where "the Spirit of truth" indwells, set at liberty in the fullness of the Holy Trinity who is truth itself.

They Are One and the Same Thing

In the new creature formed by the Creator, transformed by the Mediator, and matured by the Comforter, who together lead disciples into all truth, the practice of "a life worthy of God" and of truth are not separate realities. The gospel realism and personalism of English Baptists will allow no separation. The marks of a disciple's character, such as love, obedience, hope, and liberty are what truth is; truth is the marks of discipleship; they are one and the same thing.

GOD PERSUADES THE UNDERSTANDING

"There is no greater probation in the world that a proposition is true," English Baptists know, "than because God hath commanded it to be believed." Yet, in the words of John Sturgion, they know too that the God who commands persons "to believe his revelation also persuades the understanding,"[52] and necessarily so. As a result, they insist that the person who models truth must couple a life of reasonableness with a practical attunement to the scriptures, abundant life, and liberty.

A case in point is that of Andrew Wyke, who was arrested in Suffolk for preaching and dipping. When brought before the authorities he refused to give an account of his actions but challenged the authorities to produce their proofs. It happened that a woman by the name of Anne Martin had died within a few weeks after her baptism, and this the authorities charged was caused by her being dipped in cold water. This charge was strengthened by references to books which represented baptism by immersion as extremely dangerous, and which called those who administered such a practice a cruel and murdering sect. In the case of Wyke it was held that the death of the woman was due to the fact that "he held her so long in the water, that she fell sick: That her belly swell'd with the abundance of water she took in, and within a fortnight died; and upon her death-bed expressed her dipping to be the cause of her death."

The Baptist historian Thomas Crosby, nearly a century later, reflects back upon the charges lodged against Wyke: "How many children died either at baptism, or immediately after it? And yet none ever ascrib'd it to their fright at the time, or the coldness of the water thrown upon them." Moreover, Crosby asks, is it not more dangerous to dip new-born infants than mature adults? And did not a physician by the name of Sir John Floyer prove cold bathing to be both safe and useful, even helpful in curing some diseases? Besides, did not the maid's mother testify that Anne Martin told her that she was never in better health than for several days after her baptism?[53]

This small episode and commentary by themselves have little significance, but they do typically represent the classic Baptist approach to truth. English Baptists understand truth with a pronounced bent to concrete reason. In all matters, including those of the gospel, presumption requires a qualifier in the reasonableness of an enlightened conscience, an asterisk, to fix its specific meaning and provide evidence.

An Enlightened Conscience

What statements a person knows to be true and the method for determining truth's content are two considerations which can most often be found at the center of discussions of truth, and rightly so. But these concerns should not cover over the basic issue of how persons are to orient or attune themselves—how they are to be, act, choose, and think, if they are to understand truth. English Baptists seek to know what is true, and what is the best method for judging truth-claims, but all in due time. Their prime concern lies elsewhere. They seize upon the demonstrable fact that in Christ the whole person is transformed, and reason sanctified, thus allowing the new creature to think the mind of God.

General and Particular Baptists disagree over the impact of sin upon the natural conscience, which is comprised of reason, the will, and communication. General Baptists see conscience as marred by sin, though operative, while Particular Baptists think it virtually destroyed. They both agree, however, that redemption brings a new conscience and with it a sanctified reason. The redeemed obtain an "inlightened conscience, carrying a more bright and lively stampe of the kingly place and power of the Lord Jesus." In an enlightened conscience, all English Baptists aver, the Trinity does not set aside the norms of the "reasonable soule" by superseding the faculties thereof. On the contrary, God the Spirit approves "every truth to the understanding," moving at all times "without violence, with a rationall force," respecting the standards of reasonableness. God the Son clears the truth and leaves "naked the errors." And, God the Father "would have every man fully persuaded in his owne mind."[54]

The General Baptists' meeting in the Midlands (1651), probably at Leicester, speak of the specific make-up of an enlightened conscience. They observe that much can be known by an openness to the works of creation and the moral law, for the Cosmic Christ gives every person therein some light. The spiritual riches of eternal life, however, can only be found treasured up in Jesus Christ, springing solely from the grace that empowers disciples to believe in Christ and to do the truth. Disciples may thus be said to be called to a serious consideration of the mind of God in the works of creation, the moral law, and Jesus Christ.[55] This call is finally to engage in a process of thinking the very mind of God. Particular Baptists, in their confession of 1677, concur. They hold that a daily understanding appears within the enlightened conscience attuned to nature, creation, providence, the scriptures, and the work of the Spirit in the believer.[56]

The Standards of Reasonableness

Several standards that serve as God's chosen climate of truth in the reasonable soul are identified and regularly used by English Baptists. The standards test what counts as truth, doing so in a mix of standards which creates an orientation of sanctified reason to evidence.

The first standard is that of clarity, or the demand for precise meanings of terms, definitions, and criticism of alternatives. English Baptists repeatedly call for debate, which affords the opportunity for the use of the techniques of comparison and contrast, as well as those of definition and systematic evaluation of competing positions. William Kiffin, a pastor and a Member of Parliament, pleads for an M. Edwards to "give these leave whom you so brand [in error], as bubliquely to object against what you say, when the Sermon is ended."[57] Thomas Helwys asks for "equall tryall" of doctrine, by which he most likely means public debate.[58] Leonard Busher thinks that it is reasonable, if truth is to prevail, for diverse doctrines to be heard and read.[59]

English Baptists also judge truth-claims by an appeal to the standard of the historical-contemporary community. In his writings concerning the settlement of religious controversies, for instance, Thomas Grantham encourages decisions by three groups of people: by the pastors and the Church throughout the ages, by the historical records, and by individuals.[60] John Smyth observes that the delegated power and authority of Christ first came to the body of the Church.[61] John Tombes urges, "Aske not then, How shall men be preserved from errours? for if they be interested in Church-fellowship fixedly, they have the provision of many institutions, and Ordinances, to be imployed for them, and applied to them: the doctrine, practices, prayers, parts, and utmost help of Elders and Brethren, with the special blessing of the relation, in and upon all and each of these."[62]

The standard of the primitive paradigm in the canonical scriptures[63] functions as one more test of truth. English Baptists look to the whole of the scriptures for a blueprint of discipleship and of church life, and as a patent for salvation for all time, but in particular they seek the roots of truth in the life of Christ, the Gospels, the Acts of the Apostles, and the epistles of Paul. One way they do this is by looking to the primitive church as the paradigm (the standard case) from which spring coherent traditions of faith and practice. Note but one case. William Kiffin gives this reason, among several others, for joining a church pastored by John Spilsbury, "I concluded that the safest way was to follow the footsteps of the flock, namely, that order laid down by Christ and His apostles, and practised by the primitive Christians in their time."[64]

No evidence of the tenets of modern rationalism can be found among English Baptists. Nevertheless, they acknowledge that God instituted logic, and that God sanctions what can be proven by logic in the reasonable soul. When logic appears within life, as part of the life-world of the disciple in relation to the Holy Trinity, Baptists believe that it functions as a standard in the testing of truth. John Smyth, by way of illustration, assiduously applies the norms of logical consistency and rational coherence. Regarding the interpretation of the scriptures, he insists, "Againe, that can never be the true meaning of Scripture when it is expounded so as it contradicteth other Scriptures, or any sound conclusion gathered out of the Scriptures."[65]

But, perhaps, the most thorough, certainly the most evident, application of the tactics of logic by Baptists appears in the writings of Thomas Collier. He will abide no falsity: "I judge my self bound in conscience, and duty to Jesus Christ, to vindicate that truth I profess: every command and truth of Jesus being, to a lover of the truth, more precious than that of gold." In order to achieve the vindication of his beliefs, he closely scrutinizes relevant arguments. On one occasion, he begins his scrutiny of arguments in support of infant baptism with these words, "I shall rout you in all your twenty Arguments." And rout them he does—challenging the major and the minor premises of arguments, pointing to non sequitur conclusions, using the reductio ad absurdum argument, calling for proof, questioning the reliability of probability, uncovering tautologies, and exposing meaningless, vague, and ambiguous words.[66]

Truth-claims are often empirically tested by English Baptists. Vavosor Powel, an evangelist from Wales, thinks that, among the diverse ways of God's teaching, experience is one of the best. For experience, he argues, "is a Copy written by the Spirit of God upon the hearts of beleevers, the inward sense and feeling, of what is outwardly real; and the spirituall and powerful enjoyment of what is beleeved."[67] Christopher Blackwood, a Cambridge graduate and chaplain in the Parliamentary Army, appeals to the perspectival quality of experience in his argument that "it is against all equity to bid me to see with other men's eyes, they have read other books, heard other conferences and reasons than I have, yet I must see with their eyes."[68]

William Dell's empirical analysis of primitive Christianity uncovers no uniformity but a diversity in forms of prayers, preaching, and church government. His studies of nature and nations yield the same conclusion: diversity marks them both, and defines their beauty. Moreover, his investigation of religion reveals that among believers there is a unity-in-diversity, but no external uniformity. From these empirical facts Dell draws an initial conclusion, one applied to Christian faith, that external uniformity is undesirable and monstrous, stifling religious sentiment and taking away soul liberty. A final conclusion is drawn, namely, "Unity is Christian, Uniformity Antichristian."[69]

The strenuous application of the pragmatic standard is also welcomed by English Baptists. A portion of their argument for the practice of freedom serves as an illustration. Look and see, observe the consequences of coercion, they insist. Coercion produces a profession without faith. It leads to hypocrisy. It damages evangelism. Persecution also produces errors which harm genuine Christians. Constraint clearly leads to unsatisfactory consequences, and can thus be said not to work; it "produceth many mischiefs [and] no finall hazard and trouble." Besides, Leonard Busher observes, "Moslems oft tolerate Christians. Shall Christians be less merciful than the Turk?"[70]

The standard of history is frequently used as well. Thomas Helwys over-states his case, but his appeal to historical verification is sound. He contends that, in every case in which a magistrate decided a religious matter, the judgment was always wicked and abominable.[71] Samuel Richardson, a wealthy tradesman and a leader in London, argues that history shows that persecution may be applied to true Christians.[72] Christopher Blackwood appeals to history to show that it is characteristic of the false church to persecute, and of the true church to be persecuted, as well as to show that universal Christian practice demonstrates that coercion is harmful.[73]

Testimony against Testimony

Reasonableness has its limits, and these limits the wise know. But, disciples—who model truth—are not therefore lacking in knowledge. They know in part, still they know. A complete knowledge of truth escapes them but not a sufficient knowledge gained by an attunement of enlightened reasonableness which uses the full range of standards of evidence. Thus, each English Baptist confidently concludes with Thomas Grantham, "I have said enough to satisfie any reasonable man, [and] here is Testimony against Testimony." Now God who is Truth must "give some note of distinction between our Doctrine and yours."[74]

THE ONLY TRUTH THAT COUNTS

Truth, the only truth that counts, is "the truth as it is in Jesus." English Baptists know of a surety that disciples are "christed with Christ" and in Christ fellowship with the "three witnesses" of the Living God. They know too that in Christ disciples practice "a life worthy of God," one attuned to the Holy Scriptures, abundant life, liberty, and reasonableness. Truth, they know, is these realities severally and together—persons, human and divine, in relation within the life-world shaped by the gospel.

Or, in the seminal words of the very first articles of the 1609 Separatist-Baptist confession, English Baptists know of a surety that "there is one God, the best, the highest, and most glorious Creator and Preserver of all; who is Father, Son, and Holy Spirit [and who] has created and redeemed the human race to his own image, and has ordained all men to life."[75]

Chapter Four

EXPERIMENTAL ACQUAINTANCE
AMERICAN BAPTISTS I

The spirituall administration of Christs power in and over the spirits and consciences of men, in reference unto God, who will be worshipped in spirit and in truth, so far as it concerns the outward man, is managed by the sword that proceeds out of the mouth of his servants, the word of truth, and to the inward man, by the sword of the Spirit, that spirituall law and light with which these candles of the Lord are enlightened, and that by himself, who is that light that enlighteneth every man; and this spirituall admin- istration of Christs power on earth in and over the spirits, minds, and consciences of men, is committed to the Spirit of Christ, who is only able to translate them into the glorious liberty of the Saints in the light.

John Clarke, Ill Newes from New-England, 1652

A CERTAIN UNREST

A certain unrest gave rise to the classic heritage of personal truth among American Baptists in the seventeenth century. This unrest was created, in part, by a mix of ideas—some from England, others indigenous to the colonies. Many Baptists who joined the colonial churches first embraced Baptist ways in England or Wales, while letters, confessions, and books from the old world further shaped the notion of truth among Baptists in the new. The historian Robert A. Baker says of the influence of English ideas, "When English Baptists dipped snuff, Baptists in America sneezed."[1] But, at times, American Baptists didn't sneeze. Some of their ideas were parallel occurrences to those in Old England, not offshoots of them. They were extensions of sources at work in the colonies, such as those of the scriptures, Puritanism, Separatism, the emerging American mind, and the Protestant principles of faith and grace.

In the account of his refusal to baptize his infant child, Thomas Gould speaks of this mix of ideas generated by old and new world influences: "God sent out of Old England some who were Baptists; we, consulting together what to do, sought the Lord to direct us, and taking counsel of other friends who dwelt among us, who were able and godly, they gave counsel to congregate ourselves together, and so we did, being nine of us, to walk in the order of the gospel according to the rule of Christ."[2]

But a more elemental unrest than that spawned by ideas gave rise to the classic heritage among Baptists in the colonies. Ideas do not finally give rise to an ultimate concern for truth. Ideas originate in and find their meanings in a master story engaged by the heart, not in the contents of the head. They are second-order phenomena, the origins and the meanings of which can be called into question. A concern for truth finally arises out of life, in the localized event, in time and in fact. If truth is an idea, then a concern for truth arises out of an unrest caused by ideas. But if truth is not an idea but a person, someone alive and dramatically real, then a concern for truth arises out of an unrest caused by the historically precarious happenings of a life story.

One moment in their life story, American Baptists discovered, became the absolute spring of their unrest, the center point of history at which emerged the meaning of truth and their passion for it. That moment was their encounter with the gospel and the wonder of being made whole in the master story scripted by God, a story in which the Living God opened their hearts[3] and strangely unsettled them in the new world. The wonder of it all, Baptists discovered, was that God searched for them in the colonies and in the wilderness, and in that gospel reality they knew that truth is dramatic, realistic, and personal. Truth is not in the observer but the participant, not in the thinker but the agent, not in the isolate but the common, not in the universal but the singular.[4]

In brief, caught up in the radically unsettling atmosphere of life firmly rooted in the gospel story, American Baptists knew that truth is (1) Jesus Christ, the truth par excellence,[5] and (2) the "spirituall manifestation of God's presence"[6] in this sandy land of Massachusetts, in the Carolina bottoms, and throughout the multi-formed regions of the American colonies.

TRUTH IN THE FACE OF JESUS

Truth is "not fitted to your Eares, but to your Hearts,"[7] American Baptists declare with Roger Williams, for truth is the gospel reality of Jesus Christ. So they keep the face of Jesus Christ squarely in their sights, and go directly thereto, seeing truth in "the truth." It is the Contemporary Christ that they see. American Baptists see truth in the Christ whose "resurrection declares him, whose life was taken from the earth, to be alive again." They also see truth in the contemporary believer who is formed into the likeness of the Living Christ, "so as to reckon himself to be in his soul and spirit quickened, and risen with Christ, from henceforth to live unto God the fountain of life."[8]

When American Baptists make known what it means to say that truth is primarily the Contemporary Christ, "who is called Faithful and True," and derivatively those persons who "see his face,"[9] they speak of Jesus Christ as (1) the Singular, (2) All-sufficient Object and Subject, and (3) Standard of Truth.

The Logic of the Singular

In the gospel of the twice-born, one of the most significant elements of the truth in the face of Jesus is that of singularity. Truth, American Baptists say, is the "one mediator between God and men, the man Christ Jesus, who [is] the way, and the truth, and the life."[10] They say too that the truth riveted in the face of Jesus Christ—the Nazarene, one of the Galileans, the only Son of God—is directly known by Catherine Holmes of Rhode Island, John Clarke of Massachusetts, and other colonial Baptists. The faces of truth speak and claim names, the priceless name of Jesus Christ, who acts in particular events, and the matchless names of persons in this time and at that place in the colonies, who are recreated as individuals into the very likeness of Christ. Truth, in effect, is thus thought to arise from a person responding with his or her whole being to a calling of the Contemporary Christ within singularity.

Although thoroughly orthodox in their Christology,[11] American Baptists are not orthodox in their Christ-centered view of truth. The Christian tradition they know ordinarily understands truth to be a set of universal truths about Christ, repeatable statements sanctioned by the scriptures and by the Church, frequently by the state, and their acceptance required. American Baptists, to the contrary, think of truth as the singular.

American Baptists do not find truth lodged in true doctrines about the person and the work of Jesus Christ. They rather discover truth to be the actual person and work of Jesus Christ. The singular—the unique—cannot be interchanged with or reduced to the universal. Truth is the one and only Mediator, the unique Prophet, Priest, and King, deity enfleshed in human form once for all time, the full scope of the matchless person and work of Jesus Christ.

American Baptists discover another thing too. In Jesus Christ every person is a novelty—an outburst of personal singularity with something exclusive to be, say, think, or do in Christ.

An examination of the writings of American Baptists reveals a decided penchant for identifying the be-all and end-all of truth with the singular. Of special note in their use of the logic of the singular are the Confession of Faith of the First Baptist Church of Boston and Elias Keach's Confession, which added two articles to The London Confession and became the primary confession among American Baptists, especially in the Middle Colonies.[12] But the American Baptist writing most revelatory of the meaning of the logic of the singular is John Clarke's classic book, *Ill Newes from New-England*, which records the formal defense by Obadiah Holmes, John Crandall, and John Clarke before the Massachusetts authorities in 1651.

Clarke, the pastor at Newport, Rhode Island, along with Holmes, the assistant pastor (who later became pastor of the Newport church), and a layman by the name of Crandall, made a pastoral visit to William Water in Lynn, Massachusetts. Clarke preached to a small number of neighbors of the nearly blind Water. The three men from Newport were subsequently arrested and sentenced to be whipped or fined.

In their defense before the magistrates, Holmes, Crandall, and Clarke do not argue their case by an appeal to universal and orthodox truths. They rather present four dramatic conclusions about the faith and the order of the gospel of Christ. The four conclusions speak of these singular realities: (1) the actuality of Jesus as Lord and as Christ, as Prophet, Priest, King, Mediator; (2) the identification of persons with Jesus Christ in baptism; (3) the drama of abundant life or the improvement of talent; and (4) the substantial fact of individual freedom.[13]

Expanding upon these conclusions, the three men tell a simple story that is the plain truth, a truth comprised of singular persons and events, nothing else, that of the person of Jesus Christ in the gospel work of reconciling persons. They tell the story of the Anointed Priest in atonement, the drama of an Apt Mediator in the ministry of reconciliation, the account of instruction by the Anointed Prophet, and the narrative of the Anointed King who dwells in the glorious kingdom of the Father and shall return. This matchless Christ, they say, stands as the Lord, who gathers together the "company of faithful ones, that are bought with the price of his blood, knit together by his Spirit, founded wholly upon himself, built up to be a holy habitation of God."[14]

The All-Sufficient Christ

Faith is not established by American Baptists with a turn to truths of a universal stripe, but with a radical move to the singular Jesus Christ, who in person and in work is "the truth," and in whom singular persons partake of that truth. This Singular Christ American Baptists find to be the Contemporary Christ who is the All-Sufficient Object of truth, that which is declared, and the All-Sufficient Subject or the causal agent of truth.

No other proper object of truth, no other predicate that is, can be found than that of the Contemporary Christ. For one thing, American Baptists note by way of evidence, the soul's consolation resides "in the Lord Himself."[15] For another, the gospel converges upon Christ as its end. Furthermore, Christ is the object of the work of the Holy Spirit and that of the exaltation of the Father, as well as that truth predicated of all truth. And this too, the mind of the saint lays hold upon Christ as its proper object and thinks "what is the mind of Christ in this time [and] what is truth, which is but one."

Thus John Clarke can say that Christ is the fourfold object of truth: (1) Christ is the object of the work of "the Spirit of truth"; (2) the Word is the truth exalted by God; (3) "the truth" is the Truth of all truth; and (4) believers know the Christ who dwells in them. He summarizes his position and therein that of American Baptists: "the Holy Spirit who being a Spirit of truth and sent by Christ who is the truth which God will exalt, shall glorifie him, take of him and his, and shew unto them [believers], and so lead them: from truth to truth, until he hath brought them into all truth; as a comforter or Spirit of comfort, shall fill their hearts with joy in believing, by bearing witness with their spirits, that they are the children of God, and by revealing unto them the precious things which God hath prepared for them that love him."[16]

The All-Sufficient Christ is not only the proper object, American Baptists testify, but the proper subject or the causal agent of truth. Truth is the Contemporary Christ, who actively lifts the believer into the likeness of "the truth,"[17] and who intentionally transforms the believer from one degree of truth to another, until he or she bears the full imprint of truth itself. Christ does this directly, not indirectly, speaking the will of God to the believer and writing a law of the Spirit of life in the heart.[18]

American Baptists understand that Jesus Christ is the subject and the agent of truth in a most literal fashion, in a way reflective of the angry words of Roger Williams. Upon hearing of the persecution of Clarke, Holmes, and Crandall by the magistrates, Williams recalls what the authorities of Massachusetts earlier did to him. He then bitterly challenges, "the magistrate who arrogates to himself the awesome responsibility of driving out of the country every dissenter, heretic, blasphemer, or seducer" ought well consider the possibility that he "may just be persecuting Christ himself."

In the hunt for heretics, a timely question arises as to whether the magistrate does not hunt the Saviour who is "the truth" and who indwells all believers as truth's subject. Ask yourself, John Endicott, Williams queries, "I have fought against several sorts of consciences; is it beyond all possibility and hazard that I have not fought against God, that I have not persecuted Jesus in some of them?" The answer is unavoidable: if "the truth" is the subject of the believer's life, the agent who speaks directly to the believer and who is internally related to the person of faith, then the persecution of the believer for deviation from mere truths of belief is in fact the persecution of "the truth."

The Standard of Truth and Error

Jesus Christ, who is the Singular, All-Sufficient, Contemporary Truth, is also the Standard of Truth and Error. Roger Williams understands, in a way familiar to American Baptists, that Christians are often utterly wrong in the basics of the true practice of a church, and often resist every effort to correct them. Some worship God in sleepy ignorance, he notes, while others falsely understand the scriptures. Though Christians do advocate an error-filled Christianity, and quite often so, Williams contends that no one should "imagine that they are not saved, and that their soules are not bound up in the bundle of eternall life," because they live in Jesus Christ.[19] Truth (singular), he knows, is not truths (universal); error (singular) is not errors (universal).

In keeping with his desire that truth be understood as the order of the gospel of Christ, John Clarke develops a theory of truth and error, one in keeping with that of Roger Williams. If a claim be true, Clarke observes in his remarks to the English Parliament, then it finds confirmation in Christ as its standard and in the spiritual administration of Christ's power on earth in and over the spirits, minds, and consciences of individual persons, an administration of the Spirit of Christ, the viceroy of truth on earth, who transforms sinners into the glorious liberty of the saints in truth.

If truth is Jesus Christ, then error is whatever opposes Jesus Christ or, in the words of John Clarke, whatever opposes "the order of the Gospel of Christ." Something of what Clarke means can be seen in his arguments against the magistrates of Massachusetts. He calls the established worship of God false, and evil, not the order of the gospel, and the enforcement of said worship by carnal weapons equally false, "it being in no way appointed, or approved by Christ, nor yet groundedly expected or practised by Christians who first trusted Christ, and therefore upon due examination will prove most unchristian, yea Antichristian."

Clarke clarifies his idea of the order of the gospel of Christ, and therein the distinction between truth and error, when he links truth and falsity to a precept from Christ and the Apostles in the New Testament and to a precedent among those that first trusted in Christ. In Clarke's usage of the terms, a "precedent" is a practice of the primitive church, a "precept" is a principle which imposes a standard course of action or a norm of conduct, while "the order of the Gospel of Christ" is the good story itself. When these terms are applied to a testing procedure, they lead Clarke to designate precepts and precedents as the measures by which persons square their faith and practice and try all things.

But, Clarke warns, precepts and precedents guide persons not to the measures themselves, taken as ends, but to their source in the good story of Jesus Christ. The true conforms to the truth that is the gospel of Christ; the false contradicts it. Truth at its bottom is "the acknowledgement of the truth as it is in Jesus." Truth is Christ; error is antiChrist. Truth is the Christian story; error is "unchristian, yea Antichristian."[20]

John Myles, pastor of a church formed in Wales and planted by him near Swansea, Massachusetts, catalogues a number of errors, a list which helps fix the exact nature of truth and error for American Baptists. In "that foul dunghill, of the errors of men, who leave no principle of truth unassaulted," Myles finds these instances of error: spiritual pride, hypocrisy, contempt, worldly mindfulness, and the decay of love.

Why does Myles count these particular phenomena as errors? Why does he not include such items as miscues of fact, inconsistent ideas, incoherent statements, or doctrinal weaknesses? The answer is obvious. Myles understands truth and error in personalistic, realistic, and gospel terms. Pride places the created above the Creator. Hypocrisy gives the semblance of what is there but isn't. Contempt replaces love with bitter disdain and scorn. Worldly mindfulness sets aside the mind of Christ and in its place makes the world the ultimate concern. If truth is the person of Jesus Christ, and if Jesus Christ be formed in the saints, as Myles contends, then clearly pride, disdain, and the like are errors. In this kind of falseness the essence of the personal is lost.[21]

Any definition of error must recognize the difference between the singular and the universal. The concept of error derives from the understanding of truth, or should in a sound approach to truth and error. If truth is a singular reality, then error pertains to the singular. If truth is a universal statement, then error has to do with the universal, and would bring a universal truth into jeopardy. The Baptists of the American colonies come down hard on the side of the singular as determinative of personal truth. The Contemporary Christ and contemporary believers in vital union with the Christ are the singular faces of truth. Their opposites are thus counted as error. Error is whatever is in principle or in fact antiChrist, antiperson, antilife, or antireality. It is the antisingular. It is without any face whatsoever.

THE STRIKING FACT OF BEING KNOWN
BY THE LIVING GOD

There is real truth for real people, American Baptists contend. Truth is an event, a happening in the life-world. Initially the conscience awakens to the truth in the face of Jesus, then it finds itself known by the Living God who is truth itself.

The conscience is made up of volition (will), reason, and communication, and all together tied to memory, the physical and the senses, moral discernment, social consciousness, wisdom, and spiritual insight. In other words, when American Baptists say that the conscience is known by the Living God, they understand the whole person to be caught up in the New Covenant and to be granted the privileges of the "children of God, a kingdom of priests, God's people."[22] This phenomenon of the gospel they image in three ways: persons of faith are seen to have privileged access to the truth of God that is (1) the story of love, (2) a walk together, and (3) a historical pilgrimage.

The Story of Love

With the written testimonies of Obadiah Holmes of Rhode Island more can be learned about the story quality of the truth of God than from any other classic source. The language and the logic of the drama of love encompass the only truth Holmes recognizes. God desires life, he writes, and "for that end has God appointed a way, a new and living way by which you may be saved: namely, the Lord Jesus Christ, and in His love unto the world has God sent Him that whosoever believes in Him should have everlasting life."[23] This is the heart of the gospel story, and this is the narrative heart of the truth of God, a narrative of love recorded by Holmes in six written testimonies.

In his first testimony, "On My Life," Holmes tells his personal story of salvation in the narrative of love. He thinks back to the prolonged spiritual crisis of his early years (1607–1630), which he characterizes as a time of disquietude created by the ambiguity of moral waywardness and skepticism alongside of strict pietistic striving. He also thinks back to 1630 when he sensed the futility of his constant striving and came to know that in the good story there is no preparation necessary to obtain Christ, for nothing whatsoever stands between God and the person, save love.[24]

Then, with plain colonial speech, Holmes remembers how God in 1630 brought him to consider that very well-grounded hope, the only basis of salvation and the core of truth, which was God's love to a lost world, a love in which sinners are cleansed and in Christ loved.[25] So immediately real this experimental knowledge of divine love that Holmes describes it as "a voyce from Heaven in my very Soul, bearing witness to my Conscience," a voice that remains his loving companion throughout his life.[26]

It would be an error to conclude that when Holmes speaks of an experimental knowledge of divine love that he speaks of a subjective state of affairs. The roles of the subjective (e.g., religious feelings, experiences, private thoughts) and those of the objective (e.g., proofs, orthodox systems, doctrines) in the gaining of a knowledge of truth in the story of love are recognized by Holmes. As a matter of fact, he uses the subjective and the objective (just as he uses the ordinances), but he trusts neither, resting in God's conveyance of truth through them.[27] Nothing, surely no subjective or objective state of affairs, stands between God and himself, except love, Holmes believes. Nothing stands between him and the Father who even before the crack of creation loved him. Nothing stands between him and the Son who was self-giving love incarnate. Nothing stands between him and the witness of the Spirit of comfort.

Holmes summarizes his position in the first testimony with words which speak of the narrative heart of the truth that is redemptive love,

> The first cause of this [redemption] was the purpose of God in His decree and counsel before the foundation of the world. Even then he found a way whereby mercy and justice might meet, truth and peace might kiss each other. And while I am in this conflict and spiritual battle I might have hope for my salvation as first appointed in that decree of God's; second it was by means of the Lord Jesus Christ; and, in the third place, [it was] witnessed to me by the Spirit and through faith in Jesus and [was] declared to man by word and deed in life and conversation to the comfort of others who were partakers of the same grace.[28]

The autobiography of the first testimony gives way to theological reflection in the second testimony, "On My Faith." In the story of love that is the truth of God, Holmes knows that life has primacy; reflection is secondary, but nonetheless essential.

Holmes begins his theological reflection in his confession of faith with articles devoted to God's reality, sovereignty, and trinitarian nature. Then, with a style and order of thought also found in the confessions of John Myles and Roger Williams,[29] he identifies the key characters and events which comprise the story of gospel love. With but thirty-five short articles he speaks of the characters in the story as those of the Father, the Son, and the Spirit, and of saint and sinner, with the central figure being that of Jesus Christ. He tells too of the events of creation, the fall, the covenant, the cross, the resurrection, redemption, sanctification, and providence. A review of the contents of the articles and of their serial order makes evident the fact that the Holy Trinity in the dramatic story of love is the absolutely essential core of truth.

In the third and the fourth testimonies to his wife and children, just as in the fifth and the sixth testimonies to the church and the world, Holmes mingles autobiography and theological reflection, but he centers upon real human faces—those of his family and those of saints and sinners.

In remarks on his family, Holmes observes that the love which characterizes his relation to his wife Catherine and to their eight children does not represent an application of truths about love to the family. He observes that the love which permeates the family is a part of divine love's substance. He thinks that truth is the family, not just any family either, but this one in Rhode Island, for a fellowship bonds together Obadiah, Catherine, their children, and the Living God. God, who is truth itself, is the foundation of the marriage and a real partner in it. Thus, the family in its love participates in the truth itself.[30]

Holmes writes in a similar vein to the church and the world of the basis of truth as a straightforward confidence in the love of God and as an internal relation with the true light, which enables a person to be born again and renewed in the spirit of the mind.[31]

Now there is nothing unusual about Holmes' recognition of love's central role in the gospel. Practically all Christians concur. It is the way that love operates in his truth-theory that makes his view unusual. Ideally love is given complete freedom to operate over the person, at least as far as finitude will permit. Every safeguard is taken to allow the encounter to be direct, undelegated, experimental. For the truth of God is love, Holmes thinks, and nothing whatsoever stands between the Living God and persons, except love. The access to truth is understood to be privileged indeed, but such is the stuff of "the truth as it is in Jesus."

Still, a caution is in order. The personal truth of the gospel is a contextual truth. Love yields a privileged truth, to be sure, but only within the context of the full gospel. Holmes cautions, "try what you hear whether it be according to truth, and take nothing from any man until you have tried it and well digested it by a good understanding." Then, "see that your evidence is good, which is alone the Spirit of God with your own spirit according to the scriptures." Above all else, recall the heart of the gospel story, and test all things by it. "Remember [Christ's] death often." And bring to memory this too, "Keep your way to the mark that is before you, and keep your feet sure upon the rock and your faith there."[32]

A Walk Together

The story of love forms a part of the classic view of the truth of God, but so too does a walk together. If persons of faith are to model truth, American Baptists hold, they must walk obediently with God, become Christlike, and fellowship warmly with kin.

The obedient walk of the disciple with God is a requisite for a privileged access to the truth of God, American Baptists say. At the outset of the Church Book of the First Church at Boston, the March 28, 1665, entry characterizes a walk together as a life in accord with the directions of Jesus Christ mediated through the Holy Spirit, the Holy Scriptures, and the Holy Community of Faith. It reads, "the Churche of Christ were gathered together And entered into fellowship & communion with each other,

Ingaiging to walke together in all the appointments of there Lord & Master, the Lord Jesus Christ as farre as hee should bee pleased to make known his mind & will by his word & Spirit."[33]

The covenant of the Seventh Day Baptists of Rhode Island (1671) begins in a similar way with the primary words of a direct relationship betwixt God and believers. It states, we did seek God's face, so that God might "direct us in a right way for us and our children to walk together in God's holy commandments and ordinances according to what the Lord had discovered to us or should discover to be his mind for us to be obedient unto."[34]

Obedience is a necessary ingredient of the truth that is a walk together and, American Baptists add, so too is a process of Christlikeness. The 1663 covenant of Swansea Baptist Church, in Rehoboth, Massachusetts, asserts that a walk together requires that Christians be conformed to Christ in all things, and that they be constrained by the matchless love and the distinguishing mercies found only in Christ. It also insists that Christians live under an imperative or "bounden duty to walk together in the visible gospel relation both to Christ, our only Head, and to each other as fellow-members and brethren of the same household of faith."

Another necessary ingredient of the truth that is a walk together is that of a warm fellowship of kin. So convinced are the Baptists at Rehoboth, Massachusetts, of the primacy of fellowship in a walk together that they draw the conclusion that, since union in Christ is the sole basis of their communion, though differing with others in such controversial points as are not necessary to salvation, they ought to hold communion with them.[35] In the final analysis, they understand, truth is the mutual fellowship of Christ and persons.

The walk in obedience to God, the process of becoming Christlike, and fellowship with one another[36] at Newport, Boston, and Kittery—this is the only kind of truth colonial Baptists know. They can thus but witness:

We believe with the heart & confess with the mouth that there is one god, Creator and governor of all things, distinguished into father, Son, & holy spirit, & that this is life eternal to know the only true god & Jesus Christ whom hee hath sent, the only foundation laid by the father, who hath perfectly revealed out of the bossom of his father the whole word and will of god which his servants are to know believe and obey.[37]

A Historical Pilgrimage

There remains but one further comment on what American Baptists mean when they say that persons of faith have a privileged access to the truth of God. A walk together in the story of love requires a common past, present, and future, all lifted into a common eternity. In other words, it requires the factuality of a historical pilgrimage.

The use of history as an interpretive key to truth can be seen in the covenant of the Baptist Church at Kittery, Maine. In 1682 Kittery Baptists witness to the growing together of the past, the present, and the future, and to that of time and eternity. The visible communion of the faithful with the Living God, an incarnate sort of truth, they recognize, is embedded in the past—in the revelation of God's sacred word; it is lodged in the present—in God's grace and light at present given to the saints; and it is rooted in the future—in that which God shall make known through the Holy Spirit. Furthermore, in the growing together of the past, the present, and the future into a temporal whole filled with eternity, Kittery Baptists perceive that the saints walk together with God and with each other all the days of their lives, for the eternal God of truth assists them by grace and the Spirit and gives them wisdom, strength, knowledge, and understanding.[38]

THE GRAND MOTIVE

In his letter to Thomas Skinner of Boston, William Screven of Maine pens the common cast of mind among American Baptists concerning the grand motive of truth. They eagerly intend to "walk with God here, and hereafter dwell with him in glory,"[39] beyond the hurting death, in eternal glorification with the Contemporary Christ in the life eternal.[40] That is the great story afoot in the lives of Baptists here and now, in this time and at that place, in the colonies.

Thus, instead of truths being final, for American Baptists, the integrity of persons, human and divine, is the final word of truth. Instead of truth being a right relationship between a statement and a fact or among true statements, truth is a right relationship betwixt God and persons. Instead of true doctrines scripting truth, God writes the story in which the chief characters are Jesus Christ, the Living God, and the saints in Charleston, Swansea, Rehoboth, Newport, and throughout the colonies.

Chapter Five

WALK ACCORDING TO TRUTH
AMERICAN BAPTISTS II

---

*Whereas, we poor creatures are, through the exceeding riches of God's infi-
nite grace, mercifully snatched out of the kingdom of darkness, there to be
partakers with all the saints of all those privileges which Christ hath
purchased for us, and that we do find our souls in some good measure
wrought on by divine grace to desire to be conformable to Christ in all
things, being also constrained by the matchless love to serve him according
to our utmost capacities, and that we also know that it is our bounden duty
to walk in visible communion with Christ and each other according to the
prescript rule of his most Holy Word, and also that it is our undoubted right
through Christ to enjoy all the privileges of God's house, we do therefore
freely offer up ourselves this day a living sacrifice unto Him, who is our God
in covenant through Christ our Lord and only Saviour.*

"Covenant," Swansea Baptist Church,
Rehoboth, Massachusetts, 1663

A PRACTICAL ATTUNEMENT

A debate between two groups of Calvinists occurred on the outskirts of
civilization in the Massachusetts Bay Colony on April 14–15, 1668. The
debate between the Baptists and the Puritans, who agreed that the
gospel ordains the proper basis of church order and worship, concerned
whether the Reformation had gone far enough or must go one step further
and abolish infant baptism. It also concerned whether the separation of the

Baptists from the Puritans was justified. Given the union of civil and religious authorities in the Bay Colony, this concern had to do with religious and civil revolution. The nature of a church was in question too. Both groups considered a church to be composed of visible saints. The Puritans deemed infants to be among the visible saints; the Baptists did not. The Puritans held a corporate view, the Baptists an individualistic one.

Another issue at stake was the viability of a corporate Christian state and of "a state of free individuals relying upon their own judgment to create the city of God upon the American hill." The Baptists and the Puritans recognized "in each other the essence of a struggle not just for the souls of men in the next world but for the truth of God in the social order of this world."[1]

William Turner, a member of the Baptist church at Boston, speaks early in the debate of his desire "to lie under the truth of God." The immediate context of his statement indicates that he means that all truth-claims are to be proven by the Holy Scriptures and, in particular, by the New Testament. The same context also shows that Turner relates the evidence of the scriptures to reasonableness. He prefaces his remarks on the scriptures by saying that each person must judge as an individual. In the latter parts of the debate, he conjoins his challenge to the Puritans to produce the rule of scripture with an affirmation of individual judgment: "Is it not a reasonable thing that every man have his particular judgment in matters of faith seeing we must all appear before the judgment seat of Christ?"[2]

Midway in the debate, the appeals by Turner and other Baptists to the scriptures and reasonableness, so as to settle truth-claims, are coordinated with a truth associated with the Holy Spirit and tied to abundant life and liberty. Benanuel Bowers observes of the role of the Spirit in the determination of truth, "The spirit of God in every Christian tells them whether the other be right or in form only."[3] John Thrumble, who with Bowers attends the Baptist church in Charlestown, links truth to an abundant life in which a person acts civilly, endures suffering, listens to God's counsel, walks in accord with Christ's rules, and daily grows in grace and truth.[4] He also appeals to the liberty of conscience to set what counts as truth, in agreement with Edward Drinker, a member of the Baptist church at Boston, who says, "it is the liberty of every believer to weigh."[5] If we do not walk according to truth but falsely, if we do not practice abundant life and liberty, Thrumble observes, then turn us aside.

Toward the end of debate, in a move that highlights the indispensable property of truth for American Baptists, John Thrumble brings truth-claims back to their only source and to the only substance out of which their meanings are made. He knows that truth is Jesus Christ, and that persons model the truth that the Living God is and does. With colonial plainness Trumble says, "It is the Lord and not you that must reduce us."[6]

An inner logic drives the Baptists in the 1668 debate, one that drives all American Baptists in the seventeenth century, a logic parallel to that of English Baptists. Truth is a practical attunement to (1) the Holy Scriptures, (2) abundant life and liberty, and (3) reasonableness—a practical truth fundamentally rooted in the Living God (Father, Son, Spirit), centered in Jesus Christ, and modeled by persons of faith.

THE PRESCRIPT RULE OF HIS MOST HOLY WORD

Truth, American Baptists declare, is necessarily, and not accidentally, a "communion with Christ and each other according to the prescript rule of his most Holy Word."[7] The disciple, they state, must have a special regard for the Holy Scriptures, which are God's word, covenant, and will.[8] This imperative rests in the awareness that the divinely inspired "Scripture of truth"[9] witnesses to the reality of Jesus as both Saviour and Lord and serves as the rule for faith and practice.[10] It also rests upon the understanding that when "the word of Truth" is preached and taught the Living Christ uniquely speaks in and through the scriptures, the believer existentially encounters the Living God, and the Holy Spirit of Truth guides the believer into truth.

The Sufficiency of the Lord Jesus Christ

The Holy Scriptures are not an objective, external authority in matters of truth. American Baptists do not think that the scriptures function either as an artifact in the world or as a depository of objectively true statements. They also refuse to depend upon a subjective source of truth, one which exists independently of the scriptures, such as that of an inner-light or a private experience. American Baptists find only emptiness in objective appeals and want in subjective twists and turns.

Faithful persons live under the urgency of a real drama of grace in which Jesus Christ speaks with tremendous power, American Baptists argue, for the Word who is the self-expression of God reveals the unadorned heart and the splendid glory of God in redemption, creation, and revelation. As a consequence of this argument, when it comes to the truth of the scriptures (the word), American Baptists passionately trust the matchless Lord and Saviour (the Living Word) who reveals truth to their hearts. The truth of the scriptures, they confess, is where Jesus Christ is, nowhere else. All things arise from and return to, find their center in, the only fountain of all truth—in Jesus Christ, who upholds all things, in whom true light will be found, and by whom all is proven that will be proven.[11]

The words of Obadiah Holmes speak eloquently of this overpowering zeal for Christ as the only way: "I have only [the scriptures] and them alone for my rule and direction, beseeching the Lord to give me understanding of them by His Holy Spirit which is the only revealer of secrets to my soul and who speaks peace to my conscience."[12]

The Only Rule of Faith and Practice

The scriptures, in the mouth of the Christ and interpreted by the Spirit, are used by American Baptists as the only rule of faith and practice.

Thomas Gould, the pastor of the First Church of Boston, in the 1668 debate, holds up the scriptures then says to the Puritans, "We have nothing to judge but this." John Watts, the pastor of the Pennepek Church, Philadelphia, in response to an Anglican overture late in the seventeenth century, invites reconciliation with the Church of England if, and only if, "it can be proved by the holy scriptures that her constitution, orders, officers, worship, and service are of divine appointment." Christ, he opts, is the only Head, Lord, and Lawgiver of the church, and Christ's laws and will are only to be known by the Holy Scriptures which are the only supreme and sufficient rule of all faith and practice.[13] Gould and Watts overstate their cases. In actual practice, both Baptists locate the ultimate authority in God, not in the scriptures, which have a mediating authority shared with reasonableness and the standards of liberty and life abundant.

Henry Dunster, president of Harvard College, also insists that truth-claims should be judged by the scriptural rule, a demand he too couples with other sources of knowledge. Dunster, when confronted in 1654 by the elders of the church as to why he did not baptize his child, answers that God makes faith and practice clear by the rule of the scriptures, and no rule of Christ can be found, for "that ordinance belongs to such as can make profession of their faith, as the scripture doth plainly hold forth." Dunster buttresses his decision by calling upon the churches for their help to hear the issue at hand. He also relies upon individual judgment, wording his reliance this way, I must "consider with myself what the Lord would have me to do." At one point he bases his decision upon a multi-faceted view of truth which includes the judgments of those persons who live holy lives, the presence of God, and the scriptural rule.[14]

In the blend of categories which verify truth-claims, American Baptists aver, the scriptures have a distinctive role to play. The words of the apostles, the prophets, and Jesus Christ serve as the only rule by which believers try all things as to whether they be of God or no.[15]

More often than not, American Baptists use the term "rule" without explanation. However, explicit uses of the term can be found. Edward Drinker of Boston conceives of a rule as a pattern laid down by Jesus Christ. Obadiah Holmes likens a rule to a testimony or a record, while John Clarke defines a rule as the order of truth.[16] When these explicit definitions of "rule" are placed alongside the linguistic contexts in which the term is used without explicit definition, it can be concluded that a rule is a standard. It is a measuring rod, a normative order, or a paradigmatic pattern for a truth-claim.

The affirmation of the scriptures as the rule is qualified by American Baptists. The rule does not yield truth apart from Jesus Christ and the Spirit of truth, they note, and it is definitely not the reality measured. The reality measured by the scriptures is that of "the only true god & Jesus Christ whom hee hath sent" to reconcile the world.[17] This reality, that of the gospel, and only it, is the primordial truth. The scriptures are but the standard measurement of this reality.

American Baptists do not allow the scriptures to usurp the ultimate authority of God in Christ reconciling the world. They rather give the scriptures a mediating role, albeit a necessary one, that of declaring the gospel and of providing a measuring rod, the only such rule, that can be laid beside any truth-claim so as to verify it. Other standards of truth exist, such as the marks of abundant life and reasonableness, and only Jesus Christ is finally sufficient. Nevertheless a sole measuring rod exists, there is one and only one measuring stick, that of the Holy Scriptures, hence the meaning of the term "rule" in the phrase "the only rule of faith and practice."

A rule measures only that for which it is designed. The plain rule in the New Testament, American Baptists think, is designed to measure truth-claims appropriate to the gospel, not those relevant to science, history, philosophy, etc. Obadiah Holmes, who holds that "the scriptures of truth" were written by people inspired by the Holy Spirit, limits the scope of the scriptures to a testimony of Christ and to matters concerning God and persons. John Myles considers "the substance of the whole Scripture, [which] was delivered by the hand of God," to tell only of the divinely appointed means for obtaining true light and salvation. John Watts observes that the scriptures measure items which pertain to faith and practice.[18]

"The rule of the knowledge faith & obedience concerning the worship & service of god & all other christian duties is the written word of god contained in [both] the old & new testaments."[19] But, although both Testaments are recognized, American Baptists think that the New Testament takes precedence over the Old. Consider two examples. In response to a dispute in the First Baptist Church of Newport, Rhode Island, about the proper day of worship, the first-day believers argue that "what was written on tables of Stone was done away as the old Covenant and that now we were to Hearken to the Law written in the heart, since now we were under the New Covenant."[20] In the debate of 1668, Baptists challenge the covenant theology of the Puritans by arguing that the use of circumcision to prove the viability of infant baptism confuses categories by mixing law and gospel. It is, they note, to "bring a new gospel."[21]

The Breathing, Sensuous, Blood-filled Tissue of Truth

The scriptures are the measure of all truth-claims pertaining to the gospel. Yet, in this firm contention, American Baptists do not imply that the scriptures are an external standard of truth, one isolated from life and woodenly authoritative. They conceive of the scriptures as the breathing, sensuous, blood-filled tissue of truth. The scriptures are intrinsically alive, American Baptists think, for the scriptures are the mind and will of the Living God. Their vitality is also relational, deriving from the vital activity of the Holy Spirit and from that of believers who existentially appropriate them.

Unquestionably, American Baptists think of themselves as a Spirit-filled people. They believe that the Spirit of God guides the believer with a true light, illumines the living and written word of God, and engenders the experimental encounter of believers with the Living God by means of the scriptures. John Clarke's statement is typical: "the Scriptures of truth [are] the two-edged sword of the Spirit," who leads believers into truth by means of "the words of the Lord himself, [as well as] out of the words of the Apostles of Christ, [and] by the enjoyments of those that first trusted in Christ."[22]

The vitality of the Holy Spirit comprises a portion of the breathing, sensuous, blood-filled tissue of the truth of the scriptures, but so too does the vitality of believers. American Baptists see themselves as a people who existentially appropriate the living and written word of God. They agree with Roger Williams, who pictures this appropriation as a twofold owning of the scriptures. The first owning Williams describes as "verbal and literal, viz., that such a writing or Declaration, or Treatise is extant, and that it proceeds from the Kings Authority and Command." The second owning he characterizes as "real and actual, when the Authority of it is in all humble obedience submitted to and obeyed." In other words, the scriptures, much like an external light or a judge, point to the truth of the gospel that must be existentially appropriated, making believers alive and thereby securing the truth of the scriptures.[23]

The scriptures function as much more than an artifact in the world; just as the Spirit serves as much more than an inner-light, and faith much more than a subjective experience or feeling. American Baptists believe that a unity of diverse parts forms the truth of the scriptures. Consequently, believers find consolation not in this part of the living word, or in that one, but in the relating of the parts into an organic whole and in God's conveyance of the divine presence through that lively unity-in-diversity. United together the diverse parts portend nothing less than an experimental encounter with the Living God. Believers have the scriptures for a rule; and beseeching God to grant an understanding of them through Jesus Christ and the Holy Spirit, the living word of the Holy Scriptures reveals truth itself to the troubled souls of believers who personally lay hold of the scriptures and are filled with their light and life.

A HEARTY CHRISTIAN

In conjunction with the truth that is the "communion with Christ and each other according to the prescript rule of his most Holy Word," a divine blessedness permeates the lives of believers, American Baptists discern, creating "a lively consimilitude or likenesse"[24] of Christ and a "walk according to truth."[25] The enjoyment of the heart-warming, soul-shaking encounter with divine blessedness fills the lives of believers with the gifts of faith, hope, and love, with freedom, and with the ardor of discipleship. This enjoyed abundance of life and liberty has the unmistakable ring of an incarnate truth, of a truth that is a definite practice of life, not that of a realm of truth outside of time or apart from a geographical location, certainly not the ring of a realm of universal truths separate from events or beyond the lives of real people. When American Baptists ask about the nature of truth, their answer is firm. Truth, they say, is the practice of abundant life and liberty in Christ!

To Be a Holy Spouse unto Christ

Truth is an abundant life and liberty of such intimacy with Jesus Christ that American Baptists often describe it in terms suitable to marriage. Elias Keach, who ministered in Pennsylvania and New Jersey before returning to England in 1692, speaks of Christians as immersed in "the Truth of Grace" to such an extent that they become "a Holy Spouse unto [Christ], and serve him in our Generation, and wait for his second Appearance, as our glorious Bridegroom." Christians, he continues, are to enter into a holy union with Christ and submit themselves to the discipline of the gospel required of a people in such a spiritual union.[26]

The covenant of the Swansea Church of Rehoboth, Massachusetts, describes this holy union as composed of those persons who are conformed to Christ in all things, constrained by the matchless love and fruits of grace, and who walk in visible gospel relation with Jesus Christ and each other, and perform all duties, including obedience to the government of Christ and Christian charity.[27]

Believers journey with Christ and towards Christ, intimately related in life to Christ, born anew into an eternal life which becomes for those who pursue it as natural as breathing. In that newness of life, American Baptists identify essential marks of truth. Their list of marks includes such unconventional items as love, faith, freedom, hope, and other virtues essential to Christian character.

Obadiah Holmes describes true faith as a working faith, which exhibits the marks of a person truly turned to Christ in character, deed, thought, and speech.[28] The 1682 covenant of Kittery Baptist Church, Maine, commits the church to those marks of truth relevant to the "faithfull observance of all [God's] most holy & blessed Commandmtts Ordinances Institutions or Appointments."[29] The Keach covenant spells out the particular marks of truth as those of holiness, Godliness, humility, and love, as well as bearing one another's burdens, failings, and sufferings with much tenderness, and striving for "the Truths of the Gospel, and Purity of God's Ways, to avoid Causes, and Causers of Division, to keep the Unity of the Spirit in the Bond of Peace."[30]

The conclusion can hardly be missed. Abundant life and liberty are not realms to which believers apply truths. That's the rationalistic approach to truth assiduously rejected by American Baptists who are first and foremost a gospel people. Truth is not applied to life. Truth is abundant life and liberty. It is a practical attunement to "walk according to the truth as it is in Jesus Christ," just as it is a practical attunement to live in obedience to "the prescript rule of [God's] most holy word" and to act reasonably.

Receive the Truth in the Love of It

Not content to identify the nature of truth by means of the marks of a life attuned to God, American Baptists use the marks of abundant life and liberty as tests of truth. John Clarke writes of verifying wisdom by means of works, and of falsifying untruth by unfruitful works, with these words, "every believer in Christ Jesus ought in point of duty to improve that Talent his Lord hath given unto him, yea ought to walk as a Child of God, justifying wisdom with his ways, and reproving folly with the unfruitful works thereof." He clarifies this test: "It is not words now Christian, when that worthy name is every where well spoken of, but faith that works by love, and love by works that will distinguish a heady from a hearty Christian."[31]

Obadiah Holmes also distinguishes between the assent to truths by a heady Christian and the truth of good works, love, and faith in a hearty Christian. He realizes that the life of Christ distills itself into every faculty of the soul and members of the body, manifesting itself in obedience and works, which can be used to test for truth.

Do not break the truth, Holmes cautions, avoid error, by which he does not mean a theoretical, logical, or factual mistake, but a failure to receive "the truth in the love of it." If truth is abundant life, he reasons, then error is the lack or the disrepair of life. Error is irreverence, an inconsiderate spirit, the conceit of pride and vain glory, the absence of love. Holmes counsels of this kind of error, "Let nothing below the Lord satisfy your souls and spirits; covet not; be content with your own condition and portion; envy no man's condition." Furthermore, he urges, do not boast, bear patiently the discipline of the Lord. In nothing be anxious, realizing that the Lord cares for you. Beware of hypocrisy, and watch carefully over another person for good and not for evil. At all times and upon all occasions, receive "the truth in the love of it."[32]

Truth and Liberty

Truth is the practice of the full range of the marks of a hearty Christian. But, among the marks, the practice of liberty is central for American Baptists.

The Puritan John Cotton contends that such a clear difference exists between truth and error that "one of them will be rooting out the other, either lies or the truth will be banished." Hence, he finds liberty of conscience unwarranted.[33] American Baptists argue, on the contrary, that since God is the only Lord of the "persuasion fixed in the mind and heart of a man, which enforceth him to judge,"[34] all persons must be free if truth is to prevail. Not only is liberty a necessary condition for truth's appearance, they resolutely insist, but it is truth's nature and a primary test, that is, if liberty is a just liberty grounded in the gospel and counted as the truth of God.[35]

Roger Williams refers to liberty's central role when he writes in opposition to the use of civil and ecclesiastical power in matters of conscience, "But so did never the Lord Jesus bring any unto his most pure worship, for he abhorres an unwilling Spouse, and to enter into a forced bed: The will in worship, if true, is like a free Vote: JESUS CHRIST compells by the mighty persuasions of his Messengers to come in, but otherwise with earthly weapons he never did compell nor can be compelled."[36]

The absolute centrality of liberty in the determination of truth is diligently upheld by American Baptists, with but one exception. John Myles and the members of the Swansea Church restrict liberty. They hold that the civil government of Swansea has the right to interfere with religious belief and to exclude erroneous persons who hold damnable heresies. Such a contention deviates from the historic Baptist position on freedom. Still, the deviation holds a clue as to the personal nature of error in the classic heritage. The Swansea Baptists limit access to the new town only for a particular sort of heretic—to the one whose errors violate something essentially personal and are thus inconsistent with the faith of the gospel,[37] for example, errors about the trinitarian nature of God and the union of the human and divine in Jesus Christ.

Nevertheless, this restriction of freedom does not accord with the classic heritage which holds that God's people shall be free and not coerced. Nor does it accord with the classic view that the lively experiment of the state guarantees liberty in religious affairs.[38] It also fails to perceive that truth itself and the truth that is the practice of liberty arbitrate among competing truth-claims. American Baptists know, in keeping with the classic view, that "it is the Lord and not you that must reduce us." They think themselves competent to "stand before God to hear what God hath commanded; to show us the error of our way: and the means for to reduce us therefrom."[39]

A GOOD UNDERSTANDING

American Baptists audaciously forward the claim that not only is truth a person walking in conversation with the scriptures of truth and partaking of abundant life and liberty, it is a person whose critical faculty can competently judge truth-claims.

Soul-Competency

The soul is seen by American Baptists as thoroughly competent. Thus, they argue, a person, standing apart from all civil and church authorities in matters of conscience, is directly responsible to God for the correctness of his or her faith and practice, and bound necessarily to walk within the practical attunement of an enlightened reason. Thomas Gould exemplifies this understanding of the rational dimension of soul-competency in his insistence that each person must exercise individual judgment in matters of faith.[40] Obadiah Holmes, too, would have all things tried by the good understanding of the individual.[41] Roger Williams thinks search and trial to be necessary for faith and right persuasion. He implores each and every person to "try all things, [lest] having bought Truth deare, we sell it cheap."[42]

A sound understanding is not an add-on to personal truth or an overlay which guarantees the truths of a belief system gathered from life or the scriptures. It is rather one of the crown jewels of the gospel. Each and every person must give an account of himself or herself before God. Each must repent, each must believe, and each must think for himself or herself. American Baptists accept this demand for sound reasoning as no less an imperative of the gospel than that of the injunction to follow the Spirit or to obey the scriptures.

Significantly, the gospel provides what it demands, American Baptists note. Each person in Christ has a renewed life which includes a renewed mind. Obadiah Holmes writes of this renewal, we are "born again, and the old man mortified and you renewed in the spirit of your mind, accepting the grace tendered."[43] John Clarke testifies to the same efficacious results of the gospel, "Christian, stand thou upon thy watch, and know, that if Christ be formed in thee, thou canst not but be transformed by him." Know too, he says, that the "spirit of truth shall guide the saints to worship the father, as in spirit, so likewise in truth."[44] As a result of the influence of Christ and the Spirit, the redeemed mind brings light to the soul and secures both the ability and the liberty of every believer to judge the evidence with ever increasing soundness.[45]

The Boundaries of Enlightened Reasonableness

American Baptists trust enlightened reasonableness; however, they do so within established boundaries, both broad and narrow. The boundaries are set broadly enough to encompass the common person of faith. John Russell, pastor of the Boston church, counsels Baptists to esteem learning, but not to lock up the spirit of God within the narrow limits of college-learning.[46] Russell's sentiment represents that of American Baptists, who do not restrict the exercise of sanctified reason to the few, but vigilantly guard the rights of plain persons to think soundly and to know truth. Common men and women, not just the educated or the ecclesiastical elite, are privy to a reasonable knowledge of truth and have the competency to reason soundly.

The boundaries of reasonableness are also narrowly established. With their insistence upon the abilities of all saints, American Baptists so exalt soul-competency that they appear to lose sight of reason's limits. They claim that further light upon God's word arises when the Spirit illumines the minds of believers, whose individual and collective competencies are unassailable. The fearlessness of this claim is decided. Each person, a new being in Christ, is said to think anew and aright with an enlightened reason, one capable of the hard work and guarantees of rational understanding. Yet the fearlessness of this claim is tempered by sensitivity to limits.

American Baptists identify three kinds of knowledge (natural, moral, heavenly), and they recognize pronounced limits in all three. All persons receive natural and moral light from the Creator, and "Christ, as the eternal word, by whom all things were made, hath placed and doth still preserve, in some measure, a light in the understanding of everyone that cometh into the world." Nevertheless, despite this light, both natural and moral knowledge are limited to the created and the socio-political orders. This too is a limit, John Myles cautions; the natural light gives historical, but not experimental knowledge. Furthermore, an anonymous Baptist observes, the human heart is dark, deceitful, and desperately evil,[47] and thereby it distorts the moral and the natural knowledge provided by Christ. Thus, Roger Williams can claim, in his normally colorful way, that "it is impossible for naturall man to bee capable of Gods worship, and to feed, be nourished and edified by any spirituall ordinance, no more than a dead childe can sucke the breast, or a dead man feast."[48]

An understanding of heavenly knowledge has limits too. American Baptists hold that sin marred the image of God so completely that persons "hath not as much freedom to will, or power to act, or saving knowledge to apprehend and judge of any thing that is good and acceptable to God." The mind must be created anew by God if it is to receive new light and life.[49] Furthermore, they hold, although a believer receives supernatural impressions, the reception of heavenly knowledge must of necessity conform itself to the essential structures of the human knower and to the human ways of acquiring knowledge.

In fact, all knowledge (natural, moral, or heavenly), which has the same form but not the same content, comes from an external source, and is received by a human faculty according to its capacity and standards of judgment. Therefore, all knowledge is limited by its conformity to human comprehension and experience. But, the knower should not despair, American Baptists observe, for these limitations are respected by the God who created them.[50]

The Norms of Evidence

Even though limited in its origin and in its ability to receive knowledge, an enlightened reason plays for American Baptists a divinely ordained role both in the essential composition of truth and in the testing for truth. In an enlightened reason created anew by "the truth" and indwelled by "the Spirit of truth," the person of faith models the mind of "the one, only living and true God," securing evidential integrity by the steady application of the full range of the norms of evidence, in particular, by the tests of experience, reason, utility, the community, the primitive pattern, and history.

An empirical standard is regularly used by American Baptists as a test of truth. John Clarke, for example, compares and contrasts empirical facts and seeks the agreement of his ideas with experience.[51] While John Russell, a Baptist leader in Boston, argues in an empirical way that Baptists "have never yet been found making any disturbance; by raising any tumults, or causing any Sedition, either in Church or Commonwealth."[52]

John Pierce, in his trial for joining a Baptist church, sounds the universal American Baptist injunction that all things should be founded upon sound reason.[53] Arguments must be logically consistent and coherent, he says, as well as linguistically meaningful and syllogistically valid. John Clarke carefully analyzes the meaning of the word "baptism," and uses analogies and the modus ponens argument in defense of liberty.[54] Moreover, Thomas Gould's narrative of his experience of discipline by the church shows a remarkable ability to think clearly and discursively.[55]

Persistently a utilitarian people, American Baptists regularly appeal to the pragmatic standard, often combining it with empirical and rational standards. Consider the case of Mrs. Gould, who offers as evidence against the use of civil power in religion the fact that worldly weapons never did convince any person of error.[56] Interestingly, the use of the pragmatic standard at times leads Baptists to conflicting conclusions. John Myles and the Baptists at Swansea argue that liberty ought at times to be restricted, else disastrous practical consequences befall "the well-being of the place."[57] John Clarke points to the opposite conclusion. He observes that the use of force makes people dissemblers and hypocrites and disrupts the peace of the commonwealth, as well as its property and safety.[58]

Clarke's position on liberty, not that of Myles, carries the day, for American Baptists do not depend upon any one standard to finally set what counts as truth. They resolve conflicting conclusions and determine the legitimacy of truth-claims with appeals to the full range of standards used in conjunction with the teachings of the Holy Scriptures, the leadership of the Holy Spirit, the reality of liberty, the witness of the Holy Trinity with the person of faith, and the judgments of individual and collective consciences.

Debate, a community oriented norm, often serves as a test of truth too. American Baptists, who champion soul-competency, do not rest satisfied with personal opinion, heartfelt religious experience, or private belief. The public arena offers them the give and take of the market-place of ideas necessary to establish truth-claims. Debate insures that hypotheses are stated, alternatives considered, evidence adduced and evaluated, meanings and definitions clarified, comparisons and contrasts made, and inferences drawn. Obadiah Holmes appeals to such a marketplace when he challenges any and all who speak untruths concerning him to "come forth before any to meet me in private or public, [and not] reproach me behind my back."[59]

The use of the primitive pattern as a precedent also serves as a standard of truth for American Baptists. In their conflicts with the Puritan establishment in New England, Obadiah Holmes, John Crandall, and John Clarke represent the position of American Baptists in their resolute contention that the correct view is one in agreement with the norm of the primitive pattern (the paradigm) set by the New Testament church. Clarke writes, in his brief discourse touching New England, "Let him that readeth it consider, which Church is most like the Church of Christ, the Persecuted, or Persecuting."[60]

Historical precedent, just as that of the primitive church, functions as a normative standard of evidence among American Baptists. In defense of liberty John Clarke argues that God "did neither speak to, nor yet make use of the Kings of the earth to make him disciples; but made use of the Sword of the Spirit."[61] In the debate with the Puritans concerning the separation of the Baptists, Thomas Gould observes of the Puritans that they too separated when they came from England and that even now many separate when dissatisfied.[62] In their appeal to history, American Baptists not only affirm a norm of evidence but reject the civil and the ecclesiastical traditions as properly constituted authorities. Roger Williams typifies this rejection when he declares, "the truth and faith of the Lord Jesus Christ must not bee received with respect of faces, be they ever so high, princely and glorious."[63]

A STRATEGIC TURN TO THE GOSPEL

A strategic turn to the gospel as the foundation of truth is made by American Baptists in the seventeenth century, a turn that determines not to let truth be reduced to the cut of the cloth of modern knowledge with its true statements, but which relentlessly focuses the problem of truth in terms of a practical attunement within the fellowship of the Living God, the Contemporary Christ, and persons in the life-world of the gospel story. Truth is a worthy walk, not simply something known, though it has a reasonable side. Truth is rather something that a person is, just as it is something to be obeyed and to be acted upon in life.

How a believer is attuned, the practical orientation of the heart, his or her way of being-in-the-world, opens the person to the personal truth, or so fails. If a person lives in obedience to the living word of the Holy Scriptures, within the abundant life and freedom found in the Spirit, oriented to reasonableness as a mode of living, the Baptists of the American colonies proclaim, then that person can be said to live, think, do, and be truth—that person walks according to truth.

A TIME OF NEGATION
THE EARLY–EIGHTEENTH CENTURY

AN OVERVIEW

Part Three—"A Time of Negation: The Early-Eighteenth Century"—chronicles a turning away from "the truth as it is in Jesus" by the General and the Particular Baptists of England and by the Regular and the Separate Baptists of America in the first half of the eighteenth century. It offers documentary evidence that Baptists negated their seventeenth-century legacy, and did so by covering over personal truth with the truths of reason, experience, and intuition.

Chapter Six—"Ideas and Experiences: English Baptists"—demonstrates that English Particular Baptists buried personal truth under the ideas of a hyper-Calvinism shaped in the image of modern rationalism, while English General Baptists covered over truth with an empirical starting-point which evaluated truth-claims by means of subjective experiences.

Chapter Seven—"Facts and Forgetfulness: American Baptists"—examines the ways in which the Regular and the Separate Baptists of America hid personal truth under an assemblage of intuited truths fashioned in the shape of facts. It also analyzes the essential contents of forgetfulness among English and American Baptists alike, identifying four abstractions (the given, the general, the theoretical, and the egocentric) which cover over personal truth and bring declension.

Chapter Six

IDEAS AND EXPERIENCES
ENGLISH BAPTISTS

There is a vast difference between the knowledge of the gospel which a temporary professor hath, and that of a real Christian. The former doth not understand the nature of evangelical truths. All he knows about them is, that they are true principles, and must necessarily be so, because they are revealed of God, who is truth. The spiritually enlightened person understands the things themselves; he knows the things of the Spirit, and those things which are freely given to us of God.
John Brine, A Treatise on Various Subjects, rev. ed., 1813

DECLENSION

The Baptist legacy of the seventeenth century was rich, and as a consequence, the eighteenth century held great promise.[1] But, instead of fulfilling that promise, a declension occurred among English and American Baptists in the first half of the eighteenth century. So extreme was the decline, particularly in England, that the Baptists were "almost destitute of vital religion."[2] One eye-witness describes Baptists as devoid of practical goodness.[3] Another observes, "Had matters gone on but a few years, the Baptists would have become a perfect dunghill in society."[4]

Historians variously identify the causes of the decline,[5] noting such causes as political change and moral decay. But one never mentioned, yet definitely a cause, is the fact that Baptists, in the old and in the new world, forgot the personal truth.

The seventeenth-century forbearers of the Baptists of the declension had spoken of a unity in Jesus Christ of truth and grace in which there was no possible division. They had kept their truth-theory subordinate to the gospel. In the gospel all their words of truth and grace were spoken, all heard too, and they were the same words.

But the Baptists of the declension drove a wedge between grace and truth, radically splitting them apart. Then they reduced truth to the truths of ideas, experiences, and facts, which they in turn used to interpret the gospel, subjecting it to alien ways of thinking. With these truths ready at hand, they covered over the personal truth, passing it off as something which it is not, showing it in disguise, or burying it over, forgetting the personal truth. The bright hopes of the seventeenth century thus began to grow dull, and Baptists entered "the most stagnant and lethargic period of Baptist history."[6]

IN THE HEAD NOT IN THE HANDS

The forgetting of personal truth takes various forms. English Particular Baptists cover over truth with the ideas of a hyper-Calvinism shaped by modern rationalism. They begin with an axiomatic starting-point, then they infer a rational system of ideas from the axiom secured by arguments. English General Baptists first embrace an empirical starting-point, then evaluate truth-claims by means of subjectively given experiences, thus disguising and burying personal truth. While English Baptists secure their ground with the systems of rationalism and empiricism, American Regular and Separate Baptists disdain all systems, preferring an assemblage of intuited truths fashioned as facts, but all the same, they too forget personal truth.

Although different in its forms, the declension has a common core. Baptists of the declension turn away from the truth in their hands to truths in their heads. Instead of centering upon the drama of being "christed with Christ," or upon the witness of the Holy Trinity with the competent soul, instead of walking attuned to the scriptures, abundant life, liberty, and reasonableness, they count as truth things in the head. Truth is no longer the story of their lives in the gospel drama but a set of true statements to which they must subscribe. They think that if they have the right experiences, arrive at right ideas, or get the facts straight, then they can discover truth.

A Time of Negation: The Early–Eighteenth Century

NO GOOD STORY TO PREACH: ENGLISH GENERAL BAPTISTS

Throughout the declension, a remnant of English General Baptists commit themselves to a salvation open to all, to personal faith in Christ, and to an acceptance of all who obey Christ according to their light.[7] Their commitment, which centers in the Standard Confession of 1660 and the six principles of Hebrews 6:1–2 (repentance, faith, baptism, laying on of hands, resurrection, judgment), secures a solid place for the remnant within the classic heritage. The remnant agrees with all classic Baptists: "Religion arises from a principle of Love, wrought in the Soul by the Word and Spirit of GOD, and has its Seat in the Heart, whereby the Christian converses with GOD in all religious Duties and exercises."[8]

But, howsoever classic the remnant's testimony, the majority of General Baptists fall into declension, for they have "no gospel to preach, and they preach no gospel."[9]

Empiricism

Enthralled by the immediacy of individual experience, the General Baptists of the declension increasingly question the truth of the orthodox doctrines concerning Christ. Their questioning of the deity of Christ leads them to an Arianism which accepts the preexistent but created status of Christ, who was more than a man but less than God. The demand that true statements correspond to the inner light of experience leads some of them to a Socinianism which denies the preexistence and the deity of Christ and affirms that Christ was just a good man. By 1750 many hold a Unitarian teaching which explains the Trinity as one person in three manifestations, rather than as three persons in one God.

The doctrines of the deity of Christ and the Trinity just do not correspond to the subjective experiences of the General Baptists of the declension, and failing such verification, they judge them to be false. Nothing, it seems, is so mysterious that it cannot be evaluated by the agreement of a propositional truth-claim and experience—if the experience is present, the truth-claim is true, but if not, it is false.

The Inner Voice Versus the Living Voice

The declension that inflicts widespread destruction among General Baptists in the first half of the eighteenth century begins with Matthew Caffyn, following his expulsion from Oxford University upon becoming a

Baptist and his acceptance of the pastorate of the church at Horsham in Sussex. Caffyn espouses (as early as 1656) the reliability of an inner voice or a light in every person that leads into all the ways of God. But, unlike the Quakers and the rationalists, Caffyn holds that the voice is tempered by the scriptures, which show things that are more excellent.[10]

Although he checks truth-claims by the scriptures, Caffyn's reliance upon individual experience leads him to explain inexplicables, and unable to penetrate the empirical core of the doctrines of the Trinity and the deity of Christ with the light of his own subjective experience, he concludes that these doctrines cannot be true.[11] As a result, he moves from an orthodox Christology, which affirms the humanity and the deity of Jesus Christ, to a view that denies Jesus' deity, a view he openly preaches.

Joseph Wright, pastor at Maidstone and a friend of Caffyn, presses charges against Caffyn during the General Assembly of Baptists in 1686, but the charges are set aside. Caffyn, who is emboldened by his exoneration, preaches his views even more openly. In response, the Baptists of the General Assembly finally condemn Caffyn's heresy in 1693, but they protect the accused by refusing to expel him from their fellowship. The Assembly, met at Goswell Street in London, intentionally values unity and peace above doctrinal integrity and truth. Baptists enter into their minutes these words, "Bror Caffyn was acquitted by the greater part of the Assembly."[12]

From this point on, the majority of General Baptists steadily fails to heed the Living Voice of personal truth, and among those Baptists who do not drift off into Quakerism, Unitarianism, or nondenominational churches, emphasis is placed upon the mystical and subjective elements of faith to the neglect of the gospel story with its demand of personal truth. They cannot distinguish the personal from the individual, or the experimental from the experiential. As a result, they elevate the individual and subjective experience over the personal and the experimental, thereby covering over truth.

The decline does not go unnoticed. A remnant of General Baptists in 1696 leaves the General Assembly and forms the General Association. By this act the members of the Association mindfully separate themselves from the gross errors of Caffyn and the Caffynites in the Assembly. In their formal document of separation, the Baptists of the Association establish truth by a classic appeal to the Living Voice formed by the Lordship of Jesus Christ and the relation of believers to God—by "a due regard for the honour of God, and of our Lord Jesus Christ, the purity of the churches, and the discharge of our own consciences."[13]

In an effort to lessen the divisions and to prevent further schism, the Assembly and the Association, which exist as two separate denominations, express their fidelity to the scriptures, and thus to part of the classic view. The Assembly at Goswell Street in London (1697) insists that its members are obliged to try all truth-claims about the Trinity and the Christ, not by experience, but by biblical referents and by no other. At Dunning's Alley (1704) in London, General Baptists say that only those claims are true which are contained in and proven by the scriptures, while in 1728, again meeting at Goswell Street, they state that the scriptures are the only rule of faith and practice.[14]

The appeal to the scriptures as a category of truth is repeated in the meeting at White's Alley (1733) with these words: the "Sacred Scriptures of Truth" are the authority, when interpreted by "the Light wch God giveth" to the individual, for the "Lord & Saviour Jesus Christ & his holy Apostles [have] the only Power & Right to prescribe Laws & Rules." But, General Baptists caution, care must be exercised not to elevate the light or the individual experience above the scriptures. For, in the elevation of experience to the place of final authority, the believer usurps the authority of Christ and the apostles and assumes that he or she "can infallibly determine ye Sense of Scripture, & can give a Proof of their Infallibility, wch no Protestant Christian will pretend to." Truth, the General Baptists at White's Alley know, is a Living Voice, that of God, Jesus Christ, and the plain words of the scriptures, and they would have all people try every work, both of faith and practice, by that Living Voice.[15]

During their time of declension, General Baptists not only appeal to the scriptures, but they repeatedly testify to the contents of the Standard Confession of 1660 and to the six principles of Hebrews 6:1–2, as well as to their belief in the one Lord Jesus Christ and in the "one living and true God—three persons the Father Word and Holy Ghost of one substance power and Eternity."[16] Admittedly, in this testimony, they focus upon true doctrines and not upon the truth of the true doctrines. Still, they do grasp the significance, if not the full essence, of personal truth. The turn to basic beliefs represents an awareness that the search for truth begins with the reality of the Holy Trinity, the actual Lordship of Jesus Christ, and a life of repentance and faith in the drama of resurrection and judgment—with personal realities in hand rather than with matters in the head. The classic heritage is obviously not totally forgotten.

Another element of the classic heritage surfaces among General Baptists in their time of division and declension, that of reasonableness. In their 1711 meeting at Dunning's Alley, for example, they recommend the truth-test of the community. They think that parties in a dispute may, with the consent of the church or the churches, be brought before the assembly.[17] At the 1731 Assembly, General Baptists judge it advisable to verify truth-claims with reference to a council or an assembly, which is considered to be a community of faith, and to have the right to act in Christ's name. However, they advise, the rights of the council are not without qualification, for a local church is autonomous and may disregard the council's decision. Still, the community aspect of truth-judgments isn't abnegated with this qualification. The local church, itself a community of faith, is merely allowed the final decision.

Even amidst their division and declension, the evidence shows, General Baptists at times recall some classic elements. They know, in these moments of recollection, that truth is not set by the inner voice of experience, no matter how self-authenticating, but by the Living Voice—the Voice of Jesus Christ, the Holy Trinity, the Holy Scriptures, Faith, and Reasonableness. In this knowledge, General Baptists upon occasion testify to the classic equation of truth and gospel, and thereby express their "great Assurance that all our former Misunderstandings will Remain Effectually Covered & that wee shall Quickly come into the Unity of the ffaith to a more perfect State to a greater Measure of the Stature & fulness of Christ [and to a] Compassion one of another."[18]

Abstractions

Although they at times disclaim "Mens Inferences and Compositions as a test or Boundary of any Christians Faith," preferring instead the Living Voice, General Baptists as a whole most often, and as a matter of course, cover over any remembrance of the classic heritage with the abstractions of modern empiricism.

A subjective temper spawned by the abstractions of the subject-object dichotomy holds sway among the majority of General Baptists, a subjectivism which identifies the content of knowledge with truths known, not by human explanations, but by an inner light informed and directed by subjective experience. The General Baptists of the declension feel that God will direct them into all truth and keep them from error both in faith and in life.[19] They also feel that the faithful, who follow the inner light and "hold fast truth in Every Branch of it," are obligated to use the "Standard of God's inerring Word [as] the only Standard of truth," and as the only rule.[20]

Yet, as illustrated by the Assembly met in London in 1773, by the Barbican Assembly of 1777, and throughout the whole of their writings, General Baptists shift from realities to statements, from the experimental to the experiential, from the personal to the subjective, in the setting of truth. In their use of the standard of the scriptures, they see no necessary reason to check the inner leadings and the truths of the scriptures by means of the domain of the personal. Individuals, they think, should apply the truths of God and the scriptures to their minds. That is, they should apply the true statements, mere objects in the world, to themselves as experiencing subjects and to their own individual liberty, and correlate them with their experience, which finally sets what counts as truth.[21] In this way they subjectivize all truth-claims, even those known by the leadership of God in conjunction with the scriptures.

The covering over of the Living Voice of truth by truths, experience, and subjectivity is so thorough that the primary order of personal truth gives way to the secondary order of abstract truths verified in subjective experience; then, the secondary gives way to the abstract trivialities of the tertiary. General Baptists concern themselves with the propriety of card playing, dancing, singing, and fox hunting. Quarrels and party interest over such trivialities, according to John Hursthouse of Lincolnshire, leave unity broken and anarchy let in like a flood.[22] This experience is pitted against that one, individually autonomous believers vie one with another, while propositional truths fragment into myriads of pieces, each seemingly right.

With Yorkshire bluntness, Thomas Gibbon observes of this state of affairs that "much iniquity and little, little true religion" can be found, though there is a "pious remnant among several denominations."[23] The Goswell Street minutes of 1740 describe the situation as that of the decay of religion and the absence of spirituality.[24]

The Living Voice of truth is thus forgotten. General Baptists in their declension move from the primary order of truth to the secondary order of truths, then to tertiary concerns. They aggravate these moves by means of two abstract concerns—an extreme form of individual freedom coupled with an overriding desire for peace.

General Baptists of the declension champion freedom, of this there can be no doubt whatsoever. But they do not champion a liberty set within the dynamics of persons in relation in the gospel drama. They champion an abstract individualism, one more at home with modern empiricism than with the gospel and the classic heritage. They think of the believer as an isolated center of experience (as a perceiver), rather than as a person constituted by internal relationships with the Living God, Jesus Christ, and the beloved community. So basic the isolation of the believer, and so insurmountable, that General Baptists cannot fathom, much less engage, the communal and the historical dimensions of liberty, but embrace a liberty suited to the individual subject set apart from other subjects, equally isolated and independent.

In the classic Baptist understanding of liberty, the center of reality, and thus of truth, is persons in relation, not the individual subject isolated from other subjects. The other person, human or divine, is key, as is the mutuality at the heart of the community. Each person intends and acts for the other person, and in this interconnection of persons, liberty is born and brought to maturity, or not at all. But in the dark midnight of their forgetfulness, General Baptists center reality and truth in the individual subject. Consequently, an extreme independence holds sway, not mutuality. Each individual subject realizes himself or herself in splendid isolation from the other individual, who is something of a threat to the individual subject and its freedom.

In addition to the value placed on an abstract freedom, General Baptists in their declension also value an abstract denominational peace more than the rich blend of fundamentals and categories at the heart of personal truth. What is relevant is a liberality and a laxity that lead them to squander their energies on the maintenance of a loosely connected grouping of individuals and on a determination not to make differences a breach of love. The bottom line is not to "Preach, Write or Urge in discourse, such Controversie about the Doctrine of the Trinity, which shall be unto the Disturbance of the Churches Peace."[25] Again, in the melancholy of their self-imposed fate, General Baptists cover over the Living Voice of truth by yet another abstraction.

SALVATION IS OF THE LORD
ENGLISH PARTICULAR BAPTISTS

The immediately given enchants English Baptists in the declension. The given of individual subjective experience charms General Baptists, while the given of universal reason charms Particular Baptists. The result is the same. Both groups forget the personal truth, the former by means of empiricism, the latter by means of rationalism.

Rationalism

In a world grown weary of systems, English Particular Baptists, in the first half of the eighteenth century, who seek to "defend God and truth" by a quest for certainty, cast a systematic theology, for they think that "the man without a system [is] little more than a sceptic."[26] If certain knowledge is obtainable, they assert, it must begin with an axiom from which other statements in the system of belief should be logically derived.

English Particular Baptists find their starting-point in the only universally recognized axiom thought worthy—in the apprehension that "salvation is of the Lord." So acutely aware are they of the depth of the sinful depravity of humanity, so radically sensitive to the onrush of sublime truths into the life of the saint from a point outside, not in word only, but in power, that thoughts of sovereignty gradually overshadow all else. Particular Baptists think of God as the Exalted Ruler over all—the Creator, Lawgiver, Saviour, and Master of all that happens, and with this key-category they structure their system of truths. Nothing human suffices, all things human are too far removed from truth, "an unworthy part of the dust of Zion,"[27] a Nottingham church covenant states. Hence it is that Particular Baptists begin their system with the axiom of God's sovereignty, just an axiom, albeit one that allows for a defense of "the cause of God and truth."

But why accept the axiom as true? Particular Baptists do not secure their starting-point by the ways inherent in the classic heritage. Nor do they justify it by a Cartesian appeal to a self-evident, indubitable axiom. They rather marshall deductive and inductive arguments so as to establish God's existence and nature, as well as the veracity of the scriptures, thereby securing the axiom of sovereignty and God's truth.[28]

Tragedy

Without fear of contradiction it can fairly be said that the Particular Baptists of the declension fervently intend the preservation of traditional Baptist teachings and the classic Baptist heritage of truth in a time when modern rationalism does serious damage to the churches. But, in their fervor, they make three moves, strange and at times ironic ones, which undermine their intentions and accelerate their decline. In their defense of "the cause of God and truth," they employ the devices they oppose. First, they secure the axiom of God's sovereignty by means of argument, an all-too-human agenda and a substantial portion of the dust of Zion. Second, they define sovereignty in terms of the time-bound system of hyper-Calvinistic theology. Third, their rational starting-point deflects them away from the classic heritage which they seek to protect from the ravages of modern rationalism.

The age of Calvinistic scholasticism thus begins among Particular Baptists, and a strict orthodoxy of a decidedly rationalistic bent becomes the "cardinal virtue of the churches."[29] Theological narrowness, spiritual aridity, abstruse debate, and rigid creedalism replace the zeal for the gospel so evident among earlier Particular Baptists, with the result that "many poor sinners daily perish hereby for want of knowledge."[30] Daniel Turner of Abingdon describes the churches of the declension as destitute.[31] In the annual letter of the Western Association (1765), Benjamin Francis, burdened of heart with the lukewarm and careless Christians who have grown formal in worship and indolent in God's service, wonders of Baptists, "Is the love of Jesus changed? Is his beauty faded or has the Redeemer's gospel been deprived of its vivifying energy?"[32]

Of True Principles

Rationalism first appears in Baptist circles with John Skepp, a minister in London, and it initially takes hold in one section of Particular Baptist churches in London, yet everywhere it has an influence. The chief thinkers in the movement to rationalism and high Calvinism are John Brine (1703–1765), Skepp's successor, and John Gill (1696–1771), the more influential of the two.

John Brine, pastor at Currier's Hall in Cripplegate, ministers first at Kettering then at Coventry before locating in London, where he defends the purity of the Baptist way and the gospel. His strict Calvinism, which brings him to the point where he finds it inappropriate to offer Christ to the lost, is linked to a rationalism that evaluates truth by a new standard and prizes true principles as the content of truth.

But it is a mistake to imagine that Brine uniformly espouses rationalism. He holds in an unresolved tension both classic and rationalistic notions, a move which makes him a tragic figure, one representative of Particular Baptists in the declension.

Nowhere can this inherent tension be better seen than in Brine's view of knowledge. He speaks of two kinds of knowledge. On the one hand, he says that an intellectual assent to true principles or to truths is a kind of knowledge. On the other hand, he speaks of a spiritual acquaintance with truth itself.

Both kinds of knowledge require God's initiating action, for the sinful mind suffers from a total loss and absence of truth. It also suffers from a prejudice against divine mysteries. Truth, Brine opts, is a glorious object, and without grace no one can be "the subject of a disposition suited to view the infinitely glorious objects."[33]

In the case of an intellectual knowledge, each person already has a natural ability to know, Brine contends, namely, the ability to apprehend, judge, and intellectually assent to general truths. But, Brine also contends, this ability has been so seriously damaged by sin that it functions only by God's grace and the increase of this light occurs only by revelation. God must first graciously illuminate the natural mind before it can discern the rational structure of the true principles of the gospel by the exercise of logic, particularly by the standards of consistency and coherence—the dependence of one truth upon another and the harmony of diverse truths.

The knowledge that is an intellectual assent to true principles leads to a legal conviction of sin and to a high regard for spirituality and divine institutions. It brings certainty along with facticity to the knower, even securing a rational account of a system of doctrines. It often elicits conscientiousness as regards truth, sometimes convictions and actual change. However, this kind of knowledge is not spiritual acumen or intimate acquaintance. The individual only knows about truths and does not encounter truth. Brine at this point does not mistake orthodoxy for faith, nor soundness of judgment for a holy life.[34]

The Christian has another kind of knowledge. Brine argues that the "temporary professor doth not understand the essence of evangelical truths," knowing only that the principles are true, "and must necessarily be so, because they are revealed of God, who is truth, and cannot express a falsehood." The spiritually enlightened person, however, understands the things themselves or the things of the Spirit, and may be said to be spiritually acquainted with truth.

The person spiritually acquainted with truth grasps the meaning of truth and is grasped by it. The heart utters a lament when the person comes face to face with the malignity of sin and separation from God. Concern too grips the heart. A thorough discernment of the self emerges, along with the wisdom of God. The person is embraced by the grace of the gospel. A way of salvation by Jesus Christ appears, the person cordially receives the gospel, dwells in the glory of God the Father, the honor of the Son of God, and the power of the Spirit of God.

The Christian, Brine holds, should "never form an opinion either of the truth or of the degree of our grace from perception of the evidence of the truth of gospel doctrines," because persons who have not felt grace can know that evidence. The Christian should trust that knowledge which is a spiritual or an intimate acquaintance with truth or the things themselves. Only that can be trusted which "recommends itself to [the Christian's] greatest esteem, because of that glory which arises from it to the Divine Persons and unto all the Divine perfections."[35]

Although his thought here agrees with that of the classic heritage, Brine's view of the nature of the things themselves displays the tragic inroads of rationalism. The classic heritage holds that truth is what is, and what is (the things themselves) is the gospel story of God and persons in relation in the life-world. Brine transvalues the object of truth (the things themselves) from what is real to what is thought (ideas, doctrines, general truths). He thinks that the object of knowledge by acquaintance is a true principle, an evangelical principle, or an evangelical truth.[36]

For example, Brine marshals six arguments to prove the truth of the true principle of eternal justification. The axioms of his arguments, which serve as the premises of syllogistic proofs, Brine abstracts from the scriptures interpreted by the system of Calvinism, the reliability of which he secures rationally. Then he arranges the axioms in logical relations (disjunction, conjunction, etc.). Finally, he infers necessary conclusions which substantiate the truth of the doctrine of eternal justification. One disjunctive argument runs as follows: either justification is immanent and eternal or transient; it isn't transient; therefore, it is eternal.[37]

Brine does not speak of the doctrine of eternal justification in language descriptive of a person's stark encounter with the devastating experience of sin and abandonment, or with words that depict a sinner's richly warm experience of being found by a loving God who lifts the sinner from the pits of despair into the joys of salvation. Brine's object of knowledge is not experimental, personal, real. He thinks of the thing-in-itself as a true principle in statement form. He thinks that eternal justification is an idea capable of being proved true or false by strictly rational means. It is a true doctrine that secures the vitally personal relation of justification. The thing-in-itself, after all, is the conceptual and the propositional content of the revelation of a Sovereign God.[38]

Evangelical Truths

John Brine's tragic forgetfulness is great indeed. He must have his rationally certain knowledge by which he secures his true principles, even though, in so doing, he covers over the personal truth of the gospel.

Another tragic figure, one representative of Particular Baptists, is that of John Gill, the pastor at Horsleydown church in London, who grasps the personal truth yet covers it over with evangelical truths.

Thomas Craner says of John Gill, "evangelical truths did sweetly drop from his mellifluous tongue."[39] Robert Hall disagrees, describing Gill's writings as "a continent of mud."[40] Despite contrary assessments, both Craner and Hall perceive that Gill defends "the cause of God and truth [as a] patron of the doctrines of grace."

In an era when rational theology questions orthodox doctrines, when the empiricism of the General Baptists rejects the deity of Christ, while Baptist church life breeds moral apathy as well as doctrinal laxity, Gill constructs a Calvinistic system of evangelical truths so as to understand "the truth as it is in Jesus" and to defend the whole range of Calvinistic doctrines. This most able scholar crafts a defense of doctrines by presenting a justification of the principal passages of Scripture, and the arguments founded upon them, and by justifying the doctrinal truths on rational grounds, thinking that doctrines are no more disagreeable to right reason than to divine revelation.[41]

In his defense of evangelical truths, Gill subscribes to part of the classic heritage. For instance, he describes God as truth. God the Father "is not only called the God of truth, but God the truth, Christ asserts himself to be the truth, and the Spirit is likewise so called." Furthermore, Gill holds, God's works of creation, providence, and grace are all true, as are God's essential Word and written word. And, finally, he believes, God is internally truth in the persons and the relationships visible in God; God is externally truth in the works visible in the worlds of nature and the spirit.[42]

Gill's allegiance to the classic heritage can also be seen in his avowal of experimental knowledge. God, he argues, can only be known by those persons elected to eternal union with God and justified by the works of God. By contrast, while persons are in a natural and unredeemed state, they lack divine knowledge. Only the new creature, disposed in the mind toward God, finds the light of divine knowledge. This light is that of acquaintance, fellowship, or communion with the three persons of the Godhead. Gill knows that the objects of acquaintance are not "bare axioms or propositions, for the act of the believer does not terminate at an axiom but at the thing, [with] the principal term or principal object" being that of the three persons of the Godhead. The only faith that counts is not a bare assent of the mind to the truth of the Holy Trinity, but rather a special faith in God and Christ, a communion with them, and with the people of God.[43]

Furthermore, Gill's appeal to classic views can be seen in his position on revelation. He finds revelation to be both prior to the scriptures and externally made in them. But, in matters of truth, the external revelation conjoins with an "internal revelation and application of the truths of the Gospel to the souls of men, which is sometimes ascribed to the Father, sometimes to Christ, and sometimes to the Spirit of Christ."[44]

Gill's language and thought are often classic, making it appear that he is securely within the classic heritage of truth. But what lies on the surface of his thought is not what's really there. A close examination of Gill's works leads to the conclusion that he rejects his time-honored heritage in favor of another incompatible with it. Gill adopts a rational paradigm that reconstructs the domain of truth from new fundamentals, defines what counts as a problem, sets the categories which govern activity, and approves the standards by which evidence is adduced and solutions gained.

Gill begins his system with the cardinal claim that salvation is of the Lord, but he neither grounds this axiom nor understands it in a manner faithful to the classic notion of personal truth. Quite the opposite, Gill's beginning-point reveals a rationalistic orientation in which reason establishes the axiom of the system, defines the substance and the object of truth in terms of evangelical truths understood as true statements, and sets the parameters for justifying the system of truths. His overriding concern throughout the whole of his system is a care for divine truths, evangelical truths, the cardinal tenets of the faith, the principles of evangelical truth, or the doctrines of grace.

An excellent example of Gill's rationalism is found in his major work, *A Body of Doctrinal Divinity* (1769), in which Gill begins his defense of evangelical truths with the veracity of God's existence and nature. He states, "Having undertaken to write a System of Theology, I shall begin with the Being of God, and the proof and evidence of it; which is the foundation of all religion." He explicitly rejects the attempt to prove his first principle by means of a self-evident proposition, choosing instead to strengthen the mind with reasons and arguments. Gill then arranges eight arguments which purport to prove the existence of God: (1) the universality of belief, (2) the impress of Deity on the mind of every man, (3) the works of creation, (4) the sustenance and governance of the world, (5) the miraculous things done in the world, (6) the fulfillment of prophesies about contingent future events, (7) the fears of men and the tortures of a guilty conscience, and (8) the facts of judgment or retribution.

The truth of God's existence can be proven by these eight rational arguments, so Gill proposes, but he does not think that the truth of God's essence, perfections, persons, and worship can be established in this manner. Just as John Calvin before him, Gill begins his system with a statement of natural religion, as it is called, then goes on to show its inadequacy. Only the revelation of the sacred religion, a revelation contained in the scriptures, he reasons, can provide the form and the content of the nature of God and flesh out the truthfulness of the axiom that salvation is of the Lord.

But why should anyone accept the authority and the perfection of the revelation contained in the scriptures? Again, Gill finds it necessary to rationally secure the ground he goes upon by showing that the scriptures are a perfect, plain, and sure rule of faith and practice. In his exposition of the Old Testament, Gill gives thirteen proofs of the inspiration and the authority of the scriptures, chiefly relying upon the fact that since the scriptures are God-breathed, they must be perfect and authoritative. In his systematic theology he argues for the authority, the perfection, the clarity, and the necessity of the scriptures.[45] The mere fact that Gill presents rational proofs so as to secure the truthful ground of the scriptures and thus the truthfulness of the material content of the axiom of his system is a revealing insight into the depth of his rationalistic view of truth.

The substance of the proofs for the truth of the axiom of sovereignty and of the scriptures, and of the multiple proofs which underlie the whole of his thought, also reveals the extent of Gill's rationalism. For instance, note these facts which signal the rationalism at work in the proofs offered in Gill's Calvinistic system. First, Gill insists that the scriptures do not contain "general ideas but the real sense and the very words" of the revelation— exact meanings and language immune from culture and history—lest the believer should be swept away with the contingencies of time. Second, he places in opposition the word "perfect" and the words "ignorance, error, and imperfection," thus implying that anything shy of perfection, such as reasonableness or probability, comes up far short of what counts as truth. Third, Gill demands that the scriptures be logically consistent and coherent, as well as agree or correspond to fact. And, fourth, he displays the rationalistic penchant for certainty, clarity, and distinctness.

Nowhere, perhaps, can Gill's rationalism be better seen than in his discussion of the perspicuity or the clarity of the scriptures. Gill finds scriptural passages to be unequal in clarity, while some appear dark and obscure, yet in progressive revelation (an unfolding of understanding only, not a process of change from the less to the more true, or from false to true, lest truth be historical and clouded) the dim under the law of Moses becomes clearer with the prophets, most clear in the gospel, and all together stand as a coherent and clear whole. Thus, the clarity of the parts and that of the whole contribute to the perspicuity of all scriptural passages.

Not every doctrine, he continues, is expressed in so many words in the scriptures, say one about the Trinity or the atonement, but the things themselves—the evangelical principles—signified by them are clear, and they fit together within the larger coherent system of the scriptures.

At some point, Gill thinks, either in the words used or in the meanings intended, the clear message of the scriptures denotes the things them-selves, and all is light, apart from historical contingencies, cultural fabrics, and personal interpretations, all excluded from the rooms of the mind appointed with the furniture of rationalism.

An a priori argument, a way of thinking basic to rationalism, is also used by Gill to establish the perspicuity (and the perfection) of the scriptures. The source of the scriptures, he reasons, is "the Father of Lights." All that comes from God is light and clear in its parts, free too from all imperfections. Thus, Gill concludes, the scriptures must be reckoned as a "sure, certain, and infal-lible rule, since they are the Scriptures of truth, and not only contain what is truth, and nothing but truth in them: but have a true, even a divine testi-mony bore unto them, and come from the God of truth, who cannot lie."[46]

Gill carefully qualifies his view of the perspicuity of the scriptures, but in his qualification he does not escape the clutches of rationalism. He reasons that the scriptures are a sealed book to the light of nature and reason in the darkened mind. If the meanings of the words of the scriptures are to be understood with clarity and certainty, the Spirit of God, who dictated the words, must enlighten the person.

In the Horsleydown church covenant, a church Gill served for fifty years, Gill recognizes that the scriptures are the word of God, and the only rule of faith and practice. However, he also recognizes that the scriptures are not a woodenly external authority but must be correlated with an internal revelation to the believer. Revelation, the covenant says, occurs both prior to and subsequent to the scriptures. It happened with Adam and others before the writing of the scriptures. It happens now, for if a person is to know the evangelical truths (to know the universal truths, not the singular truth) of revelation, he or she must be inspired and given revela-tions internally by the Spirit of God.

Revelation, it can therefore be said of Gill's position, occurs not only in the scriptures but to individual believers. There is nothing without the scriptures, and there is equally nothing in the scriptures without the Spirit.[47] However, it can also be said of Gill's position, in the interplay of the Spirit of God and the scriptures in the individual believer, what the Spirit secures is not "the truth as it is in Jesus" but a revelation that consists of evangelical truths in the form of statements.

At times Gill senses the importance of personal truth, but the domain of personal truth does not finally supplant that of rationalism. It is subsumed under a system of true statements and lost in the intricacies of rationalism. Gill's discussion of truth appears in chapter twenty-two of book one in *A Body of Doctrinal Divinity*, a scant three pages in a work of seven books and over seven hundred pages in length. Its status is that of but one doctrine in a long list of doctrines. Indeed, throughout the whole of the seven books, Gill's concern for true doctrines set by the axiom of God's sovereignty overshadows the personal truth itself, and hardens the axiom into a hyper-Calvinistic framework.

Gill composes the first truly systematic theology in Baptist history, and he writes the first systematic exposition of the whole of the scriptures, both monumental achievements, but he does not hold to the heart of the classic heritage. Unlike John Smyth who needs only the three witnesses to establish truth, or unlike Paul Hobson who is content to be "christed with Christ," Gill (and the Particular Baptists of the declension) must secure his evangelical truths by means of rationalism.

THINGS ALONGSIDE OTHER THINGS

In the time of their declension, English General and Particular Baptists turn away from their classic heritage of "the truth as it is in Jesus," covering over or forgetting the richly realistic personal truth, preferring instead experiences and ideas. As it so happens, in Baptist circles an abstract quality attends all thinking, and either true statements of subjective experiences or true rational statements become the ultimate concern. Positive Christian faith and practice decay. Truths hold sway. English Baptists embrace true statements alongside other true statements, just things alongside other things in the world, and not the personal truth.

Chapter Seven

FACTS AND FORGETFULNESS
AMERICAN BAPTISTS

From conviction that without habitual purity of mind, divine truth cannot be clearly perceived, and consequently cannot with success be maintained, we exhort you to walk worthy of God, to all well pleasing; let your conversation be as becometh the gospel of Christ; have respect to all the divine commandments; for if any man will do his will, he shall know of the doctrine whether it be of God.

Edmund Botsford, "On the Duty of Christians," 1794

TRUTHS READY AT HAND

American Baptists reached out and touched the personal "truth as it is in Jesus," then grasped it tightly in their hands—this was their genius throughout the whole of the eighteenth century. But they still had their moments of declension. Upon occasion American Baptists equated truth with the factual truths of intuition which lay on the surface of experience. They also at times equated truth with the doctrinal truths of Calvinism and its readily available certainties. In both cases American Baptists tragically concerned themselves with truths ready-at-hand and suffered declension.

The strength of the hold of American Baptists on personal truth, along with their occasional equation of truth with truths ready at hand, can be illustrated with reference to the 1794 circular letter of the Charleston Baptist Association in which Edmund Botsford of Georgia addresses the duty of Christians in controversy.

ℳ 106 ℞

A Time of Negation: The Early–Eighteenth Century

In the first part of the circular letter, Edmund Botsford, called "the flying preacher," traces the immediate causes of disagreements among Christians to three sources. Sentiments vary, he observes, because of the sublimity of gospel truths. They also vary due to the differences of intellectual capacity for obtaining divine information. And, lastly, divisions are fostered by particular habits of thinking which arise from different social associations. But, Botsford continues, that which primarily causes controversies among Christians is not the three immediate causes but the spiritual force of sin. The moral depravity that darkens the understanding and the taste for piety gives rise to disagreements and error. Truth and unity are where God is, at the place of new life; falsity and controversy are where God is not, at the place of sin.

Little else would be expected from Botsford, of whom Daniel Marshall, who founded the first surviving church in Georgia (at Kiokee) says, "I never heard convarsion better explained in my life." Two fundamentals make up conversion for Botsford, the same two fundamentals at the core of personal truth. One fundamental is that of the primacy of Jesus Christ. Botsford writes that however Christians may be divided, there is ultimately but one Saviour and Lord. The second fundamental is that of a kind of life that has content and models the reality of Jesus Christ. A habitual purity of mind and the values of mercy, kindness, humility, meekness, and longsuffering, characteristics modeled by Christians of all denominations who are one in Christ, preclude the indulgence of opposite feelings in controversies.

These two fundamentals not only prevent Christians from "wounding the peace and drawing a veil over the dignity of their profession," they also demonstrate whether or not a truth-claim is of God. In other words, Botsford says in classic fashion, truth is one Lord, one faith, one baptism. Truth is what's real; falsity is what's unreal. Truth is Christ; falsity is antiChrist. Truth is unity with Christ; error is estrangement from Christ. Strange indeed would be any suggestion that the truths and the errors held by Christians decide a controversy.

In parts two and three of the 1794 circular letter, Botsford appends three corollaries to his classic view. First, he notes, all Christians have different admixtures of truths and errors. No saint has only truths; no saint has only errors; no saint has pure truths or pure errors. One saint stands at the forefront of the battle with falsity. Another saint, though not foremost in the battle, brings up the rear of the Lord's host. Second, those individuals who live squarely in the personal truth of the kingdom of Jesus Christ ought openly state their sentiments concerning doctrines and practices, for this is a duty owed God. To shun true statements and sound actions is either to admit that correct sentiments of religion are of no importance or that there is not love and wisdom enough among Christians to engage them in inquiries after truth.

Third, the claims of heaven take precedence over those of the head. Botsford explains, "the thought that those with whom we now cannot fully accord, will ere long, be with us in heaven in perfect love and harmony, that it is our highest honor to promote the glory of God, rather than our own selfish interests; must have a happy influence on our minds when concerned in matters of controversy, and lead us to pray earnestly to God to pour out his gracious spirit on our souls, to dispose and enable us to act aright, and to extend the divine influence to all his dear people."

Nothing can be truth in any sense that matters, Botsford summarizes, unless its meaning can be found in the coming of the great Redeemer's kingdom in the world, where Christians shall come into the unity of the faith and the knowledge of Jesus Christ, unto the fullness of the measure of the stature of truth itself, when, Botsford surely knows, "an address, like the present, will no longer be requisite."[1]

In keeping with the classic Baptist genius, Botsford does not elevate truths over truth, but his language still contains echoes or faint remembrances of a declension peculiar to American Baptists in the eighteenth century. He speaks of gospel truths and divine information, mere truths ready at hand, in such a way that his words point to those occasions when American Regular and Separate Baptists reduced truth to intuited facts and the orthodox doctrines of Calvinism.

The classic legacy cannot state the truth absolutely or in a static way. It can only state the truth by affirming, denying, surpassing, for the truth of which it speaks is that of the Living Truth in all its historical animation. This, American Baptists, just as Edmund Botsford, upon occasion forget. Whereas their primary interest lies in the dynamic quality of the gospel story, a didactic interest occurs among American Baptists in their declension, an interest focused in factual and doctrinal statements.

Although American Baptists do not use the term "statement," they do use comparable terms, such as "gospel truths, divine information, the doctrines of grace, truths, evangelical principles, divine truths, the facts, the truth of the Baptist principles." So, whenever they ask about the truth of an assertion, they ask whether or not the statement which makes a truth-claim is true. In particular, the American Baptists in their moments of declension ask: is the statement based on either (1) the factual truths of intuition or (2) the doctrinal truths of Calvinism?

The Factual Truths of Intuition

While the English General and Particular Baptists of the declension secure the ground they go upon by appeals to empiricism and rationalism, American Regular and Separate Baptists turn to self-evident, experiential facts. This turn to an intuitive knowledge deflects them away from the personal, experimental character of truth, the result being a definite, though admittedly mild, declension from truth to truths.

A new concept of knowledge born in America distinctively shapes the thought of Baptists.[2] The American love of experiences and actions, which present themselves ready at hand, frees persons from the grand foundation of systematic thinking and replaces theories with an assemblage of truths fashioned in the shape of facts. Facts seem to come naturally in small, miscellaneous packages, in collections of novelties, and in floods of impressions, which the knower intuits, then gathers into bundles, shaping the express content of a knowledge of nature and spirit.

American Baptists, who imbibe deeply from this fount, believe that a knowledge of facts comes from just looking, albeit sharply, at their daily experiences and from acting in the arenas of life. This new kind of knowledge requires no preliminary training, no elite set of experts, no premises, no discursive reasoning, no precise definitions, no testing, no systematic network. It neither begins nor proceeds with the hard work of persons in relation within the gospel. An individual person needs only the direct, self-evident facts of daily experience which readily present themselves to consciousness. Each and every individual can plunge in anywhere, and does. Popular and phenomenal language does nicely, too.

That the declension from the domain of personal truth to the sphere of intuited facts affects American Regular and Separate Baptists cannot be denied. Nevertheless, the declension appears mild in comparison with that of English General and Particular Baptists. On a scale which measures the severity of the declension, a scale from one to ten, with ten the most severe level, General Baptists top the scale with a nine, Regular and Separate Baptists hold down the bottom with a two, while Particular Baptists occupy the middle with a seven.

One reason that the English declensions are so severe, it can be argued, lies in the fact that the question before General and Particular bodies is not that of getting at the truth bit by bit within the classic heritage, but of a far-reaching revolutionary change of basic assumptions and the necessity of a new system of knowledge that enables everything to be seen in a new light. In the English declensions, all considerations of truth are guided by new systems of relations supplied by empiricism and rationalism.

The American Baptist declension, in contradistinction from that of the English, does not arise from a new system of relations, but from a new set of constituent elements. American Baptists do not invent a new system in order to interpret the old tradition and its data. They most often remain suspicious of all traditions and all systems. Their concern is that of individual units of intuited experiences which occur singly, now and then, and at widely scattered locations and in varied ways. This concern doubly affects truth: it covers over the personal truth with individual facts, but its intermittent, sporadic character spares American Baptists from the devastating declension wrought by the empirical and rational systems at work in England.

The severity of the American Baptist declension is also ameliorated by the fact that the new way of knowing, which centers in an experiential grasping of facts by individuals, is similar to the classic approach. It therefore does not require a far-reaching revolutionary change of assumptions and the necessity of a radically new way of processing truth-claims. The experimental knowledge championed in the classic heritage and the knowledge born of the American experience share several features—in particular, they share the priority of life over knowledge, the bubbling up of truth from the bottoms of history, the democratization of knowledge, the importance of liberty, the identification of truth and action, and the priority of the unique.

Nevertheless, the classic experimental and the new experiential approach are not the same. To the nondiscriminating eye, they may appear to be the same. Upon careful examination, however, basic differences can be seen. An experimental approach to truth emphasizes persons, human and divine, in relation within the gospel story. An experiential approach, on the contrary, relates truth to individual experience. The experimental approach pertains to what's real; it apprehends the face of the Living God. The experiential approach pertains to what's known, and what's known is comprehended as an array of facts in statement form.

American Baptists experience a chill in piety, no little spiritual lethargy, and some dullness of spirit prior to the Great Awakening. One commentator on the spiritual condition of the times says that "saints were in short supply."[3] But the downturn in Baptist life does not last. In the Great

Awakening, personal piety and evangelical reform, the full force of experimental religion, become commonplace.

Yet, in an ironic twist of history, the evangelical revival moves Baptists away from their heritage of truth and its insistence upon experimental knowledge. The Great Awakening stresses the individual believer, whose very own experience is thought to be the new source of authority. As a result of the revival, Baptists claim to learn divine truths by direct experience. The experience of conversion, they argue, opens a believer's eyes to the principles of a supernatural wisdom which acquires greater weight than the wisdom found in the story of personal truth. So central is individual experience among the Separate Baptists that they have a tendency to sit in judgment on those who do not have the required kind of experience. They have a definite idea of what counts as the proper kind of religious experience, and they are loath to recognize any person as truly converted who has not experienced the emotional excitement and the individual voice of conscience informed by the New Light.

But, whether American Baptists insist that a knowledge of truth can be found in only one kind of experience, or refuse to stereotype what counts as experience, in their declension they transfer the center of truth away from the domains of the personal and the gospel. They prefer to find that center in a form of religious experience which radically separates the subject from the object, and which reduces the agent, who is a participant, to an individual observer, who intuits the factual truths of experience.

The Doctrinal Truths of Calvinism

The experiential character of the American Baptist declension appears alongside of a phenomenon which at first sight contradicts it. American Baptists turn to the doctrinal truths of Calvinism so as to guarantee experientially known facts.

Shortly after mid-century, almost all General Baptist churches join the swelling ranks of Particular Baptists, and Baptists in America are henceforth predominantly Calvinistic, though their mode for expressing it varies greatly. The Regular Baptists, largely urban, are "solemn and rational," John Leland says, while the Separate Baptists, who congregate on the frontier and in small towns and embrace the emotionalism of the Awakening, are "zealous, and the work among them very noisy."[4] But, whether they pursue Calvinism with order or ardor, its doctrines are at times understood by American Baptists to be both the substance and the test of truth.

The doctrinal truths of Calvinism function as the substance of truth for American Baptists in their occasional moments of declension. Isaac Backus of Massachusetts, for instance, complains, "The Methodists earnestly strike against the most essential doctrines of the gospel. To hold up light against their errors, as others, is of great importance in this time when many have an ear to hear."[5] The light of which Backus speaks is not that of personal truth but of Calvinistic doctrines. In a letter to the Warren Association of New England, the Weston Baptist Church similarly complains, "One thing which much discourages us is the Weslian methodists appear determined to spread their tenets which appear to us contrary to truth and our articles of faith."[6]

The Warren Baptist Association voices the same concern when it protects itself from errors by a creedal test, as if truths and errors were the substance of the gospel. Its minutes read: "As it is a time of the prevalence of errors of every kind and of the apostacy of many from the faith of the gospel, it is recommended to the churches that they express in their annual letter to the Association their particular adherence to the doctrines of grace."[7] By the term "the doctrines of grace" the Warren Baptists mean the doctrines of Calvinism as expressed in the Second London Confession. These doctrines, namely, those of Christ's divinity, the perseverance of the saints, sovereign grace, and the like, are placed in opposition not only to the doctrines of the Methodists but to those of the Unitarians, Universalists, and Arminians, so as to secure the substance of truth.

The covenants of Baptist churches classically begin with the communion of God and believers as the basis for church life. But, in the declension, a few American Baptist covenants replace this personalistic starting-point with a special regard for Calvinistic doctrines as the substance of truth. The 1785 covenant of Baptists in Bent Creek, Tennessee, for example, begins with an overriding concern for Calvinistic doctrines as the substance of truth. It states that, since those who profess to be Christians are so different in their principles and practices that they cannot generally fellowship one with another, the members of the Bent Creek church do covenant together to depend on Christ for salvation and on the scriptures which contain the doctrines of justification by the imputed righteousness of Jesus Christ, sanctification through God's grace and truth, and the final perseverance of the saints in grace.[8]

American Baptists, who heed the caution of the Philadelphia Baptist Association that Christians should hold the truths declared in the gospel,[9] not only think that the substance of truth is formed by the doctrinal truths of Calvinism, but they at times use the doctrines as a standard instrument in the testing of truth-claims. For example, Aaron Leland, pastor of the First Church of Chester, Vermont, opts, the doctrine set by Jesus and the apostles is "a discriminating doctrine—it draws the golden line between truth and error."[10] Or, consider a 1752 church query as to whether a person denying unconditional election, the doctrine of original sin, and the final perseverance of the saints can fellowship with the church. The Philadelphia Baptist Association answers in a way that decisively establishes the true propositions of Calvinism as the test of truth. It states: personal election is the truth of God; original sin is one of the fundamental doctrines of Christianity; and the perseverance of the saints is a tenet upon which faith must rest.[11]

While the doctrinal truths of Calvinism are occasionally understood to be both the substance and the test of truth, they also occasionally serve as the basis of unity among American Baptists. The New England churches of the Warren Association, for instance, find their unity in an adherence to an orthodoxy shaped by the propositional truths of London Baptists, such as the imputation of Adam's sin to his posterity, the effectual calling by sovereign grace, and justification by imputed righteousness.

The Regular and the Separate Baptists of Virginia unite around similar orthodox propositions. They deny that their confession usurps individual freedom, yet they affirm that it contains the essential truths of the gospel, and that the doctrine of salvation by Christ and by free unmerited grace alone ought to be believed by every Christian. Then they add, "upon these terms we are united."[12] The reality of persons in relation within the life-world of the gospel does not unite Virginia Baptists. In a most unbaptistic way, doctrines do. The declension, although momentary, is obvious.

In a most interesting move, John Leland of Virginia initially finds, in the controversy over the doctrines of predestination and universal provision among Virginia Baptists, that the doctrines of both parties cannot be right. Nevertheless, in a way reminiscent of the classic heritage, he admits that those who have a right heart and who walk in love cannot be wrong. Then, he observes, the doctrines of the eternal purposes of God and the freedom of the will are both truths. He further observes that preaching to be most blessed and profitable which is founded upon the Calvinistic doctrine of the sovereign grace in salvation mixed with the Arminian doctrine of free will. He thereby reconciles two true statements, and reaffirms the unity of Regular and Separate Baptists in Virginia, all the while finding unity not in the domain of the personal but in the epistemic realm of doctrinally orthodox statements.[13]

Left with an Assemblage of Facts and Doctrines

The declension of American Baptists, though mild in comparison with that of their English cousins, entails a loss of the domain of the personal and, thus, of the gospel and truth itself. Baptists at times find themselves tragically left with an assemblage of facts intuitively grasped in religious experience, often secured by the orthodox doctrines of Calvinism, and therefore found to be authoritative. Upon these occasions they embrace facts and doctrines, not faces, thereby forgetting the personal truth.

THE BAPTIST HERESY: FORGETFULNESS

In the Christian rationalism espoused by the English and the American Baptists of the classic heritage, "the supreme rational agent is not man but God."[14] Human reason is understood to be limited by finitude and rendered fallible by sin. It can originate nothing. If reason is to know the truth, it must first be converted then disciplined by the rationality of God expressed within the supreme story of revelation. All human reasoning about truth thus arises in a creaturely participation in the divine reasoning, what the English People at Amsterdam, in their 1612–1614 confession, think to be the reasoning of the new creature in fellowship with the three witnesses.[15]

Thus, classic English and American Baptists disclaim the thesis that truth is a system of truths established at the outset, fixed, and possessed all at once. Their claim, a most radical one, is that truth is not a matter of a knowledge of truths and errors (plural), but a person's participation in the biography of the person of the Living God (singular). Truth is more than a group of experiences, rational ideas, or intuited facts fastened together. It is reality, and reality is the Living God—Father, Son, Spirit—in the Good Story.

That is why for classic Baptists proving the truth is so serious a matter. The voices of the settled truths of experience, ideas, or facts are not to be confused with the voice of personal truth, for the personal truth discloses itself ever anew only to those who prove it ever anew in the drama of a life firmly planted within the gospel. Truth is not what is known but what the Living God is and does. The Christian consequently cannot examine truth in any other way than that of actually entering into the life of God. Nay, more than that, the crucial precondition for proving anew the personal truth is that the Holy Trinity lives with, for, and in the Christian, occupying the space previously held by that of a knowledge of truths and errors. The initiative is that of God's.

It is the melancholy of the fate of both English and American Baptists that in their declension they set aside Christian rationalism, preferring abstract shadows of truth rather than its concrete substance. They forget that truth is the Living God and the People of God knit together in the Dynamic Communion where Truth and Grace meet. They remember only that truth which is a monument or a static thing in the world, something easily reduced to the abstractions of (1) the given, (2) the general, (3) the theoretical, and (4) the egocentric—all associated with the dualism of subject and object, itself but an abstraction of the modern mind.

The Immediately Given

In their forgetfulness, English and American Baptists of the declension are enchanted by an abstract given. English General Baptists are fascinated with the given of an inner light, and they seek to penetrate the inexplicability of the doctrines of the Holy Trinity and the deity of Christ with the light of subjective experience. They legitimize themselves, not by doctrinal uniformity, but by way of the experiential or by subjective-mystical experiences. For them truth must first be apprehended within, and directly so.

English Particular Baptists begin with the given of rationally demonstrated axioms, those of the veracity of the scriptures and the existence of the sovereign God, and with the use of logic infer principles from the axioms present to consciousness. They know that the objects of faith are not bare axioms, for the act of faith does not terminate with axioms but at the thing-in-itself, with the chief object that of God. Still, they understand the object of faith in rationalistic terms and secure its truth with axioms abstracted from the richness of the gospel.

American Regular and Separate Baptists love the facts that lie on the surface of the phenomena given directly in the immediacy of the ordinary experiences of the worlds of nature and spirit. Everything must be clearly upfront and intuitively given, solidly orthodox too, in a Calvinistic sense.

Although separated by what counts as the form and the content of the given, Baptists from England and America unite in a forgetfulness of that truth which is a "rattlin' good yarn." A story of historical proportions is afoot, God in Christ through the Spirit is reconciling the world, yet the Baptists of the declension speak only of an abstract given—the data of experience, the axioms of reason, or the facts of intuition.

In the classic heritage, truth has a history. This history is essential, not accidental to it. The believer can know God only by entering into fellowship with God in history. But Baptists in their declension abstract from the domain of personal life, and so radically isolate their knowledge from the historical drama which sustains it that the believer is understood as a pure subject, who knows only the immediately given of an object-world. The subject stands over against the living relationships of God and persons, isolated from the relationships which sustain it, not in dynamic relationship with the good story. The subject consequently knows only the specious or the shining present filled with simple elements (experiences, ideas, or facts), which are private and which fragment, offering only a representation of what exists, and an inadequate one at best.

General Truths

Classic Baptists know that truth is constituted by the acts of the Living God in the life-worlds of people in England and America. These acts are sometimes but not always marked by an extraordinary divine character. Many appear perfectly ordinary and some seemingly trivial. Of whatever magnitude, however, the acts inevitably involve singular persons in relation within the gospel story.

The Baptists of the declension fall into heresy, not when they hold false statements about the singular, relational, and gospel faces of truth, but when they substitute general or universal statements, whether true or false, for those faces. Whenever they substitute statements which relate to, are concerned with, or are applicable to every member of a class (set or group) for the singular person, relationship, or gospel, then they forget the personal truth and fall into heresy. Statements of generality that express the nature of matters spiritual, highly specialized ones too, even well-verified doctrines or beliefs of all stripes, do not take precedence over the singularity of persons and relationships in the gospel.

On both sides of the Atlantic Ocean, in their tragic forgetfulness, Baptists think of truth as the quality of a general statement. When they examine truth, or define it, they inevitably begin by analyzing a sentence known to be universally true, say, one about the attributes of God or the way of salvation, for Baptists in their declension equate truth with the contents of true statements.

The Particular Baptists of England think of truth as the relationship between the general statements expressed in scriptural texts and those in the mind of God. The scriptures, they say, truthfully reveal the mind of God. A person must believe the true statements therein revealed, ones filtered through a Calvinistic sieve, too, such as the doctrines of limited atonement and the perseverance of the saints. These general truths represent an irreducible minimum of beliefs and establish theological parameters.

English General Baptists and American Baptists love the experiences which present themselves ready at hand, yet they focus upon beloved principles or an assemblage of facts, just one more set of general truths in the world alongside other truths, all in statement form. Again, Baptists value an irreducible minimum of general truths.

In their love of general statements, the Baptists of the declension fasten upon an abstract quality of truth. As a consequent, they fasten upon the non-existent, that is to say, upon ideas, experiences, or facts in statement form which they claim are universally true. In the classic Baptist heritage, to exist is to be in dynamic interrelation with other existents. What exists is concrete, historical, vital, personal, not abstract, propositional, general. That which is isolated from its dynamic relations with the concrete is isolated from existence and thereby from truth. With the reduction of the reality of God to a generality expressed in a belief or in a doctrinal statement, Baptists do not treat God as a singular person in gospel relation with human persons. They treat God as "God." God is an experience, an idea, or a fact, a true one to be sure, still only a general truth in the mind, along with other general truths, all of which have the same status as statements, which can only be said to be representative of truth.

The Theoretical

Along with a turn to an abstract given and the general, a theoretical temper shapes the substance of the heresy of forgetfulness. In their declension, the Baptists of England and America hold a modern rationalism (not a Christian rationalism) that proceeds as if the knowing self were a pure subject for whom the world is an object, and for whom the known is a questionable matter which demands of proof or verification. The subject stands over against the object, not in dynamic relation to it, so much so that the mind never directly contacts the real but only the given (of experience, reason, or intuition) and an irreducible minimum of general truths inferred therefrom, which, if secured by the correspondence or the coherence test of truth, or by an inductive assemblage of facts, sometimes by doctrines, provide theoretical bridges to the real object, whether it be God, nature, values, or persons.

There is a great gulf between this abstractly theoretical stance and that of the classic view of an enlightened conscience illuminated by the fundamentals and the categories of "the truth as it is in Jesus." The enlightened conscience is reduced in the declension to nothing more than the deductive and the inductive workings of a technical reason, which cannot do justice to the historical gospel and its uniquely personal kind of truth.

The presupposition of the primacy of the theoretical which permeates the Baptist declension cannot even formulate the question of truth in uniquely personal terms. It must substitute an abstract dualism of subject and object for the relationships of the person and the Living God so essential to the classic heritage. God and persons are understood as mere objects of thought, with God the supreme object, to be sure, but still only an object. Furthermore, the knowledge of God and persons in a theoretical view is not an actual or an adequate knowledge of persons. For thinking about another person, or thinking about a representation of that person in terms of experiences, ideas, or facts, can never amount to an acquaintance with that person.

The adoption of the theoretical perspective, and its accompanying dualisms—those of subject and object, theoretical and practical, subjective and objective, absolute and relative—may well reveal a desire on the part of the Baptists of the declension to know the truth without the hard work of living the truth. It may just be that their secret wish is to escape from the personal and its demand that truth finally requires a continuing quest, a historical pilgrimage, of persons in the drama of the gospel story, not a possession of knowledge, no matter how sacred or how firmly secured by the theoretical apparatus of empiricism, rationalism, or intuitionism.

The Egocentric

Throughout their declension Baptists claim to know, but their claim is egocentric, because knowledge is always that of the "I know." The person in relation within the good story gives way to the knowing self or to the subject—to the "I." The person in relation also gives way to the self isolated from the object it knows. The self is withdrawn from participation in life, reflecting on the world it knows. In its reflection upon subjective experiences, rational axioms, or self-evident facts which are present to the shining present of consciousness, the self pulls back into a theoretical mode and adopts the stance of a spectator, not that of a participant. There is no place for this self in the world. And whatever world it knows consists of its own ideas.

With this egocentric turn, taking the abstract self as their starting-point for a knowledge of truth, Baptists cover over the biography of God, the concretely tangible salvation drama which serves the classic legacy so well as the paradigm of truth. Moreover, in this turn, they do not think of the person as a "thou" that is addressed in the gospel drama, but as an "I," as a self, or as the individual, and as an individual in isolation from other individuals too.

This covering over of the biography of God and the address of God by an egocentric turn is readily seen in the fact that there can arise among Baptists such questions as "How can we know that God exists?" and "How can we secure the axiom of God's sovereignty upon which we are to build our system of truths?" It is also seen in the fact that Baptists question the deity of Christ, their Saviour and Lord and the trinitarian nature of God, wonder how the truth of the scriptures might be established so as to set true beliefs, and worry the issue of how the sacred truths square with their experience.

The self so premised is a thinker in search of knowledge. It is a knower—the correlate of the object presented for cognition. Baptists forget that the person is first and foremost a pilgrim, a disciple who follows the call of Christ, one who treads the roads of history with the Living God who forever and ever runs ahead.

BAPTISTS WIN THE SMALL PRIZES
BUT GAMBLE THEIR LIVES AWAY

In their declension in England and America, Baptists are out of touch with the personal. In the place of the concretely personal truth, they substitute the abstractions of the given, the general, the theoretical, and the egocentric. The existence of truth at once becomes problematical for them and must be confirmed by means of empiricism, rationalism, or intuitionism, for all possible objects of knowledge have become equally images or representations which demand a reference beyond themselves and which clamor for verification. Thus, Baptists win the small prizes but gamble their lives away.

A TIME OF REAFFIRMATION
THE LATE–EIGHTEENTH CENTURY

AN OVERVIEW

Part Four—"A Time of Reaffirmation: The Late–Eighteenth Century"—
traces the reaffirmation of the classic heritage of personal truth by English
and American Baptists in the second half of the eighteenth century.

Chapter Eight—"Tell Us What God Says: English General Baptists"—
records the revolution in matters of truth wrought by Dan Taylor and the
New Connexion of English General Baptists who understand that truth is
primitive Christianity.

*Chapter Nine—"The Simplicity of the Gospel: English Particular
Baptists"*—unpacks the thought of Andrew Fuller, John Sutcliff, William
Carey, and other English Particular Baptists who opt that the personal
truth which shines with bright lustre is the gospel worthy of all acceptance.

Chapter Ten—"A Cordial Reception of the Gospel: American Baptists"—
chronicles the thought of Isaac Backus and American Regular and Separate
Baptists throughout the colonies in America, and in the newly emergent
states and on the frontiers of the United States, who understand truth to be
an experimental or heart-felt reality.

Chapter Eight

TELL US WHAT GOD SAYS
ENGLISH GENERAL BAPTISTS

In the new testament, our blessed Saviour calls himself the truth. This appellation belongs to him, as he is the true substance of the Jewish types and shadows, which were intended to them, as emblematical representations of him, and of the blessings that flow from him to believers. He is also the author and fountain of truth, in all things that relate to the happiness of man. He only gives true and solid satisfaction to a soul oppressed with a sense of sin, and enquiry after everlasting felicity. He was likewise the great "teacher sent from God," to give a full account of his heavenly Father's will to us poor ignorant sinners, and to give us those true and infallible directions in the way to heaven, which whoever follows, will assuredly arrive safe at the regions of never-ending glory.

Dan Taylor, *The Consistent Christian*, 1784

REPENTANCE

English and American Baptists in the second half of the eighteenth century took to heart the meaning of the first word in the Christian message of salvation, that of "repentance." Immersed in declension, they did not consider a call to make a minor adjustment in their faith and practice, which would amount to nothing more than accepting what they already had. The only outlook adequate for them was one open to the revolutionary change wrought by the reality of the simple gospel in their hands.

Dan Taylor led the return of English General Baptists to the gospel of primitive Christianity. His New Connexion of 1770 saved General Baptists from the ravages of subjective experience and most likely from extinction, although its reforms proved to be partial, for within a century the New Connexion languished in the same problems which plagued General Baptists in their declension.

Weary of hyper-Calvinism and the rationalism which undergirded it, English Particular Baptists, under the leadership of Andrew Fuller, Robert Hall Sr., and William Carey, recovered not only a gospel but a truth worthy of all acceptance. The dismal picture of the declension thus brightened considerably. Particular Baptists adopted a modified Calvinism, regained spiritual vitality, and found a missionary spirit.

The second half of the eighteenth century was a turning point for American Baptists as well. Affected only mildly by a declension from truth to truths, Regular and Separate Baptists gained new vitality. Outwardly they became the largest denomination in America; inwardly they struggled for liberty, became an evangelistic people, and appropriated the heart-felt reality of the gospel.

With separate yet united voices, Baptists of the old and the new worlds committed themselves, not to reform their ways, but to repent thoroughly and to revive experimental religion. They trusted once more the simple story of the gospel and its realistic animation as their paradigm of truth. They knew, just as did their classic forbearers, that truth is the decidedly personal and concrete "truth as it is in Jesus" in the drama of the good story.

As a result of their repentance, Robert Hall Jr. observes of English Particular Baptists at the end of the eighteenth century, an observation equally applicable to English General and American Baptists, "a considerable revolution has been effected in the sentiments of the denomination. Truth has shone with brighter lustre."[1]

PEACE OR TRUTH

The reaffirmation of the classic legacy by English General Baptists centered in Dan Taylor (1738–1816) and the New Connexion of General Baptists. Dan Taylor, a coal miner and a Methodist convert from Yorkshire, at the age of twenty-four was baptized in the river Idle following his declaration of faith, "I am a General Baptist." Shortly thereafter he gathered a small church near his home of Wadsworth, mostly made up of common people like himself. He then led them to join with the Lincolnshire General Baptists, only to be saddened by their anti-evangelical ways and rapid turn to Unitarianism. Convinced that the General Assembly was uninterested in truth itself, vital piety, and evangelism, he joined with ministers in Whitechapel, London, in 1770, to found the New Connexion of General Baptists.

The General Assembly, which valued peace above truth, opposed the new union and sought reconciliation between the old and new bodies. At their meeting at Horsleydown, the Assembly expresses this sentiment, "We heartily wish for Union & Harmony & we express our Determination not to make a Difference of private Opinion a Breach of love & Affection." Gilbert Boyce speaks for the Assembly and its desire for peace with these words, "O Lord, direct us in thy truth. Guide us in the paths of peace."[2]

Taylor, however, is not dissuaded from the value of the New Connexion. He sees in it the only hope for the restoration of the personal truth and the essential doctrines of the gospel.[3] He states his position with Yorkshire bluntness, "It is not to be doubted that some of the vilest errors are, in this age, maintained by some of the General Baptists. It behoves us therefore to take the alarm, and with all the little might we have to militate against those pernicious tenets which our forefathers so much abhorred, and which the Word of God so expressly condemns."[4]

Love peace, Taylor counsels, but take care to love solely that peace which is "a peaceful calm, and holy serenity in our own consciences." Because, he reasons, peace is subordinate to truth, which is "a most excellent and invaluable jewel, of infinite advantage to the souls of men." When the choice is between two evils, choose the least, Taylor advises; but when between two advantages, choose the best. Truth and peace are two advantages, and since "truth has most certainly the pre-eminence," it must be chosen. Taylor does not arbitrarily choose truth as the superior value. He reasons that, whatever the advantages of peace may be, it cannot bring salvation. It cannot restore fellowship with God. It does not address the problem at the heart of the personal or recreate the purity of the personal. But truth does.[5]

TRUTH AT ITS BOTTOM

Dan Taylor delights in quoting a countryman who, when the preacher kept saying, "I think," called out in the midst of the sermon, "What signifies it what thou thinkest? Tell us what God says."[6] His delight springs in part from the realization that some Baptists are coming home to a truth that at its bottom is proclaimed in the scriptures. The free grace party, Taylor knows, is coming home to "the truth as it is in Jesus."

On June 6, 1770, at Whitechapel, London, Taylor delivered a discourse based on the words, "Be not ashamed of the testimony of the Lord." That very day the New Connexion adopted his Articles of Religion as its confession of faith.

The six articles hearken back to the legacy of the Baptist confessions of faith in the seventeenth century, for their entire focus is that of the good story of Jesus Christ. They do not speak of a subjective experience or an inner voice, so loved by the Baptists of the General Assembly in their declension. The articles speak of one thing only. They tell of a series of events that form the story of Jesus Christ in the redemptive drama. That is, they tell of the fall, the moral law, the person and the work of Jesus Christ, salvation by faith, regeneration by the Holy Spirit, and the people of God.

The six articles certainly address the points in dispute between the New Connexion and the General Assembly, like that of the doctrine of the deity of Christ, which had earlier caused so much disruption in General Baptist life. But the New Connexion's concern for orthodoxy does not signal the presence of an overriding care for doctrinal truths or point to a reduction of truth to theoretical, general, and propositional truths based squarely on the given data of inner experience. Truths undoubtedly count for the New Connexion, but not ultimately or determinatively, however. Truths do not set what counts as truth. Only truth establishes truth.

Interestingly, the New Connexion does not offer a complete summary of Christian doctrines in its articles of faith. An overriding desire for orthodox truths might well require a full summary. But the New Connexion has another goal. It uses the articles to guard against the inclination of the Baptists in the General Assembly to deny the deity of Christ on the basis of the evidence of inner experience. And, while carefully avoiding a precisely defined creed, the New Connexion also uses the articles to distinguish its tenets from those of the Assembly.

The announced design of the 1770 confession of faith, however, speaks of the primary intention of the articles—namely, "to revive experimental religion or primitive Christianity." The Baptists of the New Connexion obviously believe it more important to insist upon a living encounter and relationship with Jesus Christ than to insist upon the truths associated with orthodox doctrines and denominational soundness. They accordingly craft their statement of faith so as to tell the good story and recount its personal realities and relationships. This story, they know, is truth.

Though not in strict story form, the six articles of faith have all the distinguishing features of a story. The storylike language and style of the 1770 confession of faith of the General Baptists cannot be missed. A personalistic point of view and thematic expression also pervade each of its articles. Propositions and proofs aren't needed, so they don't appear. Systematic development and doctrines aren't prized. Theories can't be found. The Baptists of the New Connexion stand in 1770, mired in a declension of immense proportions, alone in Lincolnshire, London, Kent, and Essex; and, with their very first statement of belief, at a defining event of their history, they speak only of the good story: of sin and salvation, Jesus Christ and the Holy Spirit, law and grace, universal invitation and the particular community of baptized believers.

Moreover, when the Baptists of the New Connexion speak, they do so with reference to incident, plot, and character, all ingredients of a story. The articles abound with accounts of key incidents in the good story, such as the fall, the cross, personal regeneration, and repentance. They abound too with talk of the key characters in the good story: those of the sinner, the saint, Jesus Christ, Satan, and the Spirit. They are also filled with talk of a plot predicated upon human choice and the love of God, one tied to a historical struggle between good and evil, a plot which intertwines law and grace.

And in it all—in the personal style and language, in the personalistic thesis, and in the attention to incidents, plot, and characters—the articles of the 1770 confession bring to story the personal domain of truth, and thereby reclaim the classic heritage.

The Articles of Religion tell this story. There is one God, of whom are all things, and for whom are all things, who is Father, Son, and Holy Spirit. Persons were formed in the moral image of God, created to live, think, and desire in total devotion to God, categorically commanded to love the Lord with all of mind, heart, soul, and strength, but they fell from this purity. Sin entered the world. Human nature was depraved, minds defiled, and all persons were taken captive by their own evil and by Satan. Jesus Christ, God in the flesh, in a voluntary and vicarious death, suffered to make a full atonement for the sins of every person and thereby wrought a complete salvation, bringing the love of God to all persons. Those persons who look only to Christ by faith are made children of God, regenerated by the Holy

Spirit and through the instrumentality of the word, sanctified and recreated for the enjoyment of heaven, and bound together as baptized believers in the beloved community.[7]

It's there, is it not, in the measure of six brief articles, in only 661 words in the confession, the story of the gospel that is, and truth too, but only truth at its bottom—only a concretely personal kind of truth? The declension of a remnant of General Baptists is over; the classic heritage is embraced.

TRUTH IS THE SOLE PROPERTY OF JESUS CHRIST

Dan Taylor expands upon the personalistic thrust of the Articles of Religion of the New Connexion in the short but highly significant discussion of truth found in his 1784 book, *The Consistent Christian*. Truth, he declares, is Jesus Christ, who is (1) the essence of truth, (2) the author of truth, and (3) the teacher of truth.

The Essence of Truth

"Our blessed Saviour calls himself the Truth,"[8] Dan Taylor says. This name, which belongs to Christ alone, he adds, peculiarly points to the essence of truth as the personal reality of "the truth." The name of Christ— the appellation of "the truth" ascribed to the incarnate Son of God—does not refer the believer to the statements about Christ and the atonement, which qualify as true doctrines. It rather refers the believer to the real person of Jesus Christ and to the actual work of the life, death, and resurrection of the Word become flesh, to a person and a work which together form the substance of truth. With this move Taylor positions himself squarely within the first fundamental of the classic heritage which claims that truth is the Living God.

In his posthumously published book, *An Essay on the Truth and the Inspiration of the Holy Scriptures* (1819), Taylor argues for the equation of truth with realities or facts, primarily those realities of Jesus Christ which are recorded in the New Testament.[9] The realities of Jesus Christ, Taylor recognizes, are not mere facts contained in true doctrines and confirmed by appeals to the correspondence and the coherence tests of truth, though to be sure the biblical truth-claims associated with the realities measure up to these tests. The substance of New Testament history is not factual statements about Jesus Christ's person and work at all, he observes, but rather the real person and the actual work of Jesus Christ.

The realities of which Taylor speaks are a whole "series of events and works performed [in] sacred history," for instance, such events as Christ performing miracles and doing good, voluntarily dying on the cross, being resurrected, and sending the Spirit at Pentecost. In response to the Particular Baptist Andrew Fuller, Taylor includes among the realities the historical events of the universality of God's love, the death of Jesus Christ as the propitiation for sin, and the universal invitations of the gospel. These clearly articulated events at the heart of the Christian kerygma not only provide salvation for all, with the provision that each person chooses to believe, but they constitute truth itself.[10]

Taylor obviously adopts the classic heritage's view that truth-theory is subservient to the gospel story or, in his words, to the "series of events and works performed [in] sacred history," which taken together speak richly of truth's essence.

The Author of Truth

Taylor also holds to the second fundamental of the classic heritage, which asserts that believers possess content and model the truth that God is and does. The truth that Jesus Christ—the Son of God—is and does, Taylor contends, flows from Christ to believers, who thereby participate in the kind of truth that Christ is and does. Believers build upon the essential foundation or the epitome of Christ, and can be said to live in Christ, who is the "author and fountain of truth." In particular, when persons cordially believe, they discover a turn of mind to trust in Jesus Christ[11] and receive true fulfillment and everlasting joy.[12] This relation with Christ is what truth is.

The Teacher of Truth

Jesus Christ, Taylor says, is not only the essence and the author of truth but the teacher sent from heaven, who alone gives believers a full account of God's will concerning the true and infallible way of salvation. The mind of God can be discerned by means other than the teachings of Christ—for example, by means of the teachings of Paul, in a reasonable examination of the whole of scriptures, or by the guidance of the Holy Spirit. But only Christ's teachings have the sure stamp of final completeness.

The teachings of Christ, Taylor qualifies his view, do not carry authority in and of themselves. The life of Christ gives authority to the teachings of Christ. Life is like that. Life legitimizes teachings; teachings do not legitimize life. Therefore, it is undoubtedly the case, Taylor argues, that "the great characteristic of truth, in sacred matters, is, that the Lord hath spoken it." Taylor's emphasis here falls upon the Lord. The teachings of Christ derive their authority from the Lord who reveals the will and the ways of the heavenly Father. It is the Lord, who primordially stands "in opposition to all the errors we have imbibed," Taylor says, "through the native darkness of our minds, the wildness of our fancies, our connections in life, and the traditions of men, by which we are continually surrounded, and too frequently ensnared."[13]

THE TRUTH OF THE SCRIPTURES

Taylor and the General Baptists of the New Connexion believe that "the great characteristic of truth, in sacred matters, is, that 'the Lord hath spoken it.'" The Lord, they think, has spoken in the realities of sacred history—in the divine word, and this is truth. The Lord has spoken as well in the Holy Scriptures—in the written word, and this too is truth.

The Truth in General
The Holy Scriptures, and the Gospels in particular, the New Connexion holds, "contain THE TRUTH in general." That is to say, they are a perfect guide, one that supports the soul by giving light applicable to the whole of faith and practice. They are, indeed, the "only test of divine truth, by which we are to try and examine all our own sentiments, experience, and conduct." Whatever the word of God does not express in its oracles, or whatever cannot be inferred from them by fair rules of reasoning or interpretation, Taylor avers, is not to be admitted as truth. "Thy word is truth."[14]

Foundations of the Scriptures of Truth
The scriptures of truth are said to be founded in realities or in facts. The 1770 confession affirms that the scriptures are founded in the reality of God's moral law—a law obligatory to Adam, revealed in the ten commandments, and more fully expanded throughout the whole of the scriptures. They are grounded too in the particulars of Jesus Christ, the incarnate Son of God, who made full atonement in the cross and is present in the lives of believers. It can also be said fairly that the 1770 confession anchors the scriptures in the actual leadership of the Holy Spirit, who works through the instrumentality of the scriptures in the life of the believer. The truth of the scriptures is further grounded in the rigors of reasonableness.[15]

Dan Taylor opts as well that the truth of the scriptures is based on the actuality of inspiration and in the witnesses of the leading facts, witnesses who were moved by the Spirit of God. Moreover, it is confirmed with signs and wonders and diverse miracles and by the blood of those persons slain for the word of God. The scriptures are finally founded, Taylor thinks, in the heart of every true believer who is guided by the light from above through prayer, reflection, and meditation, and by the purposes at the bottom of the scriptures (the intentional character of the scriptures), that is, to teach doctrine, convince of sin, correct errors, reveal duty, test right and wrong, and try sermons.[16]

In other words, Taylor and the New Connexion see the scriptures functioning within the whole apparatus of truth centered in the Living God. It is only when they are so founded that they can be qualified as the only guide. They are the unique guide applicable to the whole of faith and practice because they are substantially related to the Father, the Holy Spirit, the life of faith, revelation, inspiration, sacred history, the moral nature of the world, reasonableness, and above all else, Jesus Christ. Without this interpretive matrix or relational context of the gospel drama, the scriptures would not be truthful or the truth in general. They are not an abstract, self-contained kind of truth.

So convinced is Taylor that the scriptures are inextricably linked with the full gospel and the domain of the personal, flowing as they do from the Living God, that he holds the scriptures to be the "infallible and unmixed truth. They are also the complete truth, and the only rule of judgment concerning truth and falshood, right and wrong, in all matters of religion, whether respecting faith or practice." So complete, in fact, are the scriptures that Taylor thinks that the believer should "go as far as the scripture goes [and] be silent where the scripture is silent."[17]

FELLOW HELPERS TO THE TRUTH

Truth at its bottom is the gospel story of Jesus Christ and of persons who live, move, and find their being in the reality of the person of Jesus Christ. An authentic participation in this drama requires, for the New Connexion, that persons live obediently to the scriptures and that they live attuned to the people of God and to the essentials of eternal life. Truth, after all, is thoroughly practical by turn.

In a 1796 letter to church members, Dan Taylor speaks of the practical character of truth with these words: the church is "the Pillar and ground of the truth," and believers "fellow-helpers to the truth." Together, all true believers have the right and the responsibility to demonstrate in their characters and in their deeds the truthful virtues of light and life, joy and peace, strength and consolation, purity and hope. They are also obligated to practice undissembled love and to engage in mutual edification, forgiveness, cheerfulness, sacrifice, loyalty, fairness, and watchcare, "maintaining evangelical truth" and establishing one another in truth.[18] These obligations extend to individuals and to churches, as well as to associations which are to be animated by their zealous regard for the truths of God and for the truth of God's kingdom, for these obligations are of the essence of personal truth.[19]

In answer to the question as to what manner of love and esteem Christians ought to show to the truth, Taylor answers in a most practical vein that "true faith worketh by love" and displays "the grace of God in truth." Christians are to "seek earnestly to know what is truth" and to well establish themselves in it. Speak the truth, he adds, and "abide by the truth." Be vigilant and "valiant for the truth," giving every assistance to it, propagating it, converting to the truth those who do not know it, and faithfully practicing it through every scene of life.[20]

THE GRAND OFFICE OF REASON

The distinctive kind of practice that is truth, the Baptists of the New Connexion know, is an attunement of the whole person in Christ to a life obedient to the Holy Scriptures, demonstrative of love, expressive of the full range of Christian virtues, and dedicated to the community of faith. And, they add, the distinctive kind of practice that is truth involves a commitment to a life of reasonableness.

In an enlightened conscience informed by Jesus Christ, the Baptists of the New Connexion find, "the grand office of reason" uses the full range of standards found in the classic heritage, such as those of empirical adequacy, historical reliability, the pragmatic norm, consistency, coherence, and the appeal to the primitive pattern.[21] In the 1788 Worship Street meeting of the Assembly of General Baptists, for instance, Dan Taylor objects to slavery on the grounds that the "slave trade is inconsistent with every rational & humane principle."[22] Or, in his 1788 reply to the Particular

Baptist Andrew Fuller, he insists that the gospel, when cordially believed, turns the mind to Christ, a truth he asserts is evident from reason, scripture, and experience.[23]

Dan Taylor accepts the classic heritage's vision of reasonableness, but he rethinks something of its nature. In opposition to the subjective appeal to inner experience, so loved by the General Baptists of the Assembly, he sets the rugged jaw of a reasonableness shaped by two thinkers in English and Scottish philosophy.

Following the views of the English philosopher John Locke concerning the reliability of evidence,[24] Taylor argues that truth in "matters of fact depends upon the testimony of particulars"—that is, upon the number, the integrity, the skill, the understanding, and the consistent testimony of witnesses (and the evidence of contrary testimonies). Taylor also approvingly considers the Scottish philosopher James Beattie's principles of judgment,[25] which evaluate a person's word by the standards of credibility, motive, competence, and veracity (no deception).

Nothing whatsoever, Taylor contends, can be more fair and reasonable than these rules of evidence. By them he tries the sacred historians in general and those of the New Testament in particular. And, when he applies these standards of evidence to the scriptures, he finds there follows all the guarantee of authenticity that can be reasonably desired of those reports to which God "manifestly stamped the sanction of his own approbation."[26]

In the application of the rules derived from Locke and Beattie, all the evidence needed is forthcoming. Still, Taylor appeals to the test of coherence to understand and to further confirm the veracity of the scriptures. He finds scriptural truth to be a necessary truth, and he confirms the truth of the scriptures by arguing for the coherence of the parts of the scriptures and for the coherent relation of the parts to the whole.[27]

Taylor also uses the correspondence test to think through and to confirm, not to prove, the truth of the scriptures. He defines this test of truth in general as "the exact conformity of our words with the facts we relate."[28] Then he insists that "the truth of New Testament history is greatly confirmed by its agreement in the leading facts of it, as well as in many incidental circumstances, with the best ancient historians," and in the claim that the writers were eyewitnesses who personally attended Jesus.[29]

Taylor respects the power of reasonableness, yet he carefully notes its limits in keeping with the classic legacy. The revelation of God and the perfect account of God's mind and will in the scriptures alone make a person wise unto salvation through faith in Jesus Christ. Revelation is thus superior to human reason, so reason must not set up schemes of its own. Reason must find its place, a most noble one, in the faith which seeks to understand within the personal domain and in terms of the full apparatus of truth. In the final analysis, Taylor witnesses, faith seeks understanding in association with the fundamentals and the categories of personal truth.[30]

AT HOME

"I am the truth." This is the word, the revelation, the proclamation of Jesus Christ. It is what God says. It is not a conclusion which the General Baptists of the New Connexion draw from their individual or collective experiences. It is a claim that comes from the gospel drama itself and from an experimental acquaintance with the good story.

This word is addressed to the General Baptists of the New Connexion. In response they abandon their rootless words and homeless truths which negate and deliberately destroy the reality created by God. Once more the purpose of their words, in unity with the word of God and the classic heritage, expresses the truth of what God says.

And, as a result of their response to what God says, from 1770 on to the end of the eighteenth century, Dan Taylor and the Baptists of the New Connexion, the remnant of free and faithful General Baptists, are at home in the truth of the personal narrative of Jesus Christ.[31]

Chapter Nine

THE SIMPLICITY OF THE GOSPEL
ENGLISH PARTICULAR BAPTISTS

O my God, I find myself in a world where thousands profess thy name; some are preaching, some writing, some talking about religion. All profess to be searching after truth; to have Christ and the inspired writers on their side. I am afraid lest I should be turned aside from the simplicity of the gospel. I feel my understanding full of darkness, my reason exceedingly imperfect, my will ready to start aside, and my passions strangely volatile. O illumine mine understanding, "teach my reason reason," my will rectitude, and let every faculty of which I am possessed be kept within the bounds of thy service.

Andrew Fuller, *Memoir of Mr. Fuller*

REVIVAL

Revival fire burst forth in the souls of Particular Baptists around 1770 as though kindled by a flying spark. It flamed first in the Midlands. Among the Midland Baptists who were struggling against high Calvinism and the deep declension in "doctrinal, experimental and practical religion,"[1] the Kettering pastor, Andrew Fuller (1754–1815), stands preeminent. This greatest of all theologians among English Baptists purged the Particular Baptist soul, removing its forgetfulness of personal truth and the dark night of the prevailing knowledge of modern rationalism and hyper-Calvinism. It was he who most forcefully equated truth with "the simplicity of the gospel."

Fuller was not alone in his reliance upon the truth that is the unvarnished good story simply told. In Kettering he was in touch with John Sutcliff of Olney, who persuaded the Northamptonshire Association to issue its famous prayer-call for revival. He also collaborated with John Ryland of College Lane, Northampton, Robert Hall of Arnsby, and William Carey of Moulton. From Fuller's moderate Calvinism (Fullerism), which avowed that God's grace extended to all people, Carey drew the inference that the gospel must be carried to all people, and with the embodiment of that inference in missionary action, the Baptist revival of personal truth was firmly secured.

THE GOSPEL WORTHY OF ALL ACCEPTANCE

In the revival centered in "the simplicity of the gospel," English Particular Baptists devote themselves to a protracted concentration on "the truth as it is in Jesus" within the historic drama of God loving the world so much "that he gave his only begotten Son, that whosoever believeth in him should not perish, but have everlasting life." In this devotion they find truth explicitly defined in the words of Jesus, "I am the way, the truth, and the life."[2]

Through the Cross of Christ

In order to adequately penetrate into the meaning of "the truth as it is in Jesus," Particular Baptists view everything and everyone "through the cross of Christ." Andrew Fuller observes, "The whole of the Christian system appears to be presupposed by [the cross], included in it, or to arise from it: if therefore, I write any thing, it will be on this principle." In the cross Fuller specifically finds that: (1) all things are created by and are subservient to Christ; (2) all duties are connected to Christ as the one great object; (3) the providence of God centers in the glory of the Redeemer; (4) the cross is the medium from which truths, such as those of the law and holiness, derive their content; and (5) the scriptures are full of Christ. That is to say, he finds that "all Divine truth [bears] an intimate relation to Christ."[3]

The Knowledge of God

All divine truth relates to Christ, but nowhere can this fact be better viewed than in the knowledge of God. God's character can be known,

Andrew Fuller writes, in the works of creation, in the moral law given by God to all creatures, and in the providential government of the world, but only in a partial way. It is in the gospel of Jesus Christ alone that God's full character can be known. In Christ the invisible perfections of God become visible, not as true statements but as realities, primordial realities too, those associated with the incarnation, life, preaching, miracles, sufferings, resurrection, ascension, and exaltation of Jesus Christ, who is finally "the truth."

The perfections of God known in Christ are divided by Fuller into two types: the natural (those which respect God's greatness) and the moral (those which respect God's holiness). Although it is the moral perfections, not the natural, that properly constitute God's character, he argues, both sets of perfections are declared and blended together in Christ. In Christ, wisdom and power, justice and love, "mercy and truth are met together, righteousness and peace have kissed each other," and therein is found the good story of "the infinitely happy God, pouring forth his happiness upon miserable sinners."[4] Truth, most obviously, is someone real in Fuller's view, and he testifies that only "the truth as it is in Jesus" establishes what counts as the knowledge of the God of truth, while securing "the whole chain of evangelical truth."

An Engaging Divine-Human Activity

"The truth as it is in Jesus," which reveals a knowledge of God, is not presented by Andrew Fuller as a plan of artifacts to be studied and talked about, but as an engaging divine-human activity known in terms of incident, plot, character, and theme. In Christ, God acts, Fuller observes, and a good story comes to be. For instance, in his sermon, "An Intimate Knowledge of Divine Truth," he speaks of the characters in the good story as those of God, Christ, Satan, sinners, and saints who together act in a plot centered in the struggle between good and evil. The events of providence, judgment, and salvation, and those of repentance and faith,[5] are recounted as incidents in the story.

In his book, *The Gospel Its Own Witness*, Fuller presents the good story of Jesus Christ in terms of the themes of redemption, such as those of grace, propitiation, the shedding of the Savior's blood, justification, and spiritual blessings.[6] And, in the most significant book by a Baptist in the century, *The Gospel Worthy of All Acceptance*, he speaks of the Holy Trinity and the believer as the key characters in a story which unfolds as an epic conflict of good and evil that consummates in the triumph of the good in history, a story comprised of the incidents of sin, grace, atonement, saving faith, judgment, and love, with everything centered in Christ.[7]

William Carey adds his voice to that of Fuller. In the opening paragraphs of *An Enquiry into the Obligations of Christians* (1792), he speaks of the divine-human activity of the gospel story and its distinctive truth with graceful elegance tempered by brevity. In the first paragraph he says that the gospel of Christ and compassion for the lost, which together compel believers to conscientious activity, stand as "one of the strongest proofs that we are the subjects of grace, and partakers of that spirit of universal benevolence and genuine philanthropy, which appear so eminent in the character of God himself."

Then, in the next two paragraphs, Carey reveals the dialectic of the gospel story. Sin and its baneful influence form the thesis in the dialectic; the Messiah and the Kingdom of God serve as the antithesis; while the effort to bring over a lost world to God stands as the synthesis. Christians have at times heartily spread the gospel. Now, Carey implores, Baptists must obey the divine commission. Their message to a lost world can be nothing short of the cross of Christ embraced, not as the good news which conveys the cross, but as the gospel worthy of all acceptance.

In but three paragraphs a story is told, a drama of divine-human activity set, and the drama is the old, old story of gospel salvation, which is truth itself, a personal truth at once the foundation of the classic heritage and the heart of missions.[8]

THE OBJECT AND ITS CONVEYANCE

In the telling of the old, old story of the cross, Particular Baptists distinguish the object of faith from its means of conveyance. Andrew Fuller, for example, states that faith's object is not a bare proposition, for the act of faith does not end at a true statement, but at the real thing itself. True statements serve a vital function, of course, for by them knowledge may be had of things. But if a bare statement is believed, in distinction from the thing itself, the person who believes the statement is left with the bare belief "that such and such letters make certain words, and that such words put together have a certain meaning."

Faith requires more than bare belief. It requires that a person encounter and trust the thing. "Letters, syllables, words, and propositions," Fuller claims, "are only means of conveyance and not objects of faith."

Faith concerns "the thing conveyed." Still, the thing conveyed, such as the person and the work of Christ, must be conveyed, or else it cannot be encountered and trusted. And this means but one thing: it must be conveyed by the scriptures.[9]

In making this distinction, Fuller knows that the object and the statements of the scriptures that convey the object are two different, though related, matters. The reality of Christ in the good story is the primitive truth and the source of true statements about that reality, including those of the scriptures, which serve to convey the truth.

The distinction between Jesus Christ, the object of faith, and statements about Jesus Christ, which are used to tell of the object of faith, is linked by Fuller to his view of the increase of knowledge in the believer. If an increase of knowledge is to occur, Fuller holds, the believer must begin with sense experience, for knowledge principally enters at the door of the senses. But the believer must not settle for sense experience alone, for much can be learned through instruction. A caution, however, is in order with regard to instruction. Because sin is a fact of life, and because sloth often affects instruction, the believer must temper experience and instruction with the scriptures. Any increase of the knowledge of God and Jesus Christ requires consultation with the "written religion or the Bible in our hands," which conveys knowledge.

Although an absolute essential in both the acquisition and the increase of knowledge, scriptural knowledge must be distinguished from the object known, and the priority of the latter affirmed. Fuller words the point this way: "our first concern is, that we ourselves know the only true God and Jesus Christ," whose existence is prior to any conveyance of it to the believer by scriptural statements. Christ is the primitive ground; the written scriptures themselves are "imparted to believers by Him in whom is all our sufficiency."[10] The real person and the actual work of Jesus Christ, the primordial reality of the Word, take precedence over statements, even the true ones of the written scriptures, or those of the senses and instruction.

UNION WITH CHRIST

Truth is Jesus Christ, the ultimate object conveyed, and it is persons who model the truth in Christ. In the language current among the Particular Baptists, especially in an explosion of thought around 1780 and 1781, truth is union with Christ.

Visible, Vital, Virtual Union

Robert Hall Sr., pastor at Leicestershire, identifies three kinds of union with Christ: visible, vital, and virtual. A visible union, he explains in 1781, is "a credible profession of Christ, an apparent subjection to him, the embracing of the gospel, and the obeying of the laws." This kind of union is an intellectual assent to doctrinal and moral truths, and is at best an outward union that remains a step away from actual union with truth. Many who are visibly in Christ, Hall warns, will "lift up their eyes in hell."

Vital union is "a divine connexion between Christ and his people," Hall explains. It is a form of intimate participation that brings about the actual unity of Christ and the believer. In vital union the believer relates to Christ in an internal fashion, taking on the qualities of the Contemporary Christ.

Primordially antecedent to vital union is virtual union, which is a real connexion subsisting between Jesus Christ and the elect of God. Christ is the federal head of believers, as the primordial surety, the substitution, the ransom, the saviour, Hall notes, so it can be said that believers were chosen in and given to Christ. Virtual union does not supersede vital union, but functions as the secret source from which it flows. Vital union, Hall thinks, requires a point of contact prior to the living contact. Christ is the root connected with the branches, even before the blossoms appear.[11]

The Particular Baptists, assembled at Kettering in 1781, underscore Hall's view of vital union. They do so with speech about an intimate acquaintance with "the truth." "We entreat you to search the scriptures with diligence, deliberation, and prayer," they say, "in order to an encreasing acquaintance with the truth, as it is in Jesus." Their entreaty is not that believers seek cognitive knowledge or assent to bare beliefs. Their entreaty is a call for believers to walk as saints in the good story, so that they may be illumined, enlivened, and sanctified by their internal relation to Christ.[12]

Repentance and Faith

The first step to vital union with Christ, and thus of truth, is that of repentance, so say the Baptists of Bedfordshire, who are assembled at Kettering in 1781, in agreement with those met at Carleton in 1780. Rational mistakes, ignorance, or the disbelief of assorted truths—intellectual errors—do not comprise the problem. Enmity does. Enmity is a negative relationship between God and persons, something decidedly existential in character, what the Baptists met at Carleton call "the disposition of the devil." Consequently, if believers are to enter into an intimate and a truthful union with Christ, they must turn away from enmity and turn to a delightful embrace or a cordial approval of God's sovereign method of grace in saving lost sinners.[13] Once more it is evident that in the classic heritage the notion of truth is constructed out of a salvation-personal model.

If repentance is the first step in a vital union with "the truth as it is in Jesus," faith is the second. The Particular Baptists, gathered at Kettering in 1781, understand faith to have both objective and subjective modes. Objective faith concerns the object, the matter, or the truth believed, which is Jesus Christ and the substance of gospel truths understood as matters of fact. While persons do not know the whole compass of truth, God leads them into the essential truth of salvation, i. e., God leads persons to the ground of their acceptance with God, which is none other than Jesus Christ.

In its subjective mode, faith is "the act of believing or the prevalence of evidence in the mind." In point of fact, Particular Baptists assert, without real supporting evidence, there can be no act of faith. There must be the presence of a crediting report made, or some representation given, of persons and things. Faith may relate to the existence of persons, or things, without including their qualities or characteristics. However, if the qualities are described, then faith should accept the evidence about those qualities along with the evidence of their existence. An act of faith, Baptists insist, requires evidence related to the matter at hand.

With the distinction between the objective and the subjective modes of faith firmly set, the Particular Baptists assembled at Kettering further define faith as saving faith, what they often call "a cordial belief of the truth, as it is in Jesus, or related to him." The cordial reception of truth builds upon evidence and does so in two ways: saving faith respects the scriptures or "the true sayings of God," and it appeals to reasonable evidence. As is their custom, Particular Baptists see the two ways coalescing in the gathering of the report of the gospel concerning the real facts of Christ's incarnation, offices, undertakings, relations, blood, and obedience. Still, this level of faith remains deficient, for it knows about the evidence for matters of fact, and "does not influence to love and obedience, but is dead, being alone."

True or saving faith, in addition to requiring acceptance of matters of fact, entails a believing unto righteousness, what the 1781 circular letter of

Bedfordshire Baptists calls, "an approbation of Christ and the gospel." True faith trusts, accepts, approves. It participates in warm fellowship here and in uninterrupted happiness hereafter. True faith participates too in the matchless preciousness of the person of Jesus Christ and in the infinite beauty and bounty of the Living God, forever and ever. Moreover, in the believer's approbation or participation in the life of God, the Holy Spirit gives evidence of divine truth and helps believers become fully alive.

Saving faith is more than the "theory of religion or the system of established truths." It exists as an affair of the heart structured by the relationships of the people of God with the Holy Trinity, being the communion, the happiness, the beauty, and the bounty of God the Father, the richness of the indwelling of the Holy Spirit of God, and the infinite sufficiency and joy of the Son of God. Above all else, it is the receiving of Jesus Christ, not secondhand, but first, a "looking to him for cure, a living upon him as the bread of life, a coming to him and trusting in him."

Particular Baptists draw their comments on approbation and evidential faith into one sentence, truly a classic statement in the Baptist heritage of truth: "true faith consists in a cordial belief of divine truth, arising from the evidence of reality and nature."

Only this kind of faith abolishes all enmity to the truth and makes believers the friends of God. Truth ultimately has to do with fellowship, with believers becoming friends with the Living God. In the words of John Sutcliff of Olney: believers gain the knowledge of God and themselves, "with what concerns their relation to, and enjoyment of him."[14] In their "daily address to the divine throne," they cry "with holy fervour to the divine Jesus, encrease our faith." Christ hears. But Christ does not send good news. Christ himself comes in the good story. Believers thus are enabled to dwell in union with Christ, and in their dwelling enjoy truth itself, for they are one with it.

TRUTH HAS LEGS

In the revival of their heritage, Particular Baptists recognize that the truth intrinsic to union with Christ necessarily has legs, and that most of their knowledge, and all of their primary knowledge, originates in an abundant life and liberty found in Christ.

The Firstfruits of the New Enthusiasm

"The Particular Baptist Society for propagating the Gospel amongst the Heathen," 1792, was among the firstfruits of the new enthusiasm which equated truth with the practice of abundant life and liberty. Baptists responded in 1791 to William Carey's challenge to recognize "our bounden duty to attempt somewhat toward spreading the Gospel in the Heathen World."[15] Abraham Booth of Nottinghamshire, the advocate of a simple lifestyle, urged that Baptists and other friends of truth not forget the people at home, who have scarcely anything of Christianity besides the name.[16] By 1798 it was obvious that Booth's call had struck a responsive chord, for John Rippon's *The Baptist Annual Register* reported numerous societies and missions, and it concluded that "almost the whole country is open to village preaching."[17]

The awakening of Baptists to practical truth not only concerned missions but other areas of life. Caleb Evans, the president of Bristol Academy, urged his students to engage in personal evangelism by persuading others of "the ability of Christ to save; to save to the uttermost, to save all that come to God by him."[18] In London, James Dore, the pastor at Maze Pond, preached a sermon, "On the African Slave Trade" (1788), a sermon which signaled a robust opposition of Baptists to slavery. The philanthropist, John Howard, pursued prison reform and worked tirelessly in support of hospitals and other charitable enterprises.[19] In 1780 Robert Raikes, an Anglican, turned to the poor children of Gloucester. He taught them to read, as well as the catechism of the Church of England. William Fox, a Baptist deacon in London, universalized the Sunday School, and in 1785 "The Sunday School Society" took action for the first time.

Till It Has Filled the Whole Earth with Its Glory

The equation of truth and practice finds expression not only in the firstfruits of historical actions but in theory. The Particular Baptists, assembled at Wellington in 1787, by way of illustration, argue that Christianity, still in its infancy, is not a religion of one age or of one people. It has an eschatological quality, for "it is a train of light first put in motion by God [that] will continue to move and to spread till it has filled the whole earth with its glory." Its spread, they further argue, will not be the repetition of what has been put in place in full form but the unfolding of a drama which brings new life into the particulars of time and place. The gospel points forward to eternity, transforming the whole of time. "The Great Redeemer will again appear upon the earth, as the judge and ruler of it," Wellington Baptists think, gather the saints, "abolish sin, and death, and hell, and place the righteous ever in the presence of his God, and their God."

In the eschatological unfolding of Christianity, the Wellington Baptists further think, believers cannot calmly assent to truths, allowing them to slide out of their minds without leaving any impression. In the coming kingdom, believers must be doers of truth. They must attend to eternity, mindful to mingle it with "the ordinary stream of their thought, retiring often from the world, conversing with God and their own souls, so as to walk as in his sight." Believers are not counseled to spend more time in religion than in ordinary concerns. But, amidst all the ordinary affairs of life, the Particular Baptists at Wellington advise, the gospel is to be the center of hope and the end of all goals. Truth obviously is understood to have both horizontal and vertical reaches that intersect at the point of practice.

Truth Is of a Practical Nature

Not only do the Wellington Baptists equate truth with practice, but they use the equation as a test of truth and error. In the activities of life, they say, errors, appearances, and "illusions will vanish apace, and everything will appear in its true proportion and proper color." The active test of truth is this: religion can be said to be true if it is the "source of the warmest and most interesting feelings"—if it is "a spring of consolation within, which will often be full and pour itself forth." Or, in other words: "If the gospel has not taken a share in the feelings of our hearts, if it has not moved the great springs of our hopes and fears," if it doesn't keep us firm against the assaults of the world, or if we are apt to confine Christianity to seasons of worship and to shut it out from the ordinary affairs of life, then it is most assuredly the case that we have never experienced its force.[20]

"Truth is of a practical nature," Andrew Fuller contends, in agreement with Wellington Baptists. Hence, Christians ought to "walk in the truth."[21] Other kinds of truth may have a speculative nature, but not religious truth. The simple gospel is an overflow of God's goodness and blessedness.[22] So truth too is "a system of love and goodness—an overflow of Divine blessedness"—a system of joy and reconciliation. In the truth that is one with an overflow of divine life, Fuller observes, believers live abundantly, naturally attentive to all their duties, following the practice of the things that make for peace and for holiness, considering that "pure and undefiled religion is visiting the fatherless and widows in their afflictions, and in keeping ourselves unspotted from the world."[23]

A test of truth attends Fuller's understanding of practical truth. He writes, "a strong presumption must exist for or against a system, as it is found to promote or diminish the cardinal virtues of the Christian character." If anything debases the pure spirit of Christianity, if it stands as inconsistent with the Divine character or with benevolence to people, if it opposes relative duties, then the conclusion must be drawn that it is false.

The key to this practical test of truth lies in love, for love is not only a duty, Fuller argues, but the cardinal duty. Thus, he can say that a strong presumption must exist for or against any truth-claim, if it is found to promote or to diminish love.

Of any truth-claim, three specific questions must be asked regarding love, Fuller proposes. First, does it exalt God's dignity and excellence? God possesses infinite existence, so God ought to be loved without bounds. In the same proportion as persons love God, they ought to love Christ, that is, without limit or with their whole being—heart, soul, mind, and strength. The presence or absence of boundless love serves as a test of any truth-claim.

Second, Fuller notes, it must be asked of systems which claim to be true, "which of the systems places the mediation of Christ in the most important light?" In a true system Christ "appears as the soul which animates the whole body of our divinity" and as "the centre of the system, diffusing light and life to every part of it." Take away Christ, Fuller says, and practical religion cannot keep its power, the evangelical temperament is divested of its peculiar glory, heaven is without its joys, and the gospel is annihilated. The primitive gospel was full of Jesus Christ, and so too the evangelical system must be full of Christ. Which system, Fuller thus asks, has the greatest tendency to promote love to Christ? The answer to this question goes a long way towards settling the issue of truth.

A third question must also be asked of any truth-claim: does it address the sense of debt at the heart of the reception of the gospel? Fuller argues that a system is true, if it "represents us as most indebted to Christ's undertaking." The focus of the test of love here shifts away from Christ to people. The true system recognizes that the redeemed are debtors to forgiving love and engage in a return of love. If this sense of debt is present in a theoretical or a practical system, if the sense of debt requires people to return love to Christ and give it away to neighbors and enemies, then the system is true; if this sense of debt is absent, then it is false, and necessarily so.[24]

The test of practical truth is extended by Andrew Fuller to include not only love but the virtue of holiness. The minister's task, he beseeches, is to tell of "the truth as it in Jesus," and to do so not only by words, but by a holy practice of life. Fuller's proposal is that the minister ought to give testimony to truth by means of a negative and a positive test related to holiness. A passion for truth requires the application of a negative test: "a person may be assured he has no true holiness in him at all who rests contented with any degree of it short of perfection." A passion for truth also requires the use of a positive test: "he who does the will of God shall know of his doctrine." The two tests radically embolden the believer, for no person who is "in the right temper of mind can be so in the dark, respecting what truth is, as to make any essential mistake about it." Truth will always be congenial to the hearts of those who practice holiness.[25]

An adequate definition of truth should state what truth is and what it is not. Andrew Fuller knows this; therefore, he appends a discussion of the nature of error to his definition of truth and to his proposals to make love and holiness key tests of truth. In so doing, he drives home the point that truth is essentially, not accidentally, of a practical nature. Error, Fuller explains, is a moral wandering of the mind when it thinks without a guide, being deflected away from truth by an evil cause.

Three sources of moral error can be identified, Fuller observes. Each relates to a practice of life that is antilife, and necessarily precludes the doing of truth. First, an unconverted person, no matter how talented or refined of temperament, has a system of his or her own and cannot know the truth. Second, nominal Christians engage a practice of life not governed by principle, but by social custom, and thereby fall into an erroneous attunement of conscience. Third, among Christians, with a large portion of unsanctified wisdom, error arises when life is informed by "slowness of heart."[26]

Nonmoral errors exist alongside of moral errors, Fuller discerns, but they do not negate divine truth. Nonmoral errors arise from such sources as the "diversity of habits, educations and connexions, the various tastes and talents found among men, and the frailty and imbecility of the human mind." These sources give rise to numerous errors, but they do not account for the corruption of Christian doctrine and worship. Diversity and contrariety are different. People understand more or less of truth, some have more talent and more education than others, but in this diversity there is nothing discordant or contrary to the essence of personal truth.

The difference between moral and nonmoral errors is blurred, Fuller thinks, and cannot be fixed with certainty, just as the boundaries between light and shade cannot be fixed. Yet, there is a difference, he says, one that relates to the personal and the practical natures of truth. Nonmoral errors misapprehend divine truth; moral errors (unbelief) understand the content of truth yet discredit it. Only the latter, Fuller believes, is threatened with damnation. If errors arise from the lack of natural power or from the lack of opportunity to gain evidence, then they are mere mistakes with no moral consequences. But if errors arise from "prejudice, neglect, or an evil bias of heart, it is otherwise, and may endanger our eternal salvation."[27]

THE ESSENTIALITY OF THE HOLY SCRIPTURES

Truth can be known "experimentally by having made the trial," Particular Baptists hold, but finitude and evil necessitate an explicit revelation if the God of truth is to be known.[28] Insights may be learned from other quarters, even insights which "subserve the knowledge of God." But an adequate knowledge of God must be sought in the Holy Scriptures which reveal "the mind and will of God, for here only it can be found."[29]

The Inspired Word of God
The revealed scriptures are the inspired word of God, being the results of the "supernatural influence upon the mind of a rational creature, enabling him to think, and if necessary to speak, or write, in such a manner as he could not have done without it." To this definition of inspiration Particular Baptists append a qualification. They think that inspiration admits of degrees. If the writer was acquainted with the subject, the Spirit need not inspire most of what was written but only assist in recollection. In other cases, Leicester Baptists claim, the Spirit suggested the thoughts and ideas.[30] Andrew Fuller notes that when the biblical writers foretold the future they required more assistance than when they narrated facts within their knowledge—to have narrated known facts required no more than the superintendence of the Spirit. Yet, in whatever degree of inspiration, he adds, the Spirit secured the writers from error.[31]

The Scriptures Aim Directly at the Heart
It is a distinguishing property of the inspired scriptures that their precepts "aim directly at the heart," offering instruction in the story of sin and salvation and offering imperatives about life. The first aim, a salvific one, makes the scriptures a perfect rule of faith for Particular Baptists,

while the second aim, which applies to conduct, makes the scriptures a perfect rule of practice.

The scriptures speak of salvation and can be said to be a perfect rule of faith. Andrew Fuller thinks that the scriptures do not teach astronomy, geography, or civil government, or any science which relates to the present life only, but rather "contain truth, and nothing but [the] truth" which bears upon the history, prophecies, miracles, and doctrines of the gospel or upon a relation to Christ, who is the substance and the theme of the scriptures. The perfection of the scriptures as a rule of faith, he summarizes, is finally this: they are "profitable for reproof, for correction, for instruction in righteousness," effectually "disclosing the inward workings of the human mind."[32]

The Baptists assembled at Kettering in 1781 restrict the rule of faith to matters of Christ's person and work.[33] Abraham Booth thinks that the "inerring word" concerns only the singularity, character, relations (creation, providence, redemption), and trinitarian shape of God,[34] while the Baptists assembled at Leicester in 1797 witness that the scriptures instruct in matters of everlasting peace.[35]

In other words, Particular Baptists state, God gives the sort of truth in the scriptures which is suitable to an experimental knowledge of the reality of things ("the things that are"), their nature and quality, both what they are and whose they are, a truth that promotes the redemption of Christians and the glory of Christ. In these concerns of salvation, the scriptures are a perfect guide for faith or a "touchstone of truth."[36]

The Holy Scriptures are a perfect guide of practice or conduct as well as of faith. Particular Baptists hold that the scriptures provide both moral and positive rules of conduct, with each kind of rule fitted to a peculiar dimension of truth. Moral rules, such as the duty to love or to live sacrificially, bind persons with a perpetual obligation. They are inherently true, deriving as they do from the moral nature of God; hence, they are true for conduct at all times and in all places. Positive rules, on the contrary, such as the command to worship on the seventh day, are largely ceremonial in nature, applying only for specified times. Their truth is transitory. Moral rules are commanded by God because they are right eternally, while positive rules are right because they are commanded by God to meet specific needs for limited times.

Particular Baptists qualify how moral rules function in the conduct of life. Moral rules, though eternally true, must be expressed within the context of time. They function as scriptural precedents. But they are "not binding on Christians in things of a moral nature, unless the reason of the thing be the same in the case to be proved as in the case adduced." The reason of the moral rule must be correlated with the reason of the contemporary situation, which determines what the moral command now means and how it ought to be obeyed.

The Contextualized Scriptures Are Truth

The scriptures perfectly guide both faith and practice, for they are a revelation of the mind and will of God,[37] yet Particular Baptists claim that their truth is not self-contained but contextual. Four realities are understood to serve as the context of truth—those of the Holy Spirit, Jesus Christ, internal and external connexions, and faith.

The scriptures, which were "written by men who wrote as they were inspired by the Spirit," Particular Baptists contend, must be read under the guidance of the Spirit who illumines the mind and guides the believer into truth. On the one hand, "the Holy Spirit teaches nothing but what is true, and what was true antecedently to his teaching it, and would have been true though [the person] had never been taught it." On the other hand, the test of the Spirit's illumination is whether a person's enlightenment is a part of the truth revealed in the Holy Scriptures.

It cannot be said how the Spirit imparts illumination, but the ordinary way is to work in conjunction with the scriptures. Nevertheless, Andrew Fuller argues, this has not been the uniform way. Prior to Moses there was no written revelation, and till Christ came no ordinance for preaching the word. Even some extraordinary ways have been used by God. For example, "a ray of Divine revelation shot athwart the darkness of paganism into the minds of the Eastern magi, and led them to worship the Saviour."[38]

Persons who have "an inward conviction of the truth of the leading doctrines of revelation" understand the gospel "not in word only, but in power, in the Holy Spirit, in much assurance." This assurance of truth, Particular Baptists add, is heightened when the scriptures are contextualized by the reality of Jesus Christ. Contemplating Christ as the Mediator and "reading the kind invitations which he has left on record," Baptists say, believers return "to God in his name and to the truth as it is in Jesus," thus finding their minds renewed, love empowered, salvation sweet, and the stamp of divinity on the scriptures. So lively the stamp of divinity on the scriptures that the Baptists at Leicester draw a most radical conclusion about "a life that is above the wise." They conclude that "with this Bible in your hand, and this blessed experience in your heart [the encounter with

Christ], you compare them together," and their agreement convinces you that they "are of heavenly original."[39]

In addition to the contextualization of the scriptures in the realities of the Spirit and the Christ, another reality informs the scriptures and shapes their contextualized truth. Particular Baptists argue that the scriptures are a true system[40] and must be tested in terms of their internal and external connections. A consideration of the internal connections of the scriptures, Andrew Fuller says, leads to an understanding of "truth immediately from the oracles of God." In God's light, through the study of the internally coherent structures of the scriptures, along with prayer and meditation, the student of the scriptures comes to the light of truth. An awareness of external connections also enriches the grasp of truth. The truths of the scriptures stand related to external circumstances in the world. The doctrine of sin, for example, can be seen in its worldly connections, tendencies, and consequences. In other words, this doctrine, just as all others, must be contextualized in its logical, empirical, and historical settings.

Faith too contextualizes scriptural truth. Andrew Fuller maintains that the scriptures contain a system of divine truth, which includes "the first principles, or rudiments of religion—the simple truths of the gospel and the deep things of God." Those truths which concern the works of God approve themselves to human wisdom; those truths which concern the being and the glories of God surpass it. In both instances, however, a knowledge of truth requires the believer to "go on unto perfection" by means of faith or by means of "A DEEP AND INTIMATE KNOWLEDGE OF DIVINE TRUTH."

God has not revealed in the scriptures a set of principles arranged in a scheme, Fuller explains of the role of faith in the contextualization of the scriptures. And, neither has God revealed a creed which includes all necessary beliefs. Fuller knows that truth appears scattered from one end to the other in the inspired writings, being introduced rather incidentally than systematically. Moreover, divine truth does not appear in the scriptures as an abstract proposition or as a rational system of true doctrines. It appears with great energy and force and as fully embedded within some practical end. It does not "barely meet our eyes, or our understandings, but our consciences,"[41] and is discerned in life by faith. Particular Baptists of the Northamptonshire Association speak of this phenomenon this way: "divine truth must be mixed with faith, or have faith mixed with it," a faith tested by the demonstration or "the influence of the truth we profess to believe."[42]

In conclusion, only the contextualized Holy Scriptures are truth. The Holy Trinity—"the one, only living and true God, the truth, and the Spirit of truth"—animates the scriptures, and grants to the individual "a right so to judge and to form his connexions with those whose views are most congenial with his own."[43]

TRUTH REQUIRES CONCRETE EVIDENCE

A considerable role for reasonableness and its standards, along with the scriptures and the practice of abundant life, is allowed by Particular Baptists in the setting of what counts as the nature of truth and in the testing of truth-claims. They allow this considerable role because they admittedly stand "open to conviction, and acceptance of truth, by whatever means it may please God to inform [us] of it." They also think that knowledge has permanent value, being good in itself, part of the modeling of truth by the believer who thinks as well as does the truth. They admit too that presumption requires concrete evidence. "We must not content ourselves with knowing what is truth" they say, "but must be acquainted with the evidence on which it rests."[44]

Redeemed Reason

A natural reason based on the sensuous experience of the world, Particular Baptists hold, can gain knowledge, even of God. It can know the existence of God and the divine attributes of goodness, wisdom, and power. It suffers from a complete loss, however, when it applies this knowledge to the acts of God in any particular case. Confined to a specific point of life and to ideas relative to that point, seriously affected by finitude and sin, a sensuously based reason comes up short of an understanding of matters possessed of everlasting moment. Baptists assembled at Wellington in 1787 admit: "how little information we can derive from reason in enquiries of this nature."[45]

Natural reason may be limited, Particular Baptists aver, but not redeemed reason, for it is illuminated by "the supreme excellence of the Christian dispensation." God does not leave the believer to the conjectures of reason. In Jesus Christ, God gives the believer all things and actually renews the mind, transforming it and its ability to think, creating a new creature who knows the mind of Jesus Christ. The believer, as a result, mingles the things of eternity with the ordinary stream of thoughts, converses with God and the soul, and thereby comes to a knowledge of truth, "the knowledge of God and of true happiness," or a lasting impression of the gospel.[46]

Rational and Empirical Standards

William Carey uses redeemed reason in his arguments for missions. Abraham Booth does the same in his case against slavery.[47] And, Particular Baptists universally appeal to a reason enlightened by salvation in their arguments for the inspiration of the scriptures. In these instances, and in the myriads of arguments which inform their writings, Particular Baptists appeal to rational and empirical standards of evidence.

The rational standards of consistency, coherence, formal validity, and simplicity play strategic roles in ascertaining truth. By way of illustration, note the rational standards employed by John Ryland, who champions two of the logical criteria of the geometrician Euclid as applicable to all subjects but peculiarly suited to the study of divinity: first, to show that a proposition necessarily results from the premises and, second, to demonstrate the absurdity that results from denying the proposition.

While often rational, the arguments used by Particular Baptists more often have an empirical shape. This attunement to a posteriori evidence surfaces in their frequent use of the standards of empirical coherence, empirical adequacy, historicity, the correspondence test of truth, the precedent of the primitive pattern, workability (the pragmatic norm), fulfillment of prophecy, the surety of miracles, intersubjective agreement (the community), and John Locke's criteria for the reliability of witnesses.[48]

The a posteriori tone of Baptist reasonableness derives in part from the empiricism of John Locke, Jonathan Edwards, and the Great Awakening. But it primarily derives from the gospel. The good story frames truth in the life-world. No abstract test of formal validity carries the day for it. Truth-claims are rather tested by the dramatic reality of the gospel itself.

The way Particular Baptists handle their arguments shows that they settle truth-claims by means of gospel realism. Baptists display great skill in the construction of formally valid arguments (of a deductive nature). Nevertheless, they often set aside formal standards, and use instead formally invalid but empirically true arguments. For example, Particular Baptists argue that the fulfillment of prophecy gives evidence of the inspiration of the scriptures. They present this claim in the form of a hypothetical syllogism [P = the antecedent, Q = the consequent]. If the scriptures are inspired [P], they reason, then they ought to contain prophecies which have been fulfilled [Q]. They contain fulfilled prophecies [Q]. Indeed, "numerous events are foretold with astonishing exactness." Human foresight cannot account for this phenomenon. Only the reality of someone who surveys in "one glance whatever is past, present, or future" could foretell the future. Therefore, the scriptures are inspired [P].

The argument's structure—if P, then Q; Q is the case; therefore P is the case—is formally invalid [it affirms the consequent in the minor and the antecedent in the conclusion]. Yet, its material content remains realistically factual, and it is the material content that counts for Particular Baptists.[49] In a way which parallels that of science, they use a method which is not finally determined by formal validity, concerns of clarity and precision, or the presence of necessity and certainty. The rational marks of truth are not unimportant, for they help structure truth. But what finally matters is the domain of the concretely personal. Particular Baptists do not expect truth-claims to apply to anything but the reality they hold in their hands.

TO ENJOY GOD

The enjoyment of God, for Particular Baptists in the revival of their classic heritage, is finally the great animating soul of truth. Truth, they say, is "to know that God is ours, that all his perfections, are engaged to make us blest, and to have communion with him, to receive discoveries, impressions, and gracious communications from God, and to contemplate, love, praise, submit to, obey, trust, &c through a Mediator as revealed in his word."

When this enjoyment of God is absent, "divine ordinances are empty cisterns, and spiritual graces are withering flowers." When it is absent, "the greatest human abilities labour in vain, and the noblest efforts fail of success."

But, when the enjoyment of God is present, truth is engaged, offering a "source of enjoyment, superior perhaps to anything with which we are acquainted." The task of the Christian is consequently to enjoy truth, to imbibe or to possess that truth which shines with a "superior lustre, [for] the more we think of truth, in this way, the more we shall be rooted and grounded in it."[50]

Just as a melted substance poured into a mold receives its shape from the mold, and every line in one corresponds to that of the other, so truth in the soul accords with personal truth. In the soul that enjoys God, line answers to line in "a system of love, an overflow of the Divine blesedness, as is intimated in it by its being called 'the glorious gospel of the blessed God,' a system of reconciliation, peace, and forgiveness, one full of the most amazing condescension, and of spotless rectitude."[51]

Chapter Ten

A CORDIAL RECEPTION OF THE GOSPEL
AMERICAN BAPTISTS

It is the common privilege of God's people to have the divine Spirit given them, to seal his truth to their hearts. It is the Spirit of God, and that alone that enlightens our minds to understand his word aright, and that shows men their condition and their duty, and guides his people into all truth. God leads his people in duty by applying home his truth, by causing divine light to shine into our understanding.

Isaac Backus, *An Internal Call*, 1754

THE LORD IS A SUN

The Lord is a Sun, American Regular and Separate Baptists say of the personal quality of the truth that lifts them out of their declension and establishes them squarely in the classic heritage during the late–eighteenth century. The Lord is a light that shines into the inner recesses of the soul, a force sensibly present, an animating love, an acquaintance vouchsafed in the hearts of persons who find that they cannot "rest in anything short of a union with, and conformity to Jesus Christ," and who claim "the common privilege of God's people to have the divine Spirit given them, to seal his truth to their hearts."[1]

The Divine Light Incarnates Itself in the Heart

Now the sun cannot be directly seen, American Baptists observe, "but its rays appear to point as directly to us as if there was not another person in the world for it to shine upon; and we partake (as it were) of the whole benefit of its influences." In like manner, they also observe, when the believer comes to Jesus Christ in the gospel story, then that believer beholds the glory of God, and "eternal rays of light and love shine down particularly upon him, to remove his darkness, heal his wounds, and shed immortal blessings on his soul."[2] In the purity of this divine light, truth uncovers itself, illuminating the soul—the divine light incarnating itself in the heart.

The illumination wrought by the power of God is so manifestly evident, Regular and Separate Baptists alike know, that the believer can no more doubt its reality than he or she can doubt the existence of the material world. The knowledge of the material world relies on the veracity of the senses; and in a comparable way, Baptists think, the knowledge of truth rests assured in the evidence of the light of a cordial reception of the gospel. God comes sensibly near the heart and brings a particular knowledge of God, with the result that believers are assimilated to the divine nature.[3]

The Common Accents of an Experimental Knowledge

American Baptists of the north and the south, the east and the west, speak of diverse encounters with the tangible light of the truth come near to the heart, but on every occasion they speak with the common accents of an experimental knowledge. Isaac Backus (1724–1806) of Connecticut reports that, while mowing alone in the field, he was enabled by divine light to see the righteousness of Christ and the free nature of grace. He reports that he encountered first hand the truth that dispels the darkness of evil, illuminates the soul with such understanding in the heart as was never there before, a truth Backus contends, "I knew experimentally before I did doctrinally."[4]

John Taylor, a pastor on the Kentucky frontier, says (c. 1772) of experimental knowledge, "at the hanging rock I had some glimpse of Jesus Christ, but in a moment my mind was opened to see and feel the truth."[5] Thomas Memminger and David Jones of the Philadelphia Baptist Association insist that all matters are clearly established by those persons who are made alive unto God in Christ and who receive the whole mind of God and "the truth in the love of it."[6] Oliver Hart, pastor of the First Baptist Church of Charleston, posits that the members of a true church are founded upon Jesus Christ and bear a marked similarity to the foundation on which they are laid. Richard Furman, also of Charleston, speaks of a vital union wherein the Holy Spirit indwells the body of Christ and makes it a house of God or a holy state.[7]

OF INFINITE MOMENT

The starting-point for a heart-felt acquaintance with truth, and the first and the foremost reality which defines the structure of its experimental quality, is that story which is "of infinite moment."[8] For American Baptists any consideration of truth begins with the Living God of truth and finds its ultimate expression in the Living God present in the hearts of real people. With the enjoyment of this personal story "of infinite moment" as their primal source and value, and with it alone, they rest content, knowing that the Holy Trinity is their portion and guide. Their prayer of contentment is that of the final verse of a poem by Isaac Backus, "O Lord of hosts, unto my soul much of this pleasure grant! This is all; this is the whole; what else then can I want!"[9]

A Knowledge Born of the Transformed Heart

Faithful to the pietistic temper of their minds, American Baptists think of the heart as the seat of the soul, the unitive center of personality, or the personal core of knowing, feeling, willing, believing, acting, and sharing. The heart is not feeling or choosing, but the spring of human agency. Or, in the words of Samuel Stillman, pastor of the First Baptist Church of Boston, it is the "institution of life, a vital and vivifying spirit."[10]

In the redeemed person, American Baptists opt, the heart is transformed or given new life, opening it to the light of the truth of God that is of infinite moment. Samuel Jones, in a circular letter of the Philadelphia Association, finds that grace, faith, and repentance are freely given in the gospel story, and with them, a new heart, which he defines as "a new nature, new life—all is new, all is free." God breaks up the evil heart, Isaac Backus explains of the new heart, in the same way a farmer breaks up the thorns and briers in a field, removing stones which ought not be there. Then God sows the good seed, covering it with soil, producing growth, and harvest. As a result, there is an inward persuasion of the mind, without which nothing is acceptable to God. The redeemed heart is not subjectively convinced but rather persuaded under a divine impulse. Morgan Edwards of Philadelphia says of this persuasion, "the Spirit breathes, as the wind blows; and the soul catches the breeze and lives."[11]

A knowledge born of infinite moment in the transformed heart, American Baptists believe, does not occur before or afterward, but in and through particular cases and specific circumstances in the lives of real people. For instance, the imprisoned Elizabeth Backus, in a letter to her son, Isaac, writes of the coming down of heaven into the prison at Norwich, Connecticut. "I was cast into this furnace," she explains, "yet was I loosed, and found Jesus in the midst of the furnace with me."[12]

Or, consider the report of an anonymous Baptist, converted in the 1784 revival in Lincoln County, Maine, who describes his conversion in terms of particulars. At once light, life, and power came with such force and beauty, he says, "that I knew it to be the voice of my blessed Jesus, who by his Holy Spirit set that glorious seal to my soul that God is true." So convinced are Baptists that truth is incarnate in the particulars of worldly affairs that, in June of 1762, the members of the Third Baptist Church of Middleborough, Massachusetts, find the works of providence amply showered on them, not only in the form of divine influence upon their souls, but in the form of a drought-breaking rain "in the parts where people were so much engaged in religion."[13]

Certitude and Common People

Truth of infinite moment discovered here and now, at this or that place, in particular cases and specific circumstances, comes to the heart with a pronounced sense of certitude. American Baptists do not think that the heart obtains rational certainty. That would be to think of truth as a set of rational ideas, a view they disavow. On the contrary, they discover a certitude or an existential assurance in the heart. American Baptists don't have a theoretical bone in their bodies.

John Leland of Virginia describes the certitude of the heart this way: I know "for certain that I was born of God. That I know as distinctly as if a surgeon should cut open my breast with his knife, take out my heart, and wash it, put it back again and close up the flesh." My belief in Jesus, he adds, can be seen "as plainly as I could see an object of sense." David Jones, in his 1788 letter "Saving Faith," describes certitude as a truth that is plain and easy to those persons that are taught of God and have learned of Christ. James Manning, president of Rhode Island College, counsels concerning certitude that it arises from the direct work of the Spirit of Christ who creates principles in the heart.[14]

The reasons of the heart and their certitude are open to common people, American Baptists witness, for the imprisoned Elizabeth Backus and for Elisha Paine in the sandy land of Cape Cod, not for an educated or an ecclesiastical elite, nor for any privileged few alone. This is the case because Jesus Christ plainly affirmed the right of common people to judge.

The facts also speak to this conclusion, for it is evident that in everyday life God directs and supports every trusting and obedient person.[15]

The truth born of infinite moment in the heart of the common person is a living truth, unfolding in time, and for this reason American Baptists constantly and freshly examine what the truth may be. They recognize that "the person receives the truth in the love of it," and has certitude. But they also think that the Living God has more truth yet to break forth. Truth does not occur from the outset as a set of conclusions already given and certain. The Living God of truth patiently brings forth good wheat from seeds sown in the new birth wrought by divine revelation. Isaac Backus explains: "We are often ready to say, if the Baptist Principles are right, why did we not see it before, when God appeared gloriously among us? Why did he own us if we were in an error there? Answer: God opens things to his saints by degrees."[16]

Christ Died For Me

But what things does the Living God of truth open to the heart of the common saint? What is the content of experimental knowledge, and thus of truth? American Baptists reply, in the words of Hezekiah Smith, a chaplain in the revolutionary army, that a stream cannot run higher than its source, so the desires of a soul cannot rise higher than the soul and its proper objects, which are God, the perfections of deity, and eternal life. James Manning observes that the heart knows the person of God and is aware that this truth prevails, but only "in proportion to the prevalence of the religion of the heart."[17] Isaac Backus finds that his "Heart was attracted and Drawn away after God and Swallowed up with Admiration in viewing his Divine glories."[18]

The content of the heart, in short, is a direct, personal relationship with God. But, careful to confine their ebullient pietism of the heart, American Baptists also affirm that truth can be found only within the bounds of the good story and its realities. In his defense of the Separatists, Isaac Backus identifies two extremes prohibited by any reliance upon the heart. The reasons of the heart cannot be confined to the truths of a dry morality or to any objectively based standard, and the judgments of the heart cannot be set by inward feelings or by any subjectively derived experience.[19] Over against these two extremes, Backus places the gospel itself. The gospel as the good story alone is the content of the heart. It transcends all subjectivity and all objectivity, each and every subject or object. It is the primal ground of the truth of the heart, its primal support and goal, its source, meaning, and value.

The truth of infinite moment can be found in the heart, but it does not begin or arise there. It begins and arises with the union of the Holy Trinity and the individual person in the gospel story. Elisha Paine of Cape Cod speaks of the peculiar union at the center of truth, "Christ did not die for the predestined elect, Christ died for me."[20] For me! God in Christ and through the Spirit has entered the world—for me! The audaciousness of this insight is staggering. American Baptists assert that God the Father enters into holy union with my conscience, that God the Son relates to me in my faith, and that God the Spirit unites with me and sanctifies my life. In a few words, American Baptists forward the view that truth itself enters into union with me, and that I participate in the truth that the Holy Trinity is and does.

Morgan Edwards, early in his pastorate in Philadelphia, characterizes this union as a friendship with the Living God.[21] The first and the capital pole of this friendship is that of God the Father, while the second pole is that of the conscience of the person.[22] Nothing but the light and the power of the Father's divine will, brought home upon the conscience, can make a soul whole, blending truth and mercy, and bring not only the knowledge but the presence of truth so plainly that "he that runs may read it."[23]

A friendship with God is not only a friendship with the Father, American Baptists witness, but one with the infinite fullness of the Son of God. It is a friendship with Jesus Christ, who is "the only Christian altar," the reality upon which "the church is built as the pillar and ground of truth," the source too of a true knowledge of God, persons, and holiness, which "does not receive its support from earthly power, but from TRUTH."[24] Furthermore, American Baptists say, friendship with God is of the infinite fullness of God the Spirit. The church at Wilbraham, 1779, testifies that God carries on a glorious work by the Spirit, who quickens the hearts of believers and leads them into truth. The Spirit takes away the veil from the heart, revealing the glory of the Lord, changing persons into the likeness of Christ, and leading them into all truth, not at once, but gradually "in that path which shineth more and more until the perfect day."[25]

The Foundational Error

That the truth of infinite moment is the gospel known by the heart in experimental relation to the Holy Trinity, and that it is entirely personal, can readily be seen in the American Baptist understanding of error. Isaac Backus offers this classic definition of error: "Man's foundational error is an imagination that there is something better than the will of God; some way better at present to walk in than his precepts, and some interest better than to be at his disposal [and to] submit to divine government."

Backus does not understand error at its root in terms of the correspondence or the coherence test of truth. Foundational error, just as truth, cannot be reduced to the quality of a statement which must either agree (correspond) with the facts or be integrated (cohere) with other statements accepted as true. Error at its roots is a deceitful, evil heart arrayed in opposition to the revealed will of God in the gospel story. It pertains to the unitive center of personality, and can be said to be "the love of the self, and of earthly power and gain, with ignorance of the infinite perfections of God, and going about to establish a righteousness of their own." To counteract foundational error, Backus advises, the contradictions and the empirical inadequacy need not be removed from statements of doctrine, although this is desirable, for reasonableness is a mode of truth, but believers should first and foremost "fix their dependence upon God for light to direct and for power to act."[26]

At times American Baptists shift their focus from truth and error (in the singular) to truths and errors (in the plural). They do so, particularly in the latter parts of the eighteenth century, in order to address the differences between themselves and other groups. The letters to the Warren Baptist Association, and those to other associations as well, from 1780 onwards frequently express concern over errors and heresies.[27] Yet, and the "yet" rings with clarion tones, although greatly bothered by heresies, and although sometimes turning from truth to true doctrines in order to counter the errors, American Baptists understand that what they cannot spell out, they must skip,[28] for they know themselves to be caught up in the everlasting arms of the Gracious and Living God whose light brings together truth and mercy in the hearts of the twiceborn.

LET THE WORD OF GOD DWELL IN YOU RICHLY

One thing is clear: American Baptists rely solely and finally upon personal truth. William Vanhorn of the Philadelphia Association makes the point plainly, "the everlasting love of God to his people, manifested in Jesus Christ, tends to establish the truth."[29] But, if the actual presence of God with the heart is to be reckoned as truth, how do American Baptists understand the truth of the Holy Scriptures?

Those Holy Writings of God

There are not two kinds of truth, one, the truth of God acting with the heart, the other, that of the scriptures. American Baptists think that God reveals truth itself through the actual presence of God in the heart, lifting the heart to a new level of personal communion and understanding, vitalizing all things in the process, with the pure leaven of the Holy Scriptures and the firm basis of divine revelation.[30]

American Baptists uniformly witness to the fact that the scriptures are "those holy writings of God,"[31] the word of God and the mind of Christ, the inspired revelation of God's will. But this fact alone, they add, does not establish the truth quotient of the scriptures. It is only "the Bible in your hands [or] the ingrafted word" that is authoritative. The Holy Scriptures are the precious, matchless word of truth, but they remain mute and unauthoritative—silent and without efficacy—unless the Living God is present and active through them, speaking, acting, revealing truth to the heart.

By Which Principles and Conduct Must Be Tried

If God is present and active in the word of God, American Baptists infer, then the scriptures serve as the rule, the set direction, or the measure of faith and practice. Nay, not just a rule, they believe, but a perfect or an infallible one, the only "standard by which principles and conduct must be tried."[32] The Philadelphia Baptist Association, for instance, during the revision of its confession, a task begun in 1774, declares that the scriptures are "the infallible ground of faith and certain rule of obedience; full and complete in all its parts, historical, doctrinal, and prophetical; every way useful and profitable." Or, consider the Separate and the Regular Baptists of Kentucky who describe the scriptures as the infallible word of God and as the only rule of faith and practice. Isaac Backus minces no words when he finds the scriptures perfect and sufficient, the only security against error and the only perfect law of liberty.

Without doubt, from the settled regions to the frontiers of America, Baptists believe that the scriptures are a perfect rule, and the only rule, a measure affording assurance or infallible certitude.[33]

The scriptures, however, serve as a perfect rule only when they govern in religious matters. In particular, American Baptists think of the scriptures as a rule governing three areas of religious life. The scriptures contain the necessities of salvation—a knowledge of the true God and of

Jesus Christ, the object of faith. The scriptures also are the rule respecting duties toward God, neighbors, and self, "furnishing the man of God for every good work." Finally, the scriptures convey a sense of community, being "the golden oil" which enables the united church to be "the light of the world, and the pillar and ground of truth."[34]

The Written and the Ingrafted Scriptures

The Holy Scriptures, but only "the ingrafted scriptures," are the rule or the guiding measure by which faith and practice must be tried. Four personal realities, all gospel facts, American Baptists assert, form the context that constitutes scriptural truth and define the scriptures as the ingrafted word or as "a living principle in the hearts of believers."[35]

The first reality is the Holy Spirit. American Baptists concur with Morgan Edwards of Philadelphia who insists that the crucial source of scriptural truth arises from the Holy Spirit who causes the scriptures to live in the believer and who gives a right understanding of them, for this is "the only Way by which God's people in every Age have known the Truth and Certainty of his Word."

In answer to a query from the Oyster-bay Baptist Church, the Philadelphia Baptist Association in 1761 clarifies the relation of the Spirit, the scriptures, and truth. The scriptures, it holds, function as the full, sufficient, and only rule, and anything whatsoever can be considered to be false which contradicts this rule. At the same time, however, the Association holds that the Spirit may properly be called the guide who illumines the understanding to know the mind and will of God contained in the scriptures. The Holy Spirit brings to the scriptures much assurance, conjoining spiritual matters with spiritual, appealing to discernment, stripping away the veil from the heart, giving light, skill, and strength to use the scriptural principles, and leaving the clear conviction that "our full persuasion and assurance of the infallible truth and divine authority [of the scriptures] is from the inward work of the Holy Spirit bearing witness by and with the Word in our hearts."[36]

A second reality, the personal reality of Jesus Christ, sets the context of scriptural truth and defines the scriptures as the ingrafted word. Oliver Hart's words, spoken in 1782 at Charleston, typify the American Baptist position. Jesus Christ, Hart says, functions as the final authority, supremely infallible and solely sufficient, the author of truth who even now speaks in and through his word, teaching persons directly the saving knowledge of God. In Christ it is the case that persons come into the actual presence of "the truth" and hear not just the words of scripture but the voice of the Living Truth. They hear the One who "teaches powerfully and efficaciously by his word and Spirit," and who opens his word and the harmony, the truth, and the certitude thereof, so that it appears as "glorious and Infallible Truth."[37]

The everlasting scriptures uphold persons and can be said to be truth because of two realities—a loving Christ stands alongside and an indwelling Spirit walks persons through. There is a third reality which shapes the face of the ingrafted word for American Baptists—that of faith.

Faith, or an experimental acquaintance with the operation of Divine truth upon the heart, American Baptists hold, serves as a primal ground of the truth of the scriptures. Unless God brings eternal things near to the heart, persons cannot know the truth of the scriptures. A notional religion may carry persons far in Christian profession. However, American Baptists insist that persons not merely assent to the true doctrines of the gospel, but feel their sanctifying influence on their hearts, which enables them "to believe all the divine truths revealed in the holy scriptures, to believe the record that God has given of his Son, and in particular to apprehend the Lord Jesus Christ." Without faith the scriptures are mute, but "where the voice of grace is attended to, the person receives the truth in the love of it."[38]

The fourth reality, that of a free conscience, is akin to the third, arising as it does within the heart. "Liberty," American Baptists witness, "is continually the attendant of the Spirit of God leading into all truth and righteousness." If the truth of the scriptures is to be known, persons must make their own decisions concerning it. Conscience is not to be suppressed. There is no authority for a moral being, including that of the scriptures, except one freely, rationally accepted. Not only is liberty a prerequisite of scriptural truth, it offers the best chance of preventing truth's loss. John Leland of Virginia, who defines the conscience as "common science or a court of judicature," says, "truth is in the least danger of being lost, when free examination is allowed."[39]

In summary, this can be said of the truth of the Holy Scriptures. Truth begins with, and it arises from, the domain of the personal, which includes the interplay of the written and the ingrafted scriptures, and in this broad sense American Baptists know that the scriptures are the only reliable rule. All truth finally resides in the Living God, lest it be forgotten, and that includes the truth of the scriptures.

William Straughton of the Philadelphia Association, who exhorts Baptists "to labor after an enlarged acquaintance with divine truth," states the American Baptist view of the scriptures with these words:

Let the word of God dwell in you richly in all wisdom. While you implore the teaching of the Spirit of God, search the Scriptures. The religion of Jesus' courts the investigation of all, but it has a special claim on the attention of the righteous. Ye are set as a defense of the gospel, the sword of the Spirit, which is the word of God. Be aware of the invincible arguments in favor of the truth as it is in Jesus. Remember, brethren, the religion we profess is of infinite moment. When pursuing the interests of Zion, we are fellow workers with God.[40]

LIVELY STONES

It is pointless, say American Baptists, to look for the distinguishing features of truth in any kind of abstract idea or principle. Truth is a way of life. The believer, in union with Jesus Christ, who is the Word of the Living God, and guided by the ingrafted word, encounters truth in a daring feat. Truth is the courage to live abundantly and freely in "the way, the truth, and the life." Love and holiness, obedience too, and liberty, these practical fruits of the Spirit, and others of similar ilk, are what truth is.

Act as Children of God

Just as there is no truth until persons encounter the truth of infinite moment and engage the scriptures, so there can be no truth until persons act as the children of God by faith in Christ Jesus. American Baptists contend that the Living God has laid the foundation of truth, which is Jesus Christ, and that God "makes his people lively stones," laying them on the foundation, forming them into the children of God, raising up the superstructure of the Christian community until completion. The Living God is the builder of the lively stones. God the Father chooses the materials. God the Son purchases the materials by his shed blood. And, God the Spirit "hews, planes, polishes and fits them for the building." In a real sense, American Baptists aver, persons are or do the truth. They become truth, not in origin but derivatively, as children translated from the family of Satan into the family of God, receiving a radical change in the soul, a change characterized by the "lively obedience of faith."[41]

This means, in the pilgrimage to truth, that it is more essential to learn how to believe, how to attune or comport oneself, how to be, do, and live, than to learn what to believe. The carnal person, not knowing how to believe, does not discern the things of the spirit, being neither subject to the law of God nor in fellowship with the Holy God. The twice-born, however, who exhibit the qualities of mercy, kindness, humbleness of mind, meekness, and long suffering, live by and in an evangelical knowledge. It is they, and they alone, those who partake of the new covenant, who find "their faith a lively, active faith, not only purifying their hearts but working by love, whereby they become the light of the world," discerning the practical face of truth in discipleship.[42]

The Fruits of the Spirit

What then is the specific makeup of truth practically conceived? What does it mean to be and to act as children of God? The first answer of American Baptists is this: truth is love. John Leland proposes a radical test of truth: "He cannot be wrong, whose life and heart are right. He cannot walk amiss who walks in love." When religion is lively, Leland thinks, the priority of life in matters of truth holds steady, and no alienation of affection arises from a difference of judgment. Therefore, Leland urges American Baptists to walk soberly and to let love prove the power of truth. Since, in the new covenant, the law of love is written in the believer's heart, Isaac Backus similarly argues, love must be the centerpiece of the knowledge of truth. "All those professors that don't love one another with a pure heart have but the dead carcass of religion."[43]

Holiness and obedience, along with love, also define the practical essence of gospel truth. If persons act as children of God, living a truthful life, American Baptists maintain, then it is their liberty to walk in holiness and obedience. A truthful life necessarily exhibits a sense of the holy or a sense of the "sacred to the heart of a rational immortal creature." It also necessarily exhibits an awareness that one lives under the imperative of obedience—that "if there was neither heaven nor hell, the true believer would wish to live soberly, righteously, and godly in this present world."

Not only do holiness and obedience define the practical nature of truth, but they serve as telling tests of truth's presence or absence. The Baptists of South Carolina, who realize that the holy duties of the heart count in the judgment of truth, insist that "were professors more holy, their sentiments would be more uniform." The Baptists of the Philadelphia body, who observe that the motives of the children of the bondwoman and of the free are vastly different, hold that the presence of wearisome obedience in the person in bondage spells the presence of the false. They hold conversely that the presence of joyful obedience in the life of the free, who love and delight in God's law, signals the presence of the true.[44]

Within the practice of life as children of God, truth manifests itself as a sense of holiness and obedience, of awe and diligence, and as love too. In fact, it displays all the fruits of the Spirit, such as joy, peace, patience, kindness, generosity, faith, gentleness, and self-control. American Baptists do not hesitate to draw the conclusion that the fruits of the flesh or the Spirit, which "comprehend all that men bring forth out of their hearts, in their principles, experience, conversation, and conduct," are the means whereby "we are to know them." They often sum up their contention that true wisdom is from above and exhibits the fruits of the Spirit with the golden rule: "all arguments which are founded upon a violation of the golden rule are certainly false ones."[45]

Liberty too, American Baptists insist, is continually the attendant of the Holy Spirit of God, and a defining element in the practice of a truthful life. Not just any sort of liberty attends the Holy Spirit, however, certainly not the freedom associated with arbitrary deliberation and decision or with random action. The only liberty of God's people is the liberty to walk in holiness and in the precepts of God, to enjoy liberation from guilt, sin, and Satan, and to have open access to God. The words of Isaac Backus aptly pinpoint the American Baptist view: "the true liberty of man is to know, obey and enjoy his Creator, and to do all the good unto and enjoy all the happiness with and in his fellow creatures that he is capable of, in order to which the law of love was written in his heart."

The issue before American Baptists, and a defining moment in their view of truth, thus centers in their view of Christianity as "a voluntary obedience to God's revealed will." The presence of liberty gainsays the presence of the Spirit of truth and of truth itself, while "everything of a contrary nature is antichristianism" and false. Only error needs human support. "Whenever men fly to the law or sword to protect their system of religion, and force it upon others," they say, "it is evident that they have something in their system that will not bear the light, and stand upon the basis of faith."[46]

The Spirit of Adoption

In all their moves to locate the essential nature and the tests of truth in that which has practical bearing in the lives of the children of God, American Baptists understand that a peculiar temper indwells true believers. The temper is that of adoption, wherein God shapes the life and the mind of the believer into the image of Christ. Every person of truth, they know, hears the voice of Christ and is drawn by the cords of grace into Christ's likeness. If "one peculiar excellency of the knowledge of him is, that it transforms the soul into his likeness, causing a longing after conformity in heart and life," how could it be otherwise for American Baptists than to define the nature of truth and to test for it in terms of a Christlike temper found in the practice of life? Without the attunement of Christlikeness and its "purity of mind, divine truth cannot be clearly perceived and consequently cannot with success be maintained."[47]

THE SMELL OF THE LAMP

Although American Baptists recognize that finitude and sin limit the mind, just as do the mystery of God and the profundity of the gospel, and although they know that "a God which a creature can comprehend is an idol," they insist upon reasonableness both as a constituent of truth and as an essential standard in its judgment.

The following statements by Richard Furman, Elisha Paine, and Thomas Baldwin typify this insistence upon true learning. Furman, long-time pastor at Charleston, challenges Baptist ministers to make their sermons "smell of the lamp." Paine, in a letter to his brother from Long Island, calls Baptists to the same task: "I pray to God to pinch up our minds." In 1794 Baldwin, who helped launch the missionary movement, argues "that the bible exhibits a fair system of truth; supported by rational evidence; and were it not for the blindness of the human heart, and the prejudices occasioned by sinful affections, men would yield their cheerful assent to truth, in exact proportion to the evidence laid before them; and would not choose darkness rather than light."

The Sensible Baptists

In answer to calls to true learning, and naturally predisposed to reasonableness by their personalistic approach to truth, "the sensible Baptists" of America believe that the gracious God transforms the mind, informs the understanding, reveals new light, and justifies truth to the faithful and the attentive mind, doing so, not for the elite, but for the common person. Each individual, they believe, has an inalienable right to the full persuasion of reasonableness, and therefore stands supreme and personally responsible in the estimate of truth, replacing the systems of the wise and the learned, as well as the traditional authorities of church and state, desiring "to hear witnesses tell, not that a thing is so; but also how they came to know it to be so."[48]

Three requirements for a reasonable knowledge of truth are proposed by the sensible Baptists. The first essential, and the precondition of the rest, is that thinking takes place solely in a renewed mind. If persons are to live truthfully and make judgments of truth, they must overcome the form of the fallen person, that of Adam, and in faith they must conform their minds to the form of the new person, that of Christ. The second requirement is this: persons must live in unity with Christ, who occupies the space which was previously occupied by their own knowledge. The third essential requires that the full apparatus of human powers must be set in motion— intelligence, discernment, imagination, observation, judgment, analysis, synopsis, and all the rest.

James Manning, president of Brown University, and Richard Furman, in South Carolina, best represent the sensibility so loved by American Baptists. Simeon Dogget, a student of the 1788 class at Brown, records that Manning naturally and easily shifted from college exercises to discourses on moral and religious subjects. Manning can invariably be found, he writes, "holding in his left hand the classics, in his right the word of God, with his eye fixed on the good of man, widely diffusing, as he passed along, knowledge, and religion, and happiness."[49]

In his essay, "On the use of Reason in Religion," the most complete and systematic statement on reason by any Baptist in the classic heritage, Richard Furman locates the beginnings of the Christian religion in faith, service, and adoration, "which proceed from pure principles; have the true God for their object, and his glory for their end." Some of the principles, he notes, can be known by the light of nature, others by special revelation; while the whole is contained and displayed in the inspired scriptures. But whatever their origin, the pure principles require a rigorous accounting, which reason alone can provide. Reason can, and must, contemplate the nature of religious truth, assess its evidence, and relate it to particular cases in life. Furman specifically points to several uses of reason in religion: to trace the footsteps of God in the works of creation, providence, and grace; to secure self-knowledge and the Christian graces; to ascertain the genuineness of revelation; to analyze language; to offer a defense for faith; and to determine the relationships of the holy and the profane.[50]

The Full Range of Reasonable Standards

American Baptists, who often take uncommon delight in the joys of thinking,[51] use reason in humble dependence upon divine wisdom and the gracious influences of God on the heart. But they appeal no less to the high standards of reason and exhort all believers to use the full range of rational, empirical, and pragmatic standards of truth.

American Baptists accept the rational standards of logical consistency and coherence.[52] They will not, however, allow the dictates of logic to discount empirical considerations and sound historical fact. They agree with Hezekiah Smith who posits that "truth from history preponderates upon the Baptists' side." And, they robustly recite the plain facts, appealing to the standard of empirical adequacy, to support their position. For example, John Walton, pastor of the First Baptist Church of Providence, who acknowledges his debt to the philosophy of John Locke, refuses to "be persuaded to believe things contrary to common sense and experience." Furthermore, American Baptists make judgments of truth in terms of the pragmatic consequences which accrue to a claim. They often argue, for instance, that Christianity is necessary for the good order of civil society, or that history shows the imposition of a religious test to be "the greatest engine of tyranny in the world."[53]

The Role of Reason in Special and Natural Revelation

The child of God is expected as a matter of course to live a sensible life, for reasonableness is one of the constituents of truth. This expectation applies to all of life, since faith seeks understanding at every point, but American Baptists are particularly careful to apply reasonableness to the scriptures.

Although Baptists firmly hold to the inspiration and the rule of the Holy Scriptures, they never argue for the blind acceptance of the scriptures and their record of special revelation. They believe that the scriptures carry with them an apologetic for their truthfulness, which, when subjected to the standards of reasonableness, will establish their veracity. This reasonable apology, which consists of appeals to the fulfillment of prophecy, the coherence of the scriptures, the sublimity of their styles and substance, the character of their witnesses, the divinity of their subject, and their empirical adequacy, enables American Baptists to exclaim with Isaac Backus, "O, how convincing then are the evidences that we have of the verity of the Bible."[54]

In the last two decades of the eighteenth century, American Baptists increasingly apply the standards of reasonableness to the domain of natural revelation and use them to establish the compatibility of special and natural revelation. When the divine authority of the scriptures is admitted, they maintain, then persons proceed by the light thereof, together with the light of nature, and they discover the being, the perfections, and the purposes of God in the works of creation and providence. By means of the light of reason, which reflects the revealing light of nature, the two testaments of creation and providence are examined, and from natural religion that which is "much more manifest by the sure testimony of the scripture of truth" is observed.

Although persons "comprehend but a very small part of this vast whole" by natural revelation, American Baptists confess, yet they can declare: "O how august and stupendous this work of God! It is a most rich display of all the divine perfections; especially of wisdom, goodness, and power." Still, natural revelation is not enough; it must be completed by revealed faith. "It hath pleased God to make more clear and familiar displays of himself in his word."[55]

A THIRST FOR DIVINE KNOWLEDGE

In every agenda proposed, down every avenue followed, at every point of the compass of faith and practice, "a thirst for divine knowledge"[56] permeates American Baptist thinking about truth in the second half of the eighteenth century.

This thirst turns American Baptists away from the factual truths that shaped their declension. They disavow every form, everything firm, all that is custom, creedal, institution, system, Church. This thirst turns American Baptists to the Living God, to the common person, and to an undelegated, direct, experimental, cordial acquaintance with the personal truth of God come so sensibly near in heart, word, life, liberty, and thought that they can grasp it in their hands.

American Baptists seek one thing only, that being "the highest wisdom [which] is to know Jesus Christ and him crucified; and wherein things are taught in an experimental way."[57]

Part Five

THE PERSONAL TRUTH

AN OVERVIEW

Part Five—"The Personal Truth"—reflects upon the shape of personal truth as manifest in the whole of the classic Baptist heritage of truth established by English and American Baptists in the seventeenth and eighteenth centuries.

Chapter Eleven—"An Intimate Fellowship"—observes that the truth of immeasurable and everlasting moment at the core of the classic Baptist heritage is the person of the Living God—Father, Son, Spirit—and of Jesus Christ, who together fellowship with persons face-to-face, name-to-name, story-to-story within the realism of the gospel of grace.

Chapter Eleven

AN INTIMATE FELLOWSHIP

Surely, if ever people had cause to speake for the vindication of the truth
of Christ in their hands, wee have, that being indeed the maine wheele
at this time that sets us aworke. Wee know our God in his owne time will
cleere our Cause and lift up his Sonne to make him the chief cornerstone.
Wee are all one in Communion, holding Jesus Christ to be our head and
Lord; under whose government wee desire alone to walke, in following
the Lambe wheresoever he goeth; and wee believe the Lord will daily
cause truth more to appeare in the hearts of his Saints.
"London Confession," 1644, "To All That Desire"

TRUTH IS A PERSON COME NEAR

Western thought—its theology, philosophy, science, and the like—traditionally aims at defining truth in impersonal terms, for these alone are accepted as universal and verifiable. But, the classic Baptist heritage of personal truth leaves no room whatsoever for such an endeavor. Classic English and American Baptists in the seventeenth and eighteenth centuries totally commit themselves to "the truth as it is in Jesus." No passion, or loyalty, runs more broadly and more deeply throughout the whole of the Baptist way than this ultimate passion for a personal kind of truth.

In howsoever diverse forms and varying venues, classic English and American Baptists hold dear the knowledge that Jesus Christ is a person who enters into fellowship with persons of faith, a fellowship so real, so direct, so intimate, that each and every person of faith can confess, "I have been crucified with Christ; it is no longer I who live, but Christ who lives in me; and the life I now live in the flesh I live by faith in the Son of God, who loved me and gave himself for me."[1]

Around this confession each and every person of faith can also testify that "the old has passed away, the new has come," so that I fellowship with the Father who is revealed most fully in Jesus Christ, knowing of a surety that "I am of God," living fully immersed in "the grace of the Lord Jesus Christ and the love of God and the fellowship of the Holy Spirit," a tangible form of fellowship too, a "fellowship with one another in light, life, liberty, and love."[2]

It is this intimate fellowship that classic Baptists tenaciously identify as truth. Truth, they contend, is a "face-to-face fellowship."[3] It is that simple. Truth is a person come near. It is not something but someone encountered. It happens in history, comes about, so to speak, as someone dynamic, vigorous, passionate, gracious, and sometimes quite explosive. In the language of the gospel realism so loved by classic Baptists, truth is the person of Jesus Christ come so near in intimate communion that nothing stands between the Contemporary Christ and persons recreated in the image of Jesus Christ. Truth is the Father in the Son and through the Spirit come so near in face-to-face fellowship that nothing stands between the Holy Trinity and the children of God. Nothing! Nothing whatsoever!

THE LANGUAGE OF TRUTH

A particular language of truth unpacks the meaning of the claim that truth is an intimate fellowship with "the truth as it is in Jesus." It is a unique language, too, this language of truth, which cannot be considered under the game rules of other language games and be fairly judged. It is special. It is the language of the personal defined by the gospel realism of the Baptists in the classic heritage.

Upon analysis of the realistic gospel language of the personal, it is evident that three things command the attention of classic Baptists. First, they share the vision that truth is God in person, a fact expressed in the fundamentals of truth; second, they commonly describe the character of the fundamentals by means of categories derived from the gospel; third, all classic Baptists understand truth to be relational by turn.

The Fundamentals of Truth

The language of truth in the classic heritage begins with talk of fundamentals, two in number, which constitute the essence of personal truth:

1. truth is the person of God; truth is what God is and does;
2. persons can be and do the truth—persons model or participate in the truth that God is and does.

The Categories of Truth

The primary function of the categories in the classic heritage is to reveal the character of the fundamentals by dividing them into their essential parts. Baptists in the classic heritage do this by recounting gospel realities. Their categorial scheme consists of the claims that:

1. truth is Jesus Christ, the truth, the truth exalted by God, the Truth of all truth, the truth who is in union with the Father and through the Spirit with the believer;
2. truth is the Holy Trinity—God the Father is the one, only living and true God, God the Son is full of truth and grace, and God the Holy Spirit is the Spirit of truth, all in union with each other, related severally and together to those persons who voluntarily participate in the truth the Living God is and does;
3. truth is the Holy Scriptures, the God-breathed scriptures of truth, the will and the mind of God, already but not yet, in the process of becoming, ingrafted in the heart of the believer by the Living God;
4. truth is abundant life and liberty, a walk in love with the Living God in the life-world, the practice of eternal life which enables a person of faith to be and to do the truth;
5. truth is reasonableness, a truth that moves without violence, with a rational force in the reasonable soul enlightened by the Living God.

The Relations of Truth

The fundamentals and the categories, which give body and beauty to the personal quality of truth, form a network of relations. Each fundamental and category in the network has its own unique essence and integrity. However, each also has a relational essence and integrity. That is to say, each fundamental and category is constituted by its relations. As a result, the language of truth in the classic heritage achieves and maintains its unity by a harmonious balancing of diverse elements, and it judges any truth-claim contextually by the full range of fundamentals, categories, and relations.

When the fundamentals, the categories, and the relations of truth are marshalled together, they speak a language scandalously personal and earthy. They speak of truth as a critical happening in the gospel of grace, as a real event, as a concrete singular in relation, as "the truth as it is in Jesus." Truth is the sacred history that takes place or comes to pass between God and those persons born of "the only Son from the Father"[4] and by the Spirit; it is that which comes into life when the Holy Scriptures and the Holy Spirit express their unity in "the entirely new life" of faith and in the enlightened mind shaped "in union with Christ Jesus and the Father's glorious power."[5]

TRUTH IS GREATER THAN TRUTHS

Truth is always in danger of being submerged in the everydayness of impersonal truths (in true ideas, correct facts, right beliefs, high views of scripture, veritable doctrines, or proper experiences), of becoming a thing alongside other things, something known subjectively or objectively, merely a collection of universal truths. But classic Baptists finally know that to be overtaken with truth is not to entertain truths of any kind. Truth is greater than truths. It is not about something. As long as it is that, as long as it is truths, it is not truth. For truth is reality and reality is someone: it is the person of the Living God and of Jesus Christ come near in intimate fellowship.

It can be said that, properly speaking, classic Baptists stand in irreconcilable opposition to the equation of truth with universal truths. They fasten upon an actual happening in the domain of the personal which as such is opposed to every universal. Not that they deny the existence of a knowledge of universal truths. But, just as they deny that truth is universal, so too do they deny that the personal truth can be known through universals. They rather affirm that the personal truth can be known only by a voluntary and a tangible encounter with a person-come-near. This definite occurrence takes the place of the universal, of truth in general, or of valid assertions determined by the rationalistic standards of correspondence and coherence. For the person-come-near is the Singular God, who can never become an object discovered, but can nevertheless be known in the intimacy of a divine-human fellowship initiated by grace.

The classic Baptist heritage also refuses to equate truth with either objective or subjective truths. It does not focus its discourse externally on objects, such as those of doctrines, theories, rituals, facts, creeds, books, systems, institutions, or myths. Truth is not something objective, a datum at rest in itself apart from subjects. It is, however, quite erroneous to conclude from this that truth is something subjective. The classic heritage does not focus its discourse subjectively, in the belief that truth is primarily an experience, a feeling, a form of spirituality, a private voice, a mystical state, or an idea within a subject. Truth is not an abstraction drawn from either objective or subjective appearances (or, for that matter, found in either absolute or relative judgments), something objectively grasped or subjectively secured. The dualism of subject and object, so indigenous to modern thought, has no place in the deep intimacy of the holy fellowship of faces, names, and stories in the gospel of grace found only in Jesus Christ.

The whole of the noetic enterprise is undercut by the classic Baptist heritage of personal truth. To affirm the gospel of the twice-born in one breath, only to qualify it in the next by adding the condition of epistemic truths of a universal, an objective, or a subjective kind, makes knowledge the operative principle of truth, a qualification not acceptable to English and American Baptists in the classic heritage, even when the knowledge is that of true statements.

Classic Baptists know that an intimate fellowship with God depends solely upon God's gracious initiative. There is from the human side of the fellowship no way at all that leads to God, including that of a knowledge tied to universal, objective, or subjective truths. No system of truths of any kind can deal adequately with the dynamics of personal truth. If fellowship between God and persons nevertheless exists, if persons participate in the truth that the Living God is and does, this can only be due to God's grace.

OF FACES, NAMES, STORIES, PERSONS

A final word is in order. In the classic Baptist heritage of personal truth established by English and American Baptists in the seventeenth and eighteenth centuries, truth is what is real, an actual happening; and what is real is persons, human and divine, in intimate fellowship within the life-world of the gospel story of redemption. It is that simple.

Truth is "the truth as it is in Jesus." Truth, which has a name, a face, a story, is the person of the Living God—Father, Son, Spirit—and of Jesus Christ, who together fellowship with persons face-to-face, name-to-name, story-to-story within the realism of the gospel of grace.

Endnotes

Chapter One

1. H. Wheeler Robinson, *The Life and Faith of the Baptists* (London: Methuen, 1927), 3.

2. Christopher Blackwood, *The Storming of the Antechrist* (London, 1644), title page.

3. John 1:17, Isa. 43:19. All scripture references are taken from the Revised Standard Version, unless otherwise noted.

4. Ps. 139:5.

5. John 1:14; Obadiah Holmes, "On My Life," *Baptist Piety*, ed. by E. S. Gaustad (Grand Rapids, Mich.: Christian University, 1978), 82.

6. John Ryland, *Memoirs of Mr. Fuller*, 116.

7. Gabriel Fackre, *The Christian Story* (Grand Rapids, Mich.: William B. Eerdmans, 1984), 1.

8. "The Holy Gospel of Jesus Christ, According to John," *The Geneva Bible*, 1602 Edition.

9. Paul Hobson, *A Garden Inclosed: and Wisdom Justified only of her Children* (1817), quoted by Christopher Hill, *A Turbulent, Seditious, and Factious People: John Bunyan and his Church 1628–1688* (Oxford: Clarendon, 1988), 54.

10. Henry Haggar, *The Foundation of the Font Discovered* (London: Giles Calvert), 1.

11. W. T. Whitley, *A Baptist Bibliography* (London: Kingsgate, 1916), I, 20, and Leon McBeth, *The Baptist Heritage* (Nashville: Broadman, 1987), 829, ascribe *The Ancient Bounds* (London: Henry Overton, 1645) to John Tombes; while Edward Starr, *A Baptist Bibliography* (Rochester: American Baptist Historical Society, 1976), XXIII, 274–281, does not. McBeth observes that some scholars doubt whether Tombes was ever a Baptist, although he accepted believer's baptism. The thesis of this book is in no way affected by whether or not Tombes was a Baptist, or whether or not he wrote *The Ancient Bounds*, although it assumes both to be the case.

12. John Tombes, *The Ancient Bounds*, 1, 28.

13. Paul Hobson, *A Discoverie of Truth* (London: J. Coe, 1647), 21–22; John 14:9, 20.

14. Paul Hobson, *A Discoverie of Truth*, title page.

15. Paul Hobson, *Practicall Divinity* (London: R. Harford, 1646), 16.

16. Paul Hobson, *A Discoverie of Truth*, 21–22.

17. Isaac Backus, "A Discourse Showing the Nature and Necessity of an Internal Call to Preach the Everlasting Gospel" (Boston: Fowle, 1754), x; "A Fish Caught in His Own Net," 1768, William G. McLoughlin, ed., *Isaac Backus on Church, State, and Calvinism* (Cambridge, Mass.: Harvard University, 1968), 178.

18. Abel Morgan, "Of the Holy Scriptures," *Philadelphia Baptist Association Minutes*, 1774, 137.

19. William Straughton, "Infidelity," *Philadelphia Baptist Association Minutes*, 1796, 319–320.

20. Jonathan Maxcy, "Sermon: Dedication of a Meeting House" (Providence: Carter and Wilkinson, 1796), 5–7, 11–17; "A Sermon," Charleston Baptist Association, 1812, 135; and "An Address," Rhode Island College, 1801, *The Literary Remains of the Rev. Jonathan Maxcy*, ed. by Romeo Elton (NY: A. V. Blake, 1844), 321.

21. "Short Confession of Faith in XX Articles," by John Smyth, 1609; "A Short Confession," 1610; "A Declaration of Faith of English People Remaining at Amsterdam," 1611; and "Propositions and Conclusions concerning True Christian Religion," 1612–1614.

22. "Propositions and Conclusions concerning True Christian Religion," 1612–1614, Articles 8, 41, 44, 50, 52, 61, 84.

23. "Propositions and Conclusions concerning True Christian Religion," 1612–1614, Article 61; "Second London Confession," 1677, Chapter 2, Paragraph 1, Chapter 8, Paragraph 3, Chapter 22, Paragraph 6.

24. John Ryland, *Memoirs of Mr. Fuller*, 116.

25. Roger Williams, *The Bloudy Tenet*, ed. by Samuel L. Caldwell, *The Complete Writings of Roger Williams* (NY: Russell & Russell, 1963), III, 64–66, 70.

26. "The Baptist Debate of April 14–15, 1668," ed. by W. G. McLoughlin and M. W. Davidson, reprinted in *Colonial Baptists*, ed. by S. Bedney (NY: Arno, 1980), 11.

27. Andrew Fuller, *The Gospel Its Own Witness, The Complete Works of the Rev. Andrew Fuller*, ed. by Joseph Belcher (Philadelphia: American Baptist Publication Society, 1845), I, 15; Jonathan Maxcy, "Sermon at Warren Association," 1797, 10.

28. "Swansea Song," by Hezekiah Butterworth, "The Old Welsh Swansea Motto," sung to the tune of "Men of Harlech in the Hollow."

29. John Sturgion, *A Plea for Tolleration* (London: S. Dover, 1661), 9.

30. John Tombes, *The Ancient Bounds*, 1, 26, 28, 32.

31. Thomas Grantham, *The Baptist Against the Papist* (London, 1663), 4.

32. Obadiah Holmes, "On My Life," "To the World," and "To the Church," *Baptist Piety*, 77–79, 82, 110, 117.

33. Eph. 2:20.

34. John 14:9.

Chapter Two

1. Leonard Busher, *Religions Peace; or a plea for liberty of conscience*, in *Tracts on Liberty of Conscience 1614–1661*, ed. by E. B. Underhill (London: J. Hadden, 1846), 52–53.

2. Paul Hobson, *A Discoverie of Truth* (London: J. Coe, 1647), 7–8.

3. John Tombes, *The Ancient Bounds* (London: Henry Overton, 1645), 28.

4. Paul Hobson, *A Discoverie of Truth*, 8, 30, 76.

5. See J. V. Langmead Casserley, *The Christian in Philosophy* (NY: Charles Scribner's Sons, 1951), 61–68.

6. Henry Haggar, *The Foundation of the Font Discovered* (London: Giles Calvert, 1653), title page.

7. Paul Hobson, *Practicall Divinity* (London: R. Harford, 1646), 15–16.

8. Douglas Shantz, "The Place of the Resurrected Christ in the Writings of John Smyth," *Baptist Quarterly*, no. 20 (January 1984), 202, cf. 199–203. Barrie White thinks that the covenant is the center of Smyth's Theology, *The English Separatist Tradition* (Oxford: Oxford University, 1971), 125.

9. John Smyth, *The Character of the Beast*, 1609, in *The Works of John Smyth*, ed. by W. T. Whitley (Cambridge: Cambridge University, 1915), I, 574, 645.

10. In a confession whose articles number one hundred, Articles 28–39 address the atoning work of Christ, while Articles 40–63 expound upon the resurrection, if the work of the Holy Spirit is included.

11. "A Short Confession of Faith," 1610, Articles 1–3, 8–18.

12. "Propositions and Conclusions concerning True Christian Religion," 1612–1614, Article 49.

13. "Propositions and Conclusions concerning True Christian Religion," 1612–1614, Articles 30, 47, 75.

14. "Propositions and Conclusions concerning True Christian Religion," 1612–1614, Articles 50, 61.

15. Thomas Helwys, *A Short Declaration of the Mistery of Iniquity*, Flyleaf.

16. "Propositions and Conclusions concerning True Christian Religion," 1612–1614, Article 84.

17. Thomas Collier, *The Exaltation of Christ* (London: Giles Calvert, 1647), 236; Helwys, *A Short Declaration of*

Endnotes

the Mistery of Iniquity, 43–44; "A Declaration of Faith of English People," 1611, Articles 8–9, 11–12; William Dell, *Right Reformation* (London, 1646), 113–114, 119.

18. John Turner, *A Heavenly Conference for Sions Saints* (1645), 21.

19. Paul Hobson, *A Discoverie of Truth*, 3, 4, 21.

20. Paul Hobson, *A Discoverie of Truth*, 13–14, 28–29, 58. Caps mine.

21. By contrast, an external relation is a relation in which the terms are not affected by or changed by the relation.

22. Paul Hobson, *Practicall Divinity*, 15–16.

23. Lawrence Clarkson, *Truth Released from Prison to its Former Libertie* (London: Jane Coe, 1646), 1. Although introduced to Baptist ways, Clarkson later became a member of the sect of Ranters.

24. John Sturgion, *A Plea for Tolleration* (London: S. Dover, 1661), 9; Samuel Richardson, *The Necessity of Toleration* (London, 1647), in *Tracts on Liberty of Conscience 1614–1661*, 108.

25. "Second London Confession," 1677, Chapter 1, Paragraph 4.

26. "Orthodox Creed," 1678, Article I, cf. Article III.

27. I John 3:1–2.

28. "Propositions and Conclusions concerning True Christian Religion," 1612–1614, Articles 7, 30, 41, 44, 50, 52.

29. "Short Confession of Faith in XX Articles," 1609; "A Short Confession of Faith," 1610; "A Declaration of Faith of English People," 1611; and "Propositions and Conclusions concerning True Christian Religion," 1612–1614.

30. "A Declaration of Faith of English People," 1611, Preface.

31. James Leo Garrett Jr. observes, "The confessions of faith belonging to the congregations led by John Smyth and Thomas Helwys and, indeed, all General Baptist confessions prior to 1660 did not begin with an article on the Bible and usually did not contain such an article at all." "Sources of Authority in Baptist Thought," *Baptist History and Heritage*, no. 13 (July 1978), 42. Garrett notes one exception: Article 23 in the 1611 confession of Thomas Helwys.

32. "Short Confession of Faith in XX Articles," 1609, Article 1. Cf. "A Short Confession of Faith," 1610, Articles 1–3; "A Declaration of Faith of English People," 1611, Article 1; and "Propositions and Conclusions concerning True Christian Religion," 1612–1614, Articles 1–8.

33. "Propositions and Conclusions concerning True Christian Religion," 1612–1614, Articles 3–6.

34. "A Declaration of Faith of English People," 1611, Articles 1, 5, 7.

35. "A Short Confession of Faith," 1610, Article 19. Cf. "Short Confession of Faith in XX Articles," 1609, Article 11; "A Declaration of Faith of English People," 1611, Article 6; "Propositions and Conclusions concerning True Christian Religion," 1612–1614, Articles 50, 57–59.

36. "Short Confession of Faith in XX Articles," 1609, Article 2. Cf. "A Short Confession of Faith," 1610, Articles 1, 19, 20; "A Declaration of Faith of English People," 1611, Articles 2, 5; "Propositions and Conclusions concerning True Christian Religion," 1612–1614, Articles 12, 41–44.

37. L. Russ Bush and Tom J. Nettles, *Baptists and the Bible* (Chicago: Moody, 1980), 30.

38. John H. Watson, "Baptists and the Bible: As Seen in Three Eminent Baptists," *Foundations*, no. 16 (July 1973), 242, 243.

39. Thomas Helwys, *A Short Declaration of the Mistery of Iniquity* (1612), 69.

40. The 1612–1614 confession begins with articles on God (1–11) and man (12–27). Then it speaks of Jesus Christ (28–40). And it fleshes out the gospel story in terms of abundant life in sections on Regenerate Man (41–47), Repentance and Faith (57–59), Church (64–69), Ordinances (70–75), Ministries (76), Church Discipline (77–80), Succession (81–82), Magistrates (83–85), Discipleship (86–90), and Final Judgment (91–100).

41. "The Faith and Practice of Thirty Congregations," 1651, Preface.

42. "The Faith and Practice of Thirty Congregations," 1651, Article 1, cf. 2–3.

43. "The Faith and Practice of Thirty Congregations," 1651, Articles 4–16.

44. "The Faith and Practice of Thirty Congregations," 1651, Articles 17–23, 28.

45. "The Faith and Practice of Thirty Congregations," 1651, Articles 19, 46.

46. "The Faith and Practice of Thirty Congregations," 1651, Articles 24–75.

47. "The Faith and Practice of Thirty Congregations," 1651, Article 41.

48. "Second London Confession," 1677, Chapter 1, Paragraph 1.

49. Bush and Nettles, *Baptists and the Bible*, 62, cf. 63–72.

50. "Confession of Faith Put forth by the Elders and Brethren of many Congregations of Christians in London and the Country," commonly called the "Second London Confession," 1677, Chapter 1, Paragraphs 1, 6; Chapter 4; Chapter 5; Chapter 10, Paragraph 4; Chapter 22, Paragraph 1.

51. "Second London Confession," 1677, Chapter 1, Paragraph 4; Chapter 2, Paragraph 1.

52. "Second London Confession," 1677, Chapter 1, Paragraph 5.

53. "Second London Confession," 1677, Chapter 1, Paragraph 1.

54. "Second London Confession," 1677, Chapter 1, Paragraph 1.

55. "Second London Confession," 1677, Chapter 14, Paragraph 2.

56. "The London Confession," 1644 (1646, Second Edition), "To All That Desire."

57. Paul Hobson, *Practicall Divinity*, 16, 25–26, 36, 39, 42; *A Discoverie of Truth*, 31, 59.

Chapter Three

1. I Thess. 1:12, Matt. 6:10.

2. Paul Hobson, *A Garden Inclosed: and Wisdom Justified only of her Children* (1817), 5–7, 17–18, 20–30.

3. Paul Hobson, *Practicall Divinity* (London: R. Harford, 1646), 86–87.

4. "Standard Confession," 1660, Article XXIII.

5. "Sixteen Articles of Faith and Order Unanimously Assented to by the Messengers Met at Warwick, the 3rd Day of the 3rd Month," 1655, Article 3.

6. "A Declaration of Faith of English People Remaining at Amsterdam in Holland," 1611, Article 9; *Heart Bleedings for Professors Abominations* (London, 1650), 11, in Leon McBeth, *A Sourcebook for Baptist Heritage* (Nashville: Broadman, 1990), 69.

7. William Dell, *Right Reformation* (London, 1646), 121. William Dell is considered by some authorities, such as E. C. Walker and Barrie White, to be a Puritan and not a Baptist. Other authorities, such as Leon McBeth, consider Dell a Baptist. In this work Dell is held to be a Baptist, although the exclusion of his ideas from the present work would not alter the force of the argument of the book. Cf. *Heart Bleedings for Professors Abominations*, 11.

8. "A Declaration of Faith of English People Remaining at Amsterdam in Holland," 1611, Article 9.

9. "Preface: All that desire."

10. John Tombes, *The Ancient Bounds* (London: Henry Overton, 1645), 40.

11. Daniel King, *A Way to Sion* (London: Charles Sumptner, 1650), 22.

12. John Tombes, *The Ancient Bounds*, 14.

13. Thomas Collier, *The Font-Guard Routed* (1653), 59; *A General Epistle to the Universal Church of the First-Born* (London, 1651), 248, 250.

14. John Turner, *A Heavenly Conference for Sions Saints* (1645), 23–24, 33.

15. Thomas Grantham, *The Baptist Against the Papist* (London, 1663), 4, 25.

16. John Turner, *A Heavenly Conference for Sions Saints*, 19.

17. "Orthodox Creed," 1679, Article XXXVII.

18. "The London Confession," 1644 (1646, Second Edition), Article VII.

19. "Baptist Catechism," 1693; Benjamin Keach, *Tropologia* (London, 1682), viii (the page number is from the London edition published by William Otidge, 1779).

20. "The True Gospel-Faith," 1654, Introductory Letter; "Midland Confession," 1655, Article 3; "Somerset Confession," 1656, Article XXX; "Standard Confession," 1660, Article XXIII.

21. Thomas Grantham, *Christianismus Primitus* (London, 1678), Book 4, 1–2.

22. "Orthodox Creed," 1679, Article XLVI.

23. John Murton, *Objections Answered* (London, 1615), in Edward B. Underhill, *Tracts on Liberty of Conscience 1614–1661* (London: J. Hadden, 1846), 153.

24. James Leo Garrett, Jr., "Sources of Authority in Baptist Thought," *Baptist History and Heritage*, 13 (July

Endnotes

1978), 43. Cf. "Biblical Infallibility and Inerrancy According to Baptist Confessions," *Search*, 3 (Fall 1972), 42–45; and "Biblical Authority According to Baptist Confessions of Faith," *Review and Expositor*, 76 (Winter 1979), 50. See *Heart Bleedings for Professors Abominations*, 11.

25. "Propositions and Conclusions concerning True Christian Religion," 1612–1614, Article 52.

26. John Smyth, *Principles and Inferences Concerning the Visible Church* (London, 1607), in W. T. Whitley, *The Works of John Smyth* (Cambridge: Cambridge University, 1915), II, 281.

27. Thomas Murton, *An Humble Supplication* (London, 1620); Underhill, *Tracts*, 201.

28. "The London Confession," 1644 (1646, Second Edition), Article II.

29. "Second London Confession," 1677, Chapter 1, Paragraph 5, and Chapter 18, Paragraphs 2–3.

30. "The London Confession," 1644 (1646, Second Edition) , Article XXIII.

31. "Midland Confession," 1655, Article 3. Cf. "Orthodox Creed," 1678, Article 37; and "Standard Confession," 1660, Article XXIII.

32. "Second London Confession," 1677, Chapter 1, Paragraph 9; "Orthodox Creed," 1678, Article 37; Hercules Collins, *The Temple Repair'd* (London, 1702), 26–28.

33. "Second London Confession," 1677, Chapter 1, Paragraph 7.

34. "A Declaration of Faith of English People Remaining at Amsterdam in Holland," 1611, Article 23.

35. Thomas Murton, *An Humble Supplication*, 193; "London Confession," 1644, Article 7.

36. L. Russ Bush and Tom J. Nettles, *Baptists and the Bible* (Chicago: Moody, 1980), 31; William R. Estep, "Biblical Authority in Baptist Confessions of Faith, 1610–1963," *The Unfettered Word* (Waco, Tex.: Word, 1987), 162; and Gordon H. James, *Inerrancy and the Southern Baptist Convention* (Dallas: Southern Baptist Heritage Press, 1986), 34. See also Leon McBeth, "Early Baptist Hermeneutics," in Bruce Corley, Steve Lemke, Grant Lovejoy, eds., *Biblical Hermeneutics* (Nashville: Broadman & Holman, 1996), 89.

37. Richard Claridge, "Preface," in Hecules Collins, *The Sandy Foundation of Infant Baptism Shaken* (London: Will. Marshall, 1695), 1.

38. Henry Haggar, *The Foundation of the Font Discovered* (London: Giles Calvert, 1653), 1, 2.

39. "Records of the Abingdon Association, 11 January, 1656."

40. Richard Claridge, "Preface," 2, 3.

41. Richard Claridge, "Preface," 2.

42. Paul Hobson, *Practicall Divinity*, 16–17, 25–26.

43. Thomas Collier, *The Right Constitution and True Subjects of the Visible Church of Christ* (London: Henry Hills, 1654), 2, 8, 9–18.

44. "Propositions and Conclusions concerning True Christian Religion," 1612–1614, Articles 30, 63.

45. John Tombes, *The Ancient Bounds*, 25.

46. Leonard Busher, *Religions Peace; or a plea for liberty of conscience* (1614), 15.

47. Edward Barber, *To the King's Majesty* (London, 1641).

48. Samuel Richardson, *The Necessity of Toleration* (London, 1647), 275.

49. Thomas Helwys, *The Mistery of Iniquity* (1612), 69.

50. William Dell, *Right Reformation*, 329.

51. "Propositions and Conclusions concerning True Christian Religion," 1612–1614, Articles 7, 14, 17, 27, 30, 41, 50, 52, 61.

52. John Sturgion, *A Plea for Tolleration* (London: S. Dover, 1661), 329, 332.

53. Thomas Crosby, *The History of the English Baptists* (London, 1738), I, 238–239.

54. John Tombes, *The Ancient Bounds*, 1, 26, 28, 32.

55. "The Faith and Practice of Thirty Congregations," 1651, Articles 6–12, 24, 26, 28, 31.

56. "Second London Confession," 1677, Preface, "To All That Desire."

57. William Kiffin, *To M. Edwards*, 1644.

58. Thomas Helwys, *The Mistery of Iniquity*, 51.

59. Leonard Busher, *Religions Peace*, 20.

60. Thomas Grantham, *The Baptist Against the Papist*, 4, cf. 9, 14.

61. John Smyth, *Paralleles and Censures* (1609), 69.

62. John Tombes, *The Ancient Bounds*, 64–65.

63. Thomas Grantham, *The Baptist Against the Papist*, 13.

64. William Kiffin, quoted in J. Jackson Goadby, *Bye-Paths in Baptist History* (London: Elliot Stock, 1871), 35.

65. John Smyth, *The Character of the Beast*, Whitley, *Works* II, 629.

66. Thomas Collier, *The Font-Guard Routed*, "The Epistle to the Reader," 2–46.

67. Vavasor Powel, *Spiritual Experiences* (London, 1652), Preface, "To the Sober and Spiritual Readers of this Booke."

68. Christopher Blackwood, *The Storming of the Antechrist* (London, 1644), 15.

69. William Dell, *Uniformity Examined* (London: Henry Overton, 1646), 62–65, 69.

70. Leonard Busher, *Religions Peace*, 24.

71. Thomas Helwys, *The Mistery of Iniquity*, 79.

72. Samuel Richardson, *The Necessity of Toleration*, 108.

73. Christopher Blackwood, *The Storming of the Antechrist*, 14, 15.

74. Thomas Grantham, *The Baptist Against the Papist*, 22, 63.

75. "Short Confession of Faith in XX Articles," 1609, Articles 1, 2.

Chapter Four

1. W. R. Estep, "The Nature and Use of Biblical Authority in Baptist Confessions of Faith," *Baptist History and Heritage*, 22 (October 1987); 12; Robert A. Baker, *The Southern Baptist Convention* (Nashville: Broadman, 1974), pp. 15–16, 21.

2. Thomas Gould, in Peter G. Mode, *Source Book and Bibliography for American Church History* (Menasha, Wis.: George Banta, 1921), 287.

3. Humphrey Churchwood, "To the Church of Christ at Boston," in Isaac Backus, *A History of New England with Particular Reference to the Denomination of Christians Called Baptists* (Newton, Mass.: Backus Historical Society, 1871), I, 401.

4. Obadiah Holmes, "Unto the well beloved Brethren John Spilsbury, William Kiffin, and the rest that in London stand fast in that Faith," in John Clarke, *Ill Newes from New-England* (London: Henry Hills, 1652), 46.

5. Obadiah Holmes, "To the World," *Baptist Piety*, ed. by E. S. Gaustad (Grand Rapids, Mich.: Christian University, 1978), 117.

6. Obadiah Holmes, "Unto the well beloved Brethren," 48–49.

7. Roger Williams, *Queries of Highest Consideration* (London, 1644), *The Complete Writings of Roger Williams* (New York: Russell & Russell, 1963), II, 14.

8. John Clarke, *Ill Newes from New-England*, reprinted in *Colonial Baptists*, ed. by S. Bedney (New York: Arno, 1980), 84.

9. Rev. 19:11, 22:4.

10. 1 Tim. 2:5–6, John 14:6.

11. American Baptists believe that Jesus Christ is the Mediator in the threefold office of Prophet, Priest, and King. They faithfully hold to the doctrines of the deity and the humanity of Christ, as well as to the factuality and the personal appropriation of the atoning work of Jesus Christ on the cross. American Baptists also agree that "the sending of Christ, faith, holiness, and eternal life, are the effects of [God's] love, by which he manifesteth the infinite riches of his grace." John Clarke, *Ill Newes from New-England*, 84.

12. "Confession of Faith," First Baptist Church Boston, *The History of the First Baptist Church of Boston*, 65–66; and "The Articles of the faith of the Church of Christ, or congregation meeting at Horsley-down," London, 1697. See Morgan Edwards, *Materials Towards a History of the American Baptists in XII Volumes* (Philadelphia: J. Crukshank and I. Collins, 1770), I, 5–11.

13. John Clarke, *Ill Newes from New-England*, 25–26, 36–37, 70–113.

14. John Clarke, *Ill Newes from New-England*, 70–80.

15. Obadiah Holmes, "Of My Life," *Baptist Piety*, 81.

16. John Clarke, *Ill Newes from New-England*, 19, 20, 91.

17. John Myles, "Holy Covenant," in Henry Melville King, *Rev. John Myles* (Providence, R.I.: Preston & Rounds, 1905), 52.

18. John Clarke, *Ill Newes from New-England*, 81.

19. Roger Williams, *The Letters of Roger Williams*, *The Complete Works of Roger Williams*, VI, 214–228.

20. John Clarke, *Ill Newes from New-England*, 4, 6, 7, 9–16.

21. John Myles, *An Antidote Against the Infection of the Times* (London: T. Brewster, 1656), 19–27, a work attributed to Myles by Edward C. Starr, *A Baptist Bibliography*.

Endnotes

22. Rom. 8:16, Rev. 1:6, 1 Pet. 2:10.

23. Obadiah Holmes, "To the World," 117.

24. Obadiah Holmes, "On My Life," 74–76.

25. Obadiah Holmes, "On My Life," 77–78.

26. Obadiah Holmes, "Unto the well beloved Brethren," 46, 48.

27. Obadiah Holmes, "On My Life," 81.

28. Obadiah Holmes, "On My Life," 82.

29. John Myles, *An Antidote Against the Infection of the Times*, 1–17; and Roger Williams, *George Fox Digg'd out of his Burrowes* (Boston: John Foster, 1676), 236–237.

30. Obadiah Holmes, "To My Wife" and "A Letter to All My Children," *Baptist Piety*, 95, 101–102.

31. Obadiah Holmes, "To the Church" and "To the World," *Baptist Piety*, 108, 116–118.

32. Obadiah Holmes, "To the Church" and "To the World," 108–111, 116–117.

33. "Church Book," 1665, in Nathan E. Wood, *The History of the First Baptist Church of Boston* (Philadelphia: American Baptist Publication Society, 1899), 56.

34. "Covenant," Seventh Day Baptist Church, Newport, Rhode Island, 1671, in Charles W. Deweese, *Baptist Church Covenants* (Nashville: Broadman, 1990), 133–134.

35. "Covenant," Swansea Baptist Church, Rehoboth, Mass., 1663, in Charles W. Deweese, *Baptist Church Covenants*, 132–133.

36. "Covenant," Kittery Baptist Church, Kittery, Maine, 1682, in Charles W. Deweese, *Baptist Church Covenants*, 134.

37. "Church Book" and "Church Covenant," 1665, in Nathan E. Wood, *The History of the First Baptist Church of Boston*, 56, 65.

38. "Covenant," Kittery Baptist Church, Kittery, Maine, 1682, 134. Cf. Robert Baker and Paul J. Craven, Jr., *Adventure in Faith* (Nashville: Broadman, 1982), 42.

39. William Screven, "To Thomas Skinner, Boston, For the Church," in Isaac Backus, *A History of New England*, I, 404.

40. Quoted in Joan Gallagher, *The John Clarke Property* (Providence, R.I.: Brown University, 1981), 69.

Chapter Five

1. William G. McLoughlin and Martha Whiting Davidson, eds., "The Baptist Debate of April 14–15, 1668," reprinted in S. Bedney, ed., *Colonial Baptists* (New York: Arno, 1980), 104, cf. 97–104.

2. "The Baptist Debate of April 14–15, 1668," 111, 118–119.

3. "The Baptist Debate of April 14–15, 1668," 113.

4. "The Baptist Debate of April 14–15, 1668," 113.

5. "The Baptist Debate of April 14–15, 1668," 116, 117.

6. "The Baptist Debate of April 14–15, 1668," 117.

7. John Myles, "Holy Covenant," in Henry Melville King, *Rev. John Myles* (Providence, R.I.: Preston & Rounds, 1905), Appendix A, 53.

8. John Myles, *An Antidote Against the Infection of the Times* (London: T. Brewster, 1656), 13, a work attributed to John Myles by Edward C. Starr, *A Baptist Bibliography*.

9. Obadiah Holmes, "Of My Faith," E. S. Gaustad, ed., *Baptist Piety* (Grand Rapids, Mich.: Christian University, 1978), Articles 24, 89–90. Cf. John Clarke, *Ill Newes from New-England* (London: Henry Hills, 1652), reprinted in S. Bedney, ed., *Colonial Baptists*, 70.

10. John Clarke, *Ill Newes from New-England*, 70, 71; "First Instrument in Founding Rhode Island," March 7, 1638, signed by John Clarke, quoted in Isaac Backus, *A History of New England With Particular Reference to the Denomination of Christians Called Baptists* (Newton, Mass. A: Backus Historical Society, 1871), I, 427.

11. John Myles, *An Antidote Against the Infection of the Times*, 13.

12. Obadiah Holmes, "On My Life," *Baptist Piety*, 80.

13. "The Baptist Debate of April 14–15, 1668," 111; John Watts, *et al.*, "A Baptist Reply to an Anglican Overture," 1699, in H. S. Smith, R. T. Handy, and L. A. Loetscher, *American Christianity* (New York: Charles Scribner's Sons, 1960), I, 271.

14. Thomas Gould, "Letter," Isaac Backus, *A History of New England*, I, 289–297. See Isaac Backus, *A History of New England*, I, 299, footnote 3; E. S. Gaustad, ed., *Baptist Piety*, 30.

15. John Clarke, *Ill Newes from New-England*, 21.

16. "The Baptist Debate of April 14–15, 1668," 116; Obadiah Holmes, "Of My Faith," Articles 16, 89; John Clarke, *Ill Newes from New-England*, 85–99.

17. "Confession of Faith," in Nathan E. Wood, *The History of the First Baptist Church of Boston* (Philadelphia: American Baptist Publication Society, 1899), Article d, 65. The confession has two articles numbered "d." I have quoted the first.

18. Isaac Backus, *A History of New England*, I, 395.

19. Obadiah Holmes, "Of My Faith," Articles 16, 24, 89–90, 92; John Myles, *An Antidote Against the Infection of the Times*, 13; John Watts, "A Baptist Reply to an Anglican Overture," 271; "Confession of Faith," Article d, 65.

20. "Records," First Baptist Church, Newport, R. I., 1671, typescript, Archives, Seventh Day Baptist Historical Society, 1–5.

21. "The Baptist Debate of April 14–15, 1668," 127.

22. John Clarke, *Ill Newes from New-England*, 92–93, 96, 98.

23. Roger Williams, *George Fox Digg'd Out of his Burrowes* (Boston: John Foster, 1676), 137, 141; Obadiah Holmes, "To the World," *Baptist Piety*, 117, 121, 125.

24. Obadiah Holmes, "Unto the well beloved Brethren John Spilsbury, William Kiffin, and the rest that in London stand fast in that Faith," in John Clarke, *Ill Newes from New-England*, 46.

25. "The Baptist Debate of April 14–15, 1668," 115.

26. "Covenant of Benjamin and Elias Keach," 1697, in Charles W. Deweese, *Baptist Church Covenants* (Nashville: Broadman, 1990), 119–120.

27. "Covenant of Swansea Baptist Church," Rehoboth, Mass., 1663, in Charles W. Deweese, *Baptist Church Covenants*, 132–133.

28. Obadiah Holmes, "To the World," 123, 126.

29. "Covenant of Kittery Baptist Church," Kittery, Maine, 1682, in Charles W. Deweese, *Baptist Church Covenants*, 134.

30. "Covenant of Benjamin and Elias Keach," 120.

31. John Clarke, *Ill Newes from New-England*, 18, 36–37.

32. Obadiah Holmes, "To the World," "To the Church," *Baptist Piety*, 126, 111–112.

33. John Cotton, *A Practical Commentary*, in Irwin H. Polishook, *Roger Williams, John Cotton, and Religious Freedom* (Englewood Cliffs, N.J.: Prentice-Hall, 1967), 77.

34. Roger Williams, "Appendix," *Reply to Cotton*, 1652, in Isaac Backus, *A History of New England*, I, 211.

35. The words of Roger Williams concerning John Clarke, quoted in Thomas Armitage, *A History of the Baptists* (New York: Bryan Taylor, 1893), 292.

36. Roger Williams, *Christenings make not Christians*, in *The Complete Works of Roger Williams* (New York: Russell & Russell, 1963), VII, 38.

37. Isaac Backus, *The History of New England*, I, 286, editor's note (David Weston).

38. Henry Melville King, *Rev. John Myles*, 38–40, 60–62; John Clarke, *Ill Newes from New-England*, 41, 96–113; and "A Petition Addressed to the King in 1662," in W. R. Estep, *The Revolution Within the Revolution* (Grand Rapids, Mich.: William B. Eerdmans, 1990), 93.

39. "The Baptist Debate of April 14–15, 1668," 117, 124.

40. "The Baptist Debate of April 14–15, 1668," 119.

41. Obadiah Holmes, "To the Church," 110.

42. Roger Williams, *The Bloudy Tenet*, in *The Complete Works of Roger Williams* III, 13.

43. Obadiah Holmes, "To the World," 118.

44. John Clarke, *Ill Newes from New-England*, 21.

45. "The Baptist Debate of April 14–15, 1668," 111, 116.

46. John Russell, *Some Considerable Passages* (London, 1680), in William H. Brackney, ed., *Baptist Life and Thought: 1600–1980* (Valley Forge, Pa.: Judson, 1983), 113.

47. John Myles, *An Antidote Against the Infection of the Times*, 2.

48. Roger Williams, *The Examiner Defended* (London: James Cottrel, 1652), in *The Complete Works of Roger Williams*, VIII, 127, 130.

49. John Myles, *An Antidote Against the Infection of the Times*, 2.

50. John Myles, *An Antidote Against the Infection of the Times*, 2; Roger Williams, *The Examiner Defended*, VIII, 240–242, 354–355; and *George Fox Digg'd Out of his Burrowes*, V, 370–372.

51. John Clarke, *Ill Newes from New-England*, passim.

52. John Russell, *Some Considerable Passages*, 99.

Endnotes

53. John Pierce, "Petition," William G. McGlothlin, *New England Dissent 1630–1833* (Cambridge, Mass.: Harvard University, 1971), I, 88.

54. John Clarke, *Ill Newes from New-England*, 82–84, 101.

55. Thomas Gould, "Narrative," *The History of the First Baptist Church of Boston*, 42–51.

56. Mrs. Gould, "Narrative," Isaac Backus, *A History of New England*, I, 307.

57. John Myles, "Reply of the Church to the Propositions of Capt Thomas Willet," in Henry Melville King, *Rev. John Myles*, Appendix C, 60.

58. John Clarke, *Ill Newes from New-England*, 103, 109, 111.

59. Obadiah Holmes, "Letter," *Baptist Piety*, 32.

60. John Clarke, *Ill Newes from New-England*, 27.

61. John Clarke, *Ill Newes from New-England*, 102.

62. "The Baptist Debate of April 14–15, 1668," 114.

63. Roger Williams, *The Bloudy Tenet* III, 180.

Chapter Six

1. Leon McBeth, *The Baptist Heritage* (Nashville: Broadman, 1987), 151.

2. Raymond Brown, *The English Baptists of the Eighteenth Century* (London: The Baptist Historical Society, 1986), 3; Leon McBeth, *The Baptist Heritage*, 151.

3. Benjamin Wallin, *The Christian Life: In Divers of its Branches, Described and Recommended* (1746) II, ix.

4. Quoted by Simon Valentine, "A Wrestler Who Fought the Devil," *Baptist Times* (1 March 1990), 6.

5. Michael A. G. Haydin, for example, lists as causes: High Calvinism, legal restrictions, isolation, and loss of identity, "A Habitation of God, Through the Spirit," *Baptist Quarterly*, 39 (1992), 304–305; Raymond Brown identifies five causes: political change, the religious ferment of Roman Catholicism and rationalism, a moral decay in English society, ecclesiastical controversy, and sociological conditions, *The English Baptists of the Eighteenth Century*, 1–12.

6. Barrie White, *The English Baptists of the Seventeenth Century* (London: The Baptist Historical Society, 1983), 138; H. Wheeler Robinson, *Baptists in Britain* (London: Baptist Union Publication Department, 1937), 20.

7. W. T. Whitley, *Minutes of the General Assembly of General Baptists*, 2 vols. (London: Kingsgate, 1909), I, xxvi.

8. *Proceedings of the General Assembly* (Horsley-Down: J. Brown, 1790), 6.

9. Leon McBeth, *The Baptist Heritage*, 158.

10. Matthew Caffyn, *The Deceived and Deceiving Quakers* (London: R. I., 1656), 2.

11. Adam Taylor, *The History of the English General Baptists*, 2 vols. (London: T. Bore, 1818), I, 464.

12. W. T. Whitley, *Minutes*, I, 40.

13. "The Reasons for our Separation from the General Assembly," 1693.

14. W. T. Whitley, *Minutes*, I, 51, 103, 113, 149. Cf. Adam Taylor, *The History of the English General Baptists*, I, 470.

15. W. T. Whitley, *Minutes*, I, xxx–xxxi.

16. W. T. Whitley, *Minutes*, I, 88. Cf. Goswell Street, 1728, I, 149.

17. W. T. Whitley, *Minutes*, I, 103, 113.

18. W. T. Whitley, *Minutes*, I, 149–150.

19. W. T. Whitley, *Minutes* II, 32–33.

20. S. Acton, *Truth Without Disguise: An Essay for Union Among Christians* (London: J. Noon, 1732), 2, 41.

21. Gilbert Bryce, *et al.*, "Causes of Decay," *The Letter of the Committee* (London: General Baptist Assembly, 1773), 11–12; W. T. Whitley, *Minutes* II, 159.

22. John Hursthouse, *An Epistle to the Baptized Churches in Lincolnshire* (1729), 3–21. See also Strickland Gough, *An Enquiry into the causes of the Decay of the Dissenting Interest* (1730); and W. T. Whitley, *Minutes* II, 67, 95.

23. Thomas Gibbons, *The State of the World in General, and of Great Britain in Particular, as to Religion* (London: James Buckland, 1770), 23, 27, 32.

24. W. T. Whitley, *Minutes* II, 49, 58, 95–96; Gilbert Bryce, *et al.*, "Causes of Decay," 5–8.

25. W. T. Whitley, *Minutes* II, 2, 141.

26. Olin C. Robison, "The Legacy of John Gill," *Baptist Quarterly*, 24 (1971), 112.

27. Sydney F. Clark, "Nottinghamshire Baptist Beginnings," *Baptist Quarterly*, 17 (1957–58), 162–169.

28. John Gill's method is typical. See *Body of Practical Divinity* (London: Printed for the Author, 1770), I, 1–25.

29. D. Mervyn Himbury, *British Baptists—A Short History* (London: Kingsgate, 1962), 66.

30. Benjamin Keach, *The Gospel Minister's Maintenance Vindicated* (1689), 82.

31. Ernest A. Payne, *Baptists of Berkshire* (London: Kingsgate, 1951), 79.

32. J. G. Fuller, *A Brief History of the Western Association* (Bristol, 1843), 46–47.

33. John Brine, *A Treatise on Various Subjects*, revised by James Upton (London: Printed for the Editor, 1813), 39, 126, 127.

34. John Brine, *A Treatise on Various Subjects*, 169–174.

35. John Brine, *A Treatise on Various Subjects*, 175–183.

36. John Brine, *A Treatise on Various Subjects*, 195.

37. John Brine, *A Defence of the Doctrine of Eternal Justification* (London: A. Ward, 1732), reprinted by The Baptist Standard Bearer, Paris, Arkansas, 1987, 1–13.

38. John Brine, *A Treatise on Various Subjects*, 181–185, 195.

39. Thomas Craner, *A Grain of Gratitude* (London, 1771, 1757), 31–32.

40. Olinthus Gregory and Joseph Belcher, eds., *The Works of Rev. Robert Hall*, 4 vols. (New York: Harper, 1854), III, 82.

41. John Gill, *The Cause of God and Truth* (Grand Rapids, Mich.: Baker, 1980), iii; John Rippon, *A Brief Memoir of the Life and Writings of the Late Rev. John Gill* (London: John Bennett, 1838), 39–41.

42. John Gill, *A Body of Doctrinal Divinity* (London: Printed for the Author, 1769), I, 110–113.

43. John Gill, *A Body of Doctrinal Divinity*, I, 198–201, 330–340, 372–377, 525–528; and *A Body of Practical Divinity* (reprint, Paris, Ark.: The Baptist Standard Bearer, 1984), 705–713, 730–746.

44. John Gill, *Expositions of the New Testament* (London, 1810), III, 593.

45. John Gill, *A Body of Doctrinal Divinity*, I, 1–21.

46. John Gill, *A Body of Doctrinal Divinity*, I, 21–23.

47. John Gill, *Articles of Religion*, 1620, Article 1, in John Rippon, *A Brief Memoir of the Life and Writings of the Late Rev. John Gill*, 15.

Chapter Seven

1. Edmund Botsford, "On the Duty of Christians in matters of Controversy," Circular Letter, 1794, Charleston Baptist Association, in Wood Furman, ed., *A History of the Charleston Association of Baptist Churches* (Charleston, S.C.: J. Hoff, 1811), 98–104.

2. Daniel Boorstin, *The Americans* (New York: Vintage, 1958), 149–168.

3. Clarence C. Goen, *Revivalism and Separatism in New England, 1740–1800* (Archon Books, 1969), 3.

4. John Leland, "The Virginia Chronicle," (Virginia, 1790), in L. F. Greene, *The Writings of John Leland* (New York: Arno, 1969), 105.

5. Quoted in William G. McLoughlin, *New England Dissent 1630–1883* (Cambridge, Mass.: Harvard, 1971), II, 695.

6. "Warren Association Minutes," 1792.

7. "Warren Association Minutes," 1784, 4.

8. "Covenant," Bent Creek Baptist Church, Bent Creek, Tenn., 1785, in Charles W. Deweese, *Baptist Church Covenants* (Nashville: Broadman, 1990), 148.

9. "Minutes of the Philadelphia Baptist Association," 1741, in A. D. Gillette, ed., *Minutes of the Philadelphia Baptist Association, 1707–1807* (Philadelphia: American Baptist Publication Society, 1851), 44.

10. "Woodstock Association Minutes," n.d.

11. "Minutes of the Philadelphia Baptist Association," 1752, 68–69.

12. "Warren Association Minutes," 1767; Garnett Ryland, *The Baptists of Virginia 1699–1926* (Richmond, Va.: Virginia Baptist Board of Missions and Education, 1955), 139.

13. John Leland, "Letter of Valediction on Leaving Virginia, in 1791," *The Writings of John Leland*, 172.

14. J. V. Langmead Casserley, *The Church Today and Tomorrow* (London: SPCK, 1965), 27, see also 20–41.

15. "Propositions and Conclusions concerning True Christian Religion," Article 61.

Chapter Eight

1. Robert Hall Jr., *The Works of the Rev. Robert Hall, A. M.*, 2 vols., ed. Olinthus Gregory (New York: Harper, 1835), II, 452.

Endnotes

2. W. T. Whitley, *Minutes of the General Assembly of General Baptists*, 2 vols. (London: Kingsgate, 1909), II, 141.

3. Adam Taylor, *Memoirs of the Rev. Dan Taylor* (London: Printed for the Author, 1820), 72.

4. J. Fletcher, "Dan Taylor and the English Baptists," *The English Baptists* (London: E. Marborough, 1881), 112.

5. Dan Taylor, *The Consistent Christian* (Leeds: G. Wright, 1784), 57–58, 65–69.

6. J. Fletcher, "Dan Taylor and the English Baptists," 123.

7. "Articles of Religion of the New Connexion," 1770, Articles 1–6.

8. Dan Taylor, *The Consistent Christian*, 18.

9. Dan Taylor, *An Essay on the Truth and Inspiration of the Holy Scriptures* (London: P. And F. Heck, 1819), 35, 42–43, 49, 58–61, 146–147.

10. Dan Taylor, *Observations on the Rev. Andrew Fuller's Reply to Philanthropos* (London: J. Bloom, 1788), subtitle.

11. Dan Taylor, *Observations on the Rev. Andrew Fuller's Reply to Philanthropos*, 11.

12. Dan Taylor, *The Consistent Christian*, 18, 22.

13. Dan Taylor, *The Consistent Christian*, 18, 22.

14. Dan Taylor, *The Consistent Christian*, 21–34; *Duties of Ministers and People* (Leeds: G. Wright, 1775), 11.

15. "Articles of Religion of the New Connexion," Articles 2, 3, 5.

16. Dan Taylor, *A Catechism*, Questions 5–7, 9–15, 21, 23–24; *Scripture Directions and Encouragements to Feeble Christians* (Leeds: G. Wright, 1777), 14; *The Scriptural Account of the Way of Salvation* (Hallifax: E. Jacob, 1772), 4.

17. Dan Taylor, *Duties of Ministers and People*, 10–11; *Christian Baptism*, 2d ed. (London: J. W. Pasham, 1777), 8; *A Modest Inquiry* (London: G. Keith, 1772), 5; *A Catechism*, Questions 25–26, 29, 31.

18. Dan Taylor, *Letter on the Duties of Church Members* (London: R. Hawes, 1796), 3–20.

19. "On Associations," Circular Letter, New Connexion, 1779, Coventry.

20. Dan Taylor, *The Consistent Christian*, 36–47.

21. Dan Taylor, *The Scriptural Account of the Way of Salvation*, 4.

22. W. T. Whitley, *Minutes of the General Assembly of General Baptists* II, 194. For other instances of Taylor's use of reasonable standards, see *A Dissertation on Singing in the Worship of God* (London: Printed for the Author, 1786), 18, 36, 40; "On Associations," 5; W. T. Whitley, *Minutes* II, 72–73; and Adam Taylor, *Memoirs of the Rev. Dan Taylor*, 128.

23. Dan Taylor, *Observations on the Rev. Andrew Fuller's Reply to Philanthropos*, 11.

24. John Locke, *Essay Concerning Human Understanding*, L. iv. chap. 4.16.

25. James Beattie, *Evidences of the Christian Religion* (Edinburgh: Strahen & Cadell, 1786), I, 52–53.

26. Dan Taylor, *An Essay on the Truth and Inspiration of the Holy Scriptures*, 48–49, 53. An exposition of the truth of the scriptures using the empirical rules set forth by Locke and Beattie can be found in the *Essay*. A lengthy discussion of the internal and external evidence in favor of the divine revelation of the scriptures can also be found in this volume.

27. Dan Taylor, *Duties of Ministers and People*, 11; *The Consistent Christian*, 21–28; *The Essay on the Truth and Inspiration of the Holy Scriptures*, 81–83.

28. Dan Taylor, *The Consistent Christian*, 18.

29. Dan Taylor, *An Essay on the Truth and Inspiration of the Holy Scriptures*, 35, 42.

30. Dan Taylor, *The Scriptural Account of the Way of Salvation*, 4–5.

31. The "Fundamentals" or the absolute essentials of truth in personal narrative—the nature and relationships of God, Man, the Moral Law, the Fall, the Law of God, Condemnation, Salvation, Faith, Holiness, and Death—can be found systematically discussed in Dan Taylor, *Fundamentals of Religion* (Leeds: Printed for the Author, 1775), Chapters 1–15.

Chapter Nine

1. Robert Hall Sr., *Help to Zion's Travellers* (Halifax: Hartley and Walker, 1781), title page. See A. C. Underwood, *A History of English Baptists* (London: Baptist Union, 1947), 160.

2. Andrew Fuller, "Plan Proposed to be Pursued," *The Complete Works of the Rev. Andrew Fuller*, ed. Joseph Belcher (Philadelphia: American Baptist Publication Society, 1845), I, 690; "An Essay on Truth," *Works* III, 525–526.

3. Andrew Fuller, "An Essay on Truth," III, 526; "Plan Proposed to be Pursued," I, 690–692; "The Uniform Bearing of the Scriptures on the Person and Work of Christ," *Works*, I, 703.

4. Andrew Fuller, "Plan Proposed to be Pursued," I, 693, 695; "The Perfections of God," *Works*, I, 705–707; "Confession of Faith," *Life and Death of the Rev. Andrew Fuller*, ed. John Ryland, (Charlestown: S. Etheridge, 1818), 54–56.

5. Andrew Fuller, "The Nature and Importance of an Intimate Knowledge of Divine Truth," *Works*, I, 162–163, 166–167.

6. Andrew Fuller, *The Gospel Its Own Witness*, *Works*, I, 82.

7. Andrew Fuller, *The Gospel Worthy of All Acceptance*, *Works*, II, 343–367. Fuller's "Confession of Faith" tells the story in twenty articles.

8. William Carey, *An Enquiry into the Obligations of Christians* (Leicester: Ann Ireland, 1792), 3–5.

9. Andrew Fuller, *The Gospel Worthy of All Acceptance*, II, 340.

10. Andrew Fuller, "The Increase of Knowledge," *Works*, I, 417–419; "The Vanity of the Human Mind," *Works*, I, 435–438.

11. Robert Hall Sr., *Help to Zion's Travellers*, 48–60. Parts I-III present the whole gospel story.

12. "The Nature of Faith," Circular Letter, From the Baptist Ministers and Messengers, Assembled at Kettering, in Northamptonshire, 1781, 1–14.

13. "The Doctrine of Repentance," Circular Letter, From the Baptist Ministers and Messengers, Assembled at Carleton, in Bedfordshire, 1780, 2.

14. John Sutcliff, *The First Principles of the Oracles of God* (Halifax: Ewood Hall, 1783), 3.

15. William Carey, quoted in Mervyn Himbury, *British Baptists—A Short History* (London: Carey Kingston, 1962), 78.

16. Abraham Booth, "Address to the friends of Evangelical Truth in general and to the Calvinistic Churches in particular."

17. John Rippon, quoted in Charles Brown, *The Story of Baptist Home Missions* (London: Veal, Chifferieri, 1897), 13, 14.

18. Caleb Evans, "A Charge and Sermon; delivered at the ordination of Thomas Dunscombe," Bristol, 1773, 6.

19. *Baptist Magazine*, IX (London, 1817), 54, 55.

20. "The Excellence of the Christian Dispensation," Circular Letter, The Elders, Ministers, and Messengers of the Several Baptist Churches, Being met in Association at Wellington, 1787, 6–10.

21. Andrew Fuller, "Churches Walking in the Truth the Joy of Ministers," *Works*, I, 529–530.

22. Andrew Fuller, "The Being of God," *Works*, I, 695.

23. Andrew Fuller, "Churches Walking in the Truth the Joy of Ministers," I, 530–531; "The Characteristics of Pure Religion," *Works*, I, 399–402.

24. Andrew Fuller, *The Calvinistic and Socinian Systems Examined and Compared as to their Moral Tendency*, *Works*, II, 153, 189–195; "The Nature and Importance of an Intimate Knowledge of Divine Truth," I, 169; Thomas Eakins, *Life and Writings of Andrew Fuller* (London: Heaton, 1863), 165.

25. Andrew Fuller, "Spiritual Knowledge and Love Necessary for the Ministry," *Works*, II, 649–650.

26. Andrew Fuller, "An Essay on Truth," III, 531, 532–535; "The Nature and Importance of an Intimate Knowledge of Divine Truth," I, 160.

27. Andrew Fuller, *Dialogues and Letters Between Crispus and Gaius*, *Works*, II, 650–654.

28. Abraham Booth, "Confession of Faith," 1769, 14.

29. Andrew Fuller, "The Nature and Importance of an Intimate Knowledge of Divine Truth," I, 160–161; "On an Intimate and Practical Acquaintance with the Word of God," *Works*, I, 483; "The Necessity of a Divine Revelation," *Works*, I, 695; "Confession of Faith," Articles I-II, Joseph Belcher, ed., *The Last Remains of the Rev. Andrew Fuller* (Philadelphia: American Baptist Publication Society), 209.

30. "The Divinity of the Christian Religion," Circular Letter, From the Baptist Ministers and Messengers, Assembled at Leicester, 1797, 3–4.

31. Andrew Fuller, "The Inspiration of the Scriptures," *Works*, I, 699.

32. Andrew Fuller, *The Gospel Its Own Witness*, I, 15, 63, 68, 88. See also "The Nature of Faith," 1781, 4–10.

33. "The Nature of Faith," 1781, 6; and Andrew Fuller, "The Inspiration of the Scriptures," I, 699; "The Uniform Bearing of the Scriptures on the Person and Work of Christ," I, 703–704.

34. Abraham Booth, *An Apology for Baptists* (London: E. And C. Dilly, 1778), 20; "A Confession of Faith," 17–23.

35. "The Divinity of the Christian Religion," 1797, 3–5.

36. Abraham Booth, "A Confession of Faith," 17, 20–21; *An Apology for Baptists*, 17, 20.

37. Andrew Fuller, "On Moral and Positive Obedience," *Works* III, 352–353, 357; "The Nature and Importance of an Intimate Knowledge of Divine Truth," I, 160; "An Essay on Truth," III, 525.

38. Andrew Fuller, "Importance of a True System," *Works*, I, 688–689; "On an Intimate and Practical Acquaintance with the Word of God," I, 483–485; "The Necessity of a Divine Revelation," I, 698.

39. "The Divinity of the Christian Religion," 1797, 9–10.

40. Andrew Fuller, "Importance of a True System," I, 685.

41. Andrew Fuller, "The Nature and Importance of an Intimate Knowledge of Divine Truth," I, 161–167; "The Inspiration of the Holy Scriptures," I, 700.

42. "On Reading God's Word," Circular Letter, From the Ministers and Messengers of the Several Baptist Churches of the Northamptonshire Association, Assembled at Kettering, 5; Andrew Fuller, "The Nature and Importance of an Intimate Knowledge of Divine Truth," I, 165.

43. Andrew Fuller, "The Nature and Importance of an Intimate Knowledge of Divine Truth," I, 160, 166; "The Necessity of a Divine Revelation," I, 695; "Creeds and Subscriptions," *Works* III, 449–451.

44. "The Nature of Faith," 1781, 5; Abraham Booth, "Confession of Faith," 24–25; Andrew Fuller, "The Nature and Importance of an Intimate Knowledge of Divine

Truth," I, 160, 163; "The Sorrow Attending Wisdom and Knowledge," *Works*, I, 328.

45. "The Excellence of the Christian Dispensation," 1787, 2–3, 5, 7. See also Andrew Fuller's remarks on "The Magnitude of Creation," *The Gospel Its Own Witness*, I, 84–97; "The Vanity of the Human Mind," I, 434–438; and "The Sorrow Attending Wisdom and Knowledge," I, 328.

46. "Doctrine, Experience, and Practice," Circular Letter, From the Baptist Ministers and Messengers, Assembled at Leicester, 1787, 4; "The Excellence of the Christian Dispensation," 1787, 2–3.

47. William Carey, *An Enquiry into the Obligations of Christians*, 8–13; Abraham Booth, *Commerce in the Human Species*, 1792, reprinted in Leon McBeth, *Sourcebook for Baptist Heritage* (Nashville: Broadman, 1990), 138–141.

48. John Ryland, *Advice to Students of Divinity* (London: Pasham, 1770), 11–12, 14; Andrew Fuller, "The Inspiration of the Holy Scriptures," I, 699–702; *The Gospel Its Own Witness*, II, 58–97; Abraham Booth, "A Confession of Faith," 14–17; "The Divinity of the Christian Religion," 1797, 5–9.

49. For instance, see "The Divinity of the Christian Religion," 1797, 5–9.

50. "God's Kingdom," Circular Letter of the Elders, Ministers, and Messengers, Western Association, 1798, 1–11; John Ryland, *Advice to Students of Divinity*, 12–13; John Sutcliff, *Jealousy for the Lord of Hosts Illustrated* (1791), 12; Andrew Fuller, "The Nature and Importance of an Intimate Knowledge of Divine Truth," I, 163, 170.

51. Andrew Fuller, "An Essay on Truth," III, 529.

Chapter Ten

1. Isaac Backus, "Spiritual Ignorance" (Providence: William Goddard, 1763), 29; "A Discourse Showing the Nature and Necessity of an Internal Call to Preach the Everlasting Gospel" (Boston: Fowle, 1754), 15–18, 42, 69.

2. Isaac Backus, "A Discourse Showing the Nature and Necessity of an Internal Call to Preach the Everlasting Gospel," 17–18.

3. Jonathan Maxcy, "Dedication of a Meeting-House" (Providence: Carter and Wilkinson, 1796), 5–7, 16–17.

4. William G. McLoughlin, *Isaac Backus on Church, State, and Calvinism* (Cambridge, Mass.: Harvard University, 1968), 2, 55; Isaac Backus, *A History of New England with Particular Reference to the Denomination of Christians Called Baptists* (Newton, Mass.: Backus Historical Society, 1871), II, 107; "A Discourse Showing the Nature and Necessity of an Internal Call to Preach the Everlasting Gospel," x.

5. John Taylor, *The History of Ten Baptist Churches* (Louisville, 1823), quoted in W. W. Sweet, *Religion on the American Frontier: The Baptists 1783–1830* (New York: Cooper Square, 1964), 111–112.

6. Thomas Memminger, "Christian Liberty," 1797, 327–328; David Jones, "Saving Faith," 1788, 240–241; Abel Morgan, "Of the Holy Scriptures," 1774, 137; and William Straughton, "Infidelity," 1796, 319–320, in *Philadelphia Baptist Association Minutes*.

7. Oliver Hart, "A Gospel church portrayed," 749–753, 756–757; Richard Furman, "A Sermon on the Constitution and Order of the Christian Church," 1789, 759–760, 764; in Francis W. Sacks, *The Philadelphia Baptist Tradition of Church and Church Authority, 1707–1814* (Lewiston, New York: Edwin Mellen, 1989).

8. William Straughton, "Infidelity," 1796, 319.

9. Isaac Backus, "Family Prayer."

10. Samuel Stillman, "A Good Minister" (Boston: Manning and Loring, 1797), 13.

11. Isaac Backus, *A History of New England* II, 261, 264; Wood Furman, *A History of the Charleston Association* (Charleston: J. Hoff, 1811), 71; Samuel Jones, "The Gospel," Circular Letter, 1795, *Philadelphia Baptist Association Minutes*, 309; "Memorial at Philadelphia, October 4, 1774"; Morgan Edwards, *Two Academical Exercises* (Philadelphia: Dobson and Lang, 1788), 54.

12. Elizabeth Backus, "Letter, November 4, 1752," *A History of New England* II, 99.

13. Isaac Backus, *A History of New England* II, 135, 281–282.

14. John Leland, "Events in the Life of John Leland: Written by Himself," L. F. Greene, ed., *The Writings of John Leland* (New York: Arno, 1969), 12; David Jones, "Saving Faith," 1788, 240–241; James Manning, "Charge," *Life, Times, and Correspondence of James Manning* (Boston: Gould and Lincoln, 1864), 426.

15. Isaac Backus, "A Fish Caught in His Own Net," 1768, in William G. McLoughlin, ed., *Isaac Backus on Church, State, and Calvinism*, 273, 281; "The Doctrine of Sovereign Grace" (Providence: John Carter, 1771).

16. David Jones, "Saving Faith," 1788, 241; Isaac Backus, "A Discourse Showing the Nature and Necessity of an Internal Call to Preach the Everlasting Gospel," 78–79; Isaac Backus, *A History of New England* II, 261, 264; "Some Apology for My Changing My Principles Concerning Baptism," 1749–1750.

17. Hezekiah Smith, "Address," American Army, Delivered in Camp, October, 1779, in R. A. Guild, ed., *Chaplain Smith and the Baptists* (Philadelphia: American Baptist Publication Society, 1885), 232–233; James Manning, "Letter to the Rev. Dr. Stennett," *Life, Times, and Correspondence of James Manning*, 181–182.

18. Isaac Backus, "True Faith Will Produce Good Works" (Boston: D. Kneeland, 1767), 31–35, 40, 82; *The Diary of Isaac Backus* III, 1525.

19. Isaac Backus, *A History of New England*, II, 90.

20. Elisha Paine, "A Letter from the Associated Ministers of the County of Windham" (Boston, 1745), 7–8, 12.

21. Morgan Edwards, "Enoch Walked with God," Thomas R. McKibbens and Kenneth L. Smith, *The Life and Works of Morgan Edwards* (New York: Arno, 1980), 115. Cf. "Church Covenant," Meherrin Baptist Church, Lunenburg County, Virginia, 1779, Charles W. Deweese, *Baptist Church Covenants* (Nashville: Broadman, 1990) 144.

22. Isaac Backus, "Truth is Great and Will Prevail," *Isaac Backus on Church, State, and Calvinism*, 1781, 402, 424.

23. John Leland, "The Rights of Conscience Inalienable," *The Writings of John Leland*, 179, 185; "Memorial at Philadelphia, October 4, 1774"; Isaac Backus, "Government and Liberty described, and Ecclesiastical Tyranny Exposed," 1778, *Isaac Backus on Church, State, and Calvinism*, 351; "A Door Opened for Equal Christian Liberty, and No Man Can Shut It," 6.

24. Isaac Backus, *The Diary of Isaac Backus* III, 1515; "The Atonement of Christ" (Boston: Philip Freeman, 1787), 11; "Letter to a Gentleman," 1771, 5; "Evangelical Ministers Described and Distinguished from Legalists"

Endnotes

(Boston: Philip Freeman, 1772), 29; Morgan Edwards, *Res Sacra* (Philadelphia: Prichard and Hall, 1788), 8; Oliver Hart, "Circular Letter," 1782, *Philadelphia Baptist Association Minutes*, 187; John Leland, "Corresponding Letter of the Shaftsbury Association," 1796, *The Writings of John Leland*, 231.

25. "Letter," Baptist Church at Wilbraham, 1779, *A History of New England*, II, 279; Isaac Backus, "The Testimony of the Two Witnesses" (Boston: Samuel Hall, 1793), 8; "A Discourse Showing the Nature and Necessity of an Internal Call to Preach the Everlasting Gospel," 67–68; "A Fish Caught in His Own Net," 230; "A Seasonable Plea for Liberty of Conscience," (Boston: P. Freeman, 1770), 47; "Church Covenant," Dumplin Creek Baptist Church, Jefferson City, Tennessee, 1797, Charles W. Deweese, *Baptist Church Covenants*, 149.

26. Isaac Backus, "Gospel Comfort Under Heavy Tidings" (Providence: J. Carter, 1769), Appendix, xviii; *A History of New England*, II, 387; "True Faith Will Produce Good Works," 42–43; "A Fish Caught in His Own Net," 279; "The Testimony of the Two Witnesses," 26.

27. "Letter," Weston Baptist Church to the Warren Baptist Association, 1792; *Warren Baptist Association Minutes*, 1784, 4.

28. Quoted in William G. McLoughlin, *New England Dissent 1630–1883* (Cambridge, Mass.: Harvard University, 1971) II, 930.

29. William Vanhorn, "Perseverance of the Saints," 1791, *Philadelphia Baptist Association Minutes*, 274.

30. "The General Letter from the Baptist Association met in Philadelphia," 1768, *Philadelphia Baptist Association Minutes*, 11.

31. *Philadelphia Baptist Association Minutes*, 1774, 137; John Leland, "Circular Letter of the Shaftsbury Association," 1793, *The Writings of John Leland*, 196, 199; Isaac Backus, "The Sovereign Decrees of God," 295; "Spiritual Ignorance," 11.

32. "Church Covenant," Grassy Creek Baptist Church, North Carolina, 1757, Article 2, Charles W. Deweese, *Baptist Church Covenants*, 140; "Letter," Swansea, February 8, 1738–9, *A History of New England* II, 33; "A Summary of Church-Discipline" (Charleston: David Bruce, 1774), Preface.

33. *Philadelphia Baptist Association Minutes*, 1774, 137; "Terms of Union Between the Elkhorn and South Kentucky, or Separate, Associations," 1801, William L. Lumpkin, *Baptist Confessions of Faith* (Valley Forge: Judson, 1959), 359; Isaac Backus, "A Discourse Showing the Nature and Necessity of an Internal Call to Preach the Everlasting Gospel," 17; "The Atonement of Christ," 8; "Articles of Faith," 1756, First Baptist Church, Middleborough, Mass.; "Church Covenant," Beaver Creek Baptist Church, Ky., 1798; "Church Covenant," Grassy Creek Baptist Church, N. C., 1757; Abel Morgan, "Fall of Man," 1780, *Philadelphia Baptist Association Minutes*, 170–171.

34. Thomas Baldwin, *Baptism of Believers Only* (Boston: Manning and Loring, 1806), 35; Isaac Backus, *A History of New England* II, 294–295, 405; "Spiritual Ignorance," 11; *Philadelphia Baptist Association Minutes*, 1746, 50; 1774, 137; and 1795, 307–308; "Church Covenant," Beaver Creek Baptist Church, Ky., 1798; "Articles of Faith," 1756, First Baptist Church, Middleborough, Mass.; "Church Covenant," Grassy Creek Baptist Church, 1757.

35. Jonathan Maxcy, "Sermon at the Warren Association," 1797, 10.

36. "Association Book," *Philadelphia Baptist Association Minutes*, 1761, 46; *The Life and Works of Morgan Edwards*, 117; Isaac Backus, *A History of New England* II, 294, 342; "A Discourse Showing the Nature and Necessity of an Internal Call to Preach the Everlasting Gospel," 67–68, 80; "A Letter to the Rev. Mr. Benjamin Lord of Norwich" (Providence: W. Goddard, 1764), 40; "Evangelical Ministers Described and Distinguished from Legalists," 16, 20, 21; "A Fish Caught in His Own Net," 229–231.

37. Oliver Hart, "Circular Letter," 1782, 187; Isaac Backus, *The Diary of Isaac Backus*, I, 4 III, 1525; James Manning, "Circular Letter," *Life, Times, and Correspondence of James Manning*, 83.

38. Abel Morgan, "Of the Holy Scriptures," 1774, 137; Isaac Backus, *The Diary of Isaac Backus*, I, 4; Samuel Jones, "Circular Letter," 1778, 160; David Jones, "Saving Faith," 1788, 240–241.

39. Thomas Memminger, "Christian Liberty," 328; John Leland, "The Bible Baptist," 1790, 78; "The Rights

and Bonds of Conscience," *The Writings of John Leland*, 123.

40. William Straughton, "Infidelity," 1796, 318–321; William Vanhorn, "Perseverance of the Saints," 1791, 274.

41. Benjamin Foster, "Circular Letter," 1790, 262; Thomas Ustick, "Adoption," 1786, 219, 222, *Philadelphia Baptist Association Minutes*; Oliver Hart, "A Sermon on a Gospel-Church Portrayed, and Her Orderly Service Pointed Out" (Trenton: Isaac Collins, 1791); Morgan Edwards, "Enoch Walked With God," *Sermons*, X, Sermon 10; Isaac Backus, *A History of New England*, II, 263, 304; "Truth is Great, and Will Prevail," 402; "True Faith Will Produce Good Works," 40; "The Infinite Importance of the Obedience of Faith" (Boston, 1791), 4.

42. John Leland, "The Bible Baptist," 78, "The Virginia Chronicle," 111, *The Writings of John Leland*; Samuel Jones, "Circular Letter," 1778, 161; William Straughton, *A Discourse* (Philadelphia: S. C. Ustick, 1797), 14; "Infidelity," 320; Richard Furman, "On the Relation the Children of Church Members bear to the Church," 1792, 84; Edmund Botsford, "On the Duty of Christians in matters of Controversy," 1794, *A History of the Charleston Association of Baptist Churches*, 101–103; "A Summary of Church Discipline" (Charleston: David Bruce, 1774), Chapter IV.

43. John Leland, "Letter of Valediction on Leaving Virginia, in 1791," 172; "Circular Letter," 1769, *The Writings of John Leland*; Isaac Backus, *A History of New England*, II, 25, 304; "A Fish Caught in His Own Net," 222, 235, 273; "The Liberal Support of Gospel Ministers" (Boston: Samuel Hill, 1790), 23; "A Short Description of the Bond-Woman and the Free, as they are the Two Covenants" (Boston: Edes and Gill, 1770), 40.

44. "Circular Letter," 1795, *A History of the Charleston Association of Baptist Churches*, 26–27; Edmund Botsford, "On the Duty of Christians in matters of Controversy," 1794, 104; David Jones, "Saving Faith," 1788, 241; Isaac Backus, "A Short Description of the Bond-Woman and the Free, as they are the Two Covenants," 40–41.

45. Isaac Backus, "True Faith Will Produce Good Works," 75; "A Fish Caught in His Own Net," 282; "A Discourse Showing the Nature and Necessity of an Internal Call to Preach the Everlasting Gospel," iv; "A Discourse concerning the Church of Christ" (Boston: J. Boyles, 1773), 99; "A Letter to the Rev. Mr. Lord of Norwich," 3.

46. Isaac Backus, "A Discourse Showing the Nature and Necessity of an Internal Call to Preach the Everlasting Gospel," 50; "A Short Description of the Bond-Woman and the Free, as they are the Two Covenants," 12–16, 40; "An Appeal to the Public for Religious Liberty" (Boston: John Boyle, 1773), 4, 43; *A History of New England*, II, 222–223, 336; "A Door Opened for Equal Christian Liberty, and No Man Can Shut It" (Boston: Philip Freeman, 1783), 14; John Leland, "The Rights of Conscience," *The Writings of John Leland*, 185.

47. Thomas Ustick, "Adoption," *Philadelphia Baptist Association Minutes*, 220–221; Isaac Backus, "Gospel Comfort Under Heavy Tidings," 12; "A Fish Caught in His Own Net," 172, 279; Edmund Botsford, "On the Duty of Christians in matters of Controversy," 104.

48. Isaac Backus, *A History of New England*, II, 114; "True Faith Will Produce Good Works," 63, 77; "Truth is Great and Will Prevail," 402–403; John Leland, "The Virginia Chronicle," 123–124; Edmund Botsford, "On the Duty of Christians in matters of Controversy," 99–100; Thomas Baldwin, *The Baptism of Believers Only*, 120–121.

49. Simeon Dogget, "Oration on the Death of Rev. President Manning," *Life, Times, and Correspondence of James Manning*, 456–457.

50. Richard Furman, "On the use of Reason in Religion," *A History of the Charleston Association of Baptist Churches*, 125–137; Isaac Backus, "The Doctrine of Sovereign Grace," 66; "An Address to the Inhabitants of New England," 1787, *Isaac Backus on Church, State, and Calvinism*, 444; *A History of New England*, II III.

51. Jeremy Condy, "Mercy Exemplified in the Conduct of a Samaritan" (Boston, 1767).

52. Morgan Edwards, *Two Academical Exercises*, 13–14; *Materials Towards a History of the Baptists in Pennsylvania* (Philadelphia: Joseph Crukshank, 1770), 66, 103. See the splendid use of formal logic by Thomas Baldwin, *The Baptism of Believers Only*, 122.

53. Hezekiah Smith, *Doctrine of Believer's Baptism* (Boston: P. Freeman, 1766), 1; John Walton, *Remarks*

(Newport, 1731), 10–11, 68; "The Memorial of the Baptist Association, met at Sandy Creek, in Charlotte, October, 1780," 1; Isaac Backus, *A History of New England*, II, 294, 336.

54. Isaac Backus, "Spiritual Ignorance," 11.

55. Henry Smalley, "Moral Law," 1794, *Philadelphia Baptist Association Minutes*, 299; Thomas Baldwin, "Sermon at the Ordination of the Rev. David Leonard" (Boston: Joseph Bumstead, 1795), 15–16; "Sermon at the Concert of Prayer" (Boston: Manning & Loring, 1799), 5–7; Samuel Stillman, "A Sermon on Charity" (Boston: Manning & Loring, 1785), 8; Jonathan Maxcy, "Sermon at the Warren Association," 8–9; "The Existence of God Demonstrated from the Works of Creation" (Providence: Carter & Wilkinson, 1795), 5–13.

56. John Cook, "A Circular Address," Wood Furman, ed., *A History of the Charleston Association of Baptist Churches* (Charleston: J. Hoff, 1811), 19.

57. Isaac Backus, "A Fish Caught in His Own Net," 178.

Chapter Eleven

1. Gal. 2:20; Rom. 6:4.

2. 2 Cor. 5:17, 13:14; 1 John 1:3–7, 3:15, 4:1–6.

3. See John 1 and 14 in Charles B. Williams, *The New Testament in the Language of the People*.

4. John 1:14.

5. Rom. 6:3–5.

Select Bibliography of Classic Writings

Seventeenth-Century English Baptists
Claridge, Richard. Preface to *The Sandy Foundation of Infant Baptism Shaken*, by Hecules Collins (1695).

"A Declaration of Faith of English People Remaining at Amsterdam," 1611.

Hobson, Paul. *A Discoverie of Truth*. London: J. Coe, 1647.

———. *Practicall Divinity*. London: R. Harford, 1646.

"The Orthodox Creed," 1678.

"Propositions and Conclusions concerning True Christian Religion," 1612–1614.

"Second London Confession," 1677 and 1688.

"A Short Confession of Faith," 1610.

"Short Confession of Faith in XX Articles," 1609.

Sturgion, John. *A Plea for Tolleration*. London: S. Dover, 1661.

Tombes, John. *The Ancient Bounds, or Liberty of Conscience*. London: Henry Overton, 1645.

Seventeenth-Century American Baptists
"The Baptist Debate of April 14–15, 1668."

Clarke, John. *Ill Newes from New-England*. London: Henry Hills, 1652.

"Covenant," Benjamin and Elias Keach, 1697.

"Covenant," Kittery Baptist Church, Kittery, Maine, 1682.

"Covenant," Swansea Baptist Church, Rehoboth, Mass., 1663.

Holmes, Obadiah. "Of My Faith," 1775.

———. "On My Life," 1775.

———. "To the Church," 1775.

———. "To the World," 1775.

Eighteenth-Century English Baptists

"Articles of Religion of the New Connexion," 1770.

Brine, John. *A Treatise on Various Subjects*. Revised by James Upton. London: Printed for the Editor, 1813.

"The Divinity of the Christian Religion," Circular Letter, Leicester, 1797.

"The Excellence of the Christian Dispensation," Circular Letter, Wellington, 1787.

Fuller, Andrew. "An Essay on Truth."

————. *The Gospel Its Own Witness*, 1799.

————. *The Gospel Worthy of All Acceptance*, 1785.

————. "The Nature and Importance of an Intimate Knowledge of Divine Truth."

Hall, Robert Sr. *Help to Zion's Travellers*. Halifax: Hartley and Walker, 1781.

"The Nature of Faith," Circular Letter, Kettering, 1781.

Taylor, Dan. *The Consistent Christian*. Leeds: G. Wright, 1784.

————. *An Essay on the Truth and the Inspiration of the Holy Scriptures*. London: P. and F. Heck, 1819.

Eighteenth-Century American Baptists

Backus, Isaac. "A Discourse Showing the Nature and Necessity of an Internal Call to Preach the Everlasting Gospel." London: Fowle, 1754.

————. "A Fish Caught in His Own Net." Boston, 1768.

————. "True Faith Will Produce Good Works." Boston: D. Kneeland, 1767.

————. "Truth is Great and Will Prevail." Boston: Philip Freeman, 1781.

Botsford, Edmund. "On the Duty of Christians in matters of Controversy," Circular Letter, Charleston, 1794.

Furman, Richard. "On the use of Reason in Religion," Circular Letter, Charleston, n.d.

"The Philadelphia Confession," 1742.

Index of Selected Subjects

Index of Selected Subjects